Research for the Developing World

Research for the Developing World

Public Funding from Australia, Canada, and the UK

Bruce Currie-Alder

OXFORD
UNIVERSITY PRESS

OXFORD
UNIVERSITY PRESS

Great Clarendon Street, Oxford, OX2 6DP,
United Kingdom

Oxford University Press is a department of the University of Oxford. It furthers the University's objective of excellence in research, scholarship, and education by publishing worldwide. Oxford is a registered trade mark of Oxford University Press in the UK and in certain other countries

First Edition published in 2015

Published in the United States of America by Oxford University Press
198 Madison Avenue, New York, NY 10016, United States of America

British Library Cataloguing in Publication Data
Data available

Library of Congress Control Number: 2015935074

ISBN 978–0–19–874293–7

Acknowledgements

This book is the result of seven years of study, reflection, and practice of supporting research for the developing world. This journey combined formal scholarship with participant observation, as both an outsider and insider to the subject.

As a scholar, I am indebted to the wise counsel of Robert Shepherd, Lisa Mills, and Marc-Andre Gagnon. Together they forced me to ground my intellectual curiosity into a framework that draws on the literature in public management, international development, and science policy. I am particularly thankful for Robert's advice to prepare a document guide, specifying what information I needed and how it linked to the theoretical framework. This turned out to be a brilliant tactic that I recommend to anyone who wishes to stay focused and avoid getting lost in the archives. Robert also challenged me to go further, pushing beyond the obvious, to identify deeper lessons and insights. Luc Juillet and Michael Brklacich provided sage advice that sharpened the conclusions and understanding of leadership, performance, and governance.

As a practitioner, I was privileged to work with numerous colleagues at Canada's International Development Research Centre. Lauchlan Munro, Maureen O'Neil, and Tim Dottridge deserve special praise for sharing their deep knowledge of the organization's history, encouraging colleagues to question received wisdom, and providing opportunities for young people to take on new responsibility. Bruce Muirhead and Ron Harpelle provided insights on how to conduct historical research and generously shared their source materials and insights. This proved to be a point of departure for tracing a story across three countries. I am grateful for the openness of numerous people in Australia, Canada, and the United Kingdom who willingly shared their experience in, dedication to, and passion for this subject. It takes a special kind of person to set aside their professional aspirations for the benefit of others. I am humbled and privileged to have met men and women who have dedicated their professional lives to furthering science and improving lives in the developing world.

Finally, as a spouse and parent, I am indebted to Nora, Miranda, and David for their patience during the research and writing of this book. This meant tolerating far too many shortened weekends and absences from home. You accompanied me on every step of this journey, occasionally in person, and always in spirit.

Contents

List of Figures ix
List of Tables xi
List of Abbreviations xiii

1. Expecting More: Changing Governance of Public Research 1
2. Research Funders: Adapting to Government Expectations 15
3. United Kingdom: Between Haldane and Rothschild 26
4. Canada: Hopper's Vision of Empowerment 60
5. Australia: Crawford's Legacy of Partnership 96
6. Changing Context: Public Management and Research Governance 127
7. Looking Back: Program Theory and Grantmaking Practice 142
8. Looking Forward: From Foreign Aid to Global Challenges 156
9. Conclusion: The Quest for Research Impact 168

References 179
Index 189

List of Figures

1.1	Principal–agent relations	8
3.1	Timeline of UK case study	27
3.2	Performance regime surrounding DFID	45
3.3	United Kingdom's R4D spending since 1980	56
4.1	Timeline of Canada case study	61
4.2	Performance regime surrounding IDRC	78
4.3	Canada's spending since 1980	94
5.1	Timeline of Australia case study	97
5.2	Performance regime surrounding ACIAR	111
5.3	Australia's R4D spending since 1980	124

List of Tables

1.1 Variety in defining and funding research for the developing world 5

2.1 Framework used in case studies 18

6.1 Comparison of governance contexts 136

7.1 Funders as adaptive organizations 149

List of Abbreviations

ACIAR	Australian Centre for International Agriculture Research
AIMS	African Institute of Mathematical Sciences
ATSE	Academy of Technological Sciences and Engineering
AusAID	Australian Agency for International Development
BBSRC	Biotechnology and Biological Sciences Research Council
CCRD	Consultative Committee on Research and Development
CGIAR	Consultative Group on International Agricultural Research
CIDA	Canadian International Development Agency
CIFOR	Centre for International Forestry Research
CIHR	Canadian Institutes for Health Research
CRC	Cooperative Research Centres
CRD	Central Research Department
CSIRO	Commonwealth Scientific and Industrial Research Organisation
DEFRA	Department for Environment, Food and Rural Affairs
DFAIT	Department of Foreign Affairs and International Trade
DFAT	Department of Foreign Affairs and Trade
DFID	Department for International Development
DIF	Development Innovation Fund
ERA	Excellence in Research for Australia
ESRC	Economic and Social Research Council
EU	European Union
GAVI	Global Alliance for Vaccines and Immunisation
GEF	Global Environmental Facility
IAE	International Assistance Envelope
IAVI	International AIDS Vaccine Initiative
ICAI	Independent Commission for Aid Impact
ICRISAT	International Crop Research Institute for the Semi-Arid Tropics
ICT4D	information and communication technologies for development

IDRC	International Development Research Centre
IDS	Institute of Development Studies
MDG	Millennium Development Goals
NGO	non-governmental organization
NRI	Natural Resources Institute
OAG	Office of the Auditor General
ODA	Overseas Development Administration
ODI	Overseas Development Institute
PSA	Public Service Agreement
R4D	research for development
R&D	research and development
RDC	rural R&D corporations
RED	Research and Evidence Division
RQF	Research Quality Framework
S&T	science and technology
SSHRC	Social Sciences and Humanities Research Council
TBS	Treasury Board Secretariat
UKCDS	UK Collaborative on Development Sciences
UNCED	United Nations' Conference on Environment and Development
WHO	World Health Organization

1

Expecting More

Changing Governance of Public Research

The inspiration for this book came from a 2008 meeting described as a gathering of "like-minded" funders with a commitment to supporting research for the developing world. On the surface, all agreed on intent and thematic priorities: everyone wanted to improve health, resolve conflict, make governments accountable, and help poor people adapt to climate change. Yet there was no consensus on how to address these priorities. One participant urged for providing developing-country governments with budget support, another called for core funding to southern universities, and another argued for funding independent policy think tanks. Each was invested in a distinct set of programs which embodied different assumptions about how change occurs and how their organization's work contributed to it. These programs were incommensurable, departing from different first principles regarding the purpose of research, its role in development, and how the world worked. These unstated philosophies are more than an academic curiosity, as they carry real consequences for the research community, in terms of which ideas were are more attractive to the funder, and who receives their support.

From this meeting emerged a question: how do funders decide on their approach to "research for the developing world," and why do these approaches vary over time and between funders? The answer lies in the policy environment surrounding each funder. Sitting at the nexus between foreign policy and science policy, funders must be sensitive to both. Funders adopt particular program theories in part due to the performance regime in which they find themselves. This book explores how three different funders survived, and occasionally thrived, over three decades when hard questions were asked of public research. Many countries became less tolerant of curiosity-driven work with vague promises of eventual spin-offs, and began to favor more applied work predicated on more demonstrable economic and social benefits.

Chapters 3–5 delve into the parallel worlds of London, Canberra, and Ottawa, where alternate narratives of research evolved along divergent paths despite the similarities of a Westminster-style parliamentary system. The story that unfolds is one of changes in the policy environment which affect how well each funder "fits" with what government wants, and how each funder not only adapted to the changing governance but demonstrated leadership in advocating for its own ideas.

This chapter introduces the ideas of research for the developing world, and the changing governance of public research in Australia, Canada, and the United Kingdom. Chapter 2 introduces the framework used to study the governance around, and the routines inside, organizations that fund research for the developing world. Chapters 3–5 present three case studies, a funder from the United Kingdom, Canada, and Australia, identifying when and how each altered their programs and grantmaking practice. Chapters 6–8 go on to look across these experiences to discuss why funders made these decisions, and look forward to the future prospects of research for the developing world. In Chapter 9, the book concludes with critical insights on the nature of leadership with public organizations, the implementation of performance management, and the evolving definitions of research impact.

Research for the Developing World

Before delving into research for the developing world, it is useful to review the meaning of science, research, and innovation. Science is a set of procedures used to certify a claim to knowledge, or to skeptically subject ideas to argument, criticism, and empirical evidence (Merton 1942). The methods of science include observing phenomenon, formulating potential explanations, and testing hypotheses. Science is also communal as scientists share their own findings, and test and extend the findings made by others. Approaches to conducting science vary from the experimental to the speculative, depending on the use of evidence and causal explanation. Science embraces a wider range of disciplines and ways of knowing, ranging from the study and manipulation of the natural world (e.g. biology and medicine) to understanding human society (e.g. history and sociology). Scientific works are expected to be plausible, valuable, and original: attributes that contribute to the notions of scientific excellence and research quality.

Research is creative work undertaken on a systematic basis in order to increase the stock of knowledge, and the use of this stock of knowledge to devise new applications (OECD 2002). The *Frascati manual* describes surveys of research expenditures and outputs, and distinguishes activities for generating new knowledge ("research and development," or R&D) from related scientific activities for sharing knowledge, such as workshops and conferences (which together with R&D sums "science and technology," or S&T). Innovation, in contrast, is the implementation of a new or significantly improved product, process, or method (OECD/Eurostat 2005). The *Oslo manual* describes surveys of the activities intended to lead to innovations, including design, engineering, and management. While research is about new knowledge, innovation is converting knowledge into value, by making or doing things in new ways. Innovations can be entirely original (new to world) or novel for a given place or use (new to context).

Science and innovation have improved the material condition of human societies. Looking back, the development of modern Western societies stemmed from an unintentional process of adopting and refining technologies that enhanced the productive capability of the economy and improved the well-being of citizens. Whether measured as income, life expectancy, or education, human development over the past two centuries was profoundly influenced by the spread of electricity, vaccines, and telecommunications. Yet for much of that time, such advances were largely unintentional and accidental, the spontaneous diffusion of innovations that people recognized and valued. This diffusion occurred across national boundaries, as different countries learned from each other, adapted available technologies to their local conditions, and elaborated new ones to address local needs.

Following the Second World War, policy increasingly sought to intentionally direct science and innovation toward continued enhancement of life at home and addressing needs abroad. Technological advances in radar, radio, aviation, and nuclear physics had contributed to the war effort, and Western societies seized upon the promise of technology to provide freedom from want during times of peace. At home, these countries had entered an age of government science with expanded funding and institutional arrangements for public research. Abroad, the leaders of newly independent developing countries eagerly sought to establish domestic capability in key areas of science, such as agriculture, water, public health, and energy. Science and innovation had formed part of the relationship between European powers and their colonies overseas, and would become among the less controversial elements of the emerging era of foreign aid. In the United States, President Truman outlined a vision "for making the benefits of our scientific advances and industrial progress available for the improvement and growth of underdeveloped areas" (Truman 1949). The next three decades, up to the early 1970s, witnessed a period of economic growth, expanding budgets, and unbridled enthusiasm that science was improving the human condition.

The glow surrounding science and innovation lost part of its sheen between the late 1970s and 1990s. Economic crises required Western governments to cut back on public research funding, while changing ideas on the role of the state inspired divesture of government-owned laboratories in favor of stimulating science in universities and the private sector. Science entered a new period of "steady state" funding, marked by a contracting space for government science. The increased crop yields of the first green revolution in agriculture reached a point of diminishing returns, and new missions—such as the "war of cancer" or polio eradication—proved more difficult and complex than initially thought. A new awareness set in concerning the constraints of scientific progress, and its potential consequences in terms of income distribution, poverty, and environmental degradation. Yet science and innovation continued to enjoy a positive reputation and witnessed a renaissance following the Cold War, with a renewed understanding of interdependencies in a globalizing world.

These shifting perspectives on science and innovation matter because they shaped the context for public organizations that fund research for the developing world. Some of these organizations were born out of a colonial legacy of scientific cooperation with the developing world, while others were established as their countries embraced a new role in international affairs. This book traces the histories of three such organizations, one each from Australia, Canada, and the United Kingdom, and how they adapted to evolving ideas on—and government support for—science, innovation, and international development. These organizations shared the common imperative of keeping up with the times: cultivating the support of their home governments, securing the funding required to continue their work, while also maintain their credibility within the research communities at home and abroad. They also needed to define—and redefine—their position relative to other funding organizations involved in this space, including countries with different traditions—such as the Swedish Agency for Research Cooperation[1] or France's Institut de recherche pour le développement (IRD)—and philanthropic foundations—such as the Rockefeller, Ford, and Bill & Melinda Gates—that are autonomous from government expectations.

Over time, such organizations adopted diverse approaches to research for the developing world. Key among these were to provide evidence informing donors of the effects of different interventions to reduce poverty, to mobilize existing talent to design technology that serves poor people, and to build the capability of poorer countries to conduct science for their own benefit.[2] In deciding how to support research, funders must decide what knowledge to advance, what types of support to offer, and how research might be used

[1] Once an independent organization, the early twenty-first century saw SAREC merged into the Swedish International Development Agency (see King and McGrath 2004).

[2] For a fuller review of diverse approaches see Singer et al. 1970, UN Millennium Project 2005, Scoones and Leach 2006, Wagner 2008, Molenaar et al. 2009, Khagram et al. 2009; Conway and Waage 2010, Edwards 2010, and Ely and Leach 2010.

Table 1.1. Variety in defining and funding research for the developing world

Why	On what	With whom	How	For what
Inform policy	Economic policy Governance	Aid practitioners and policy researchers	Core funding Project grants	Assess interventions Reduce local poverty
Build capacity	Health systems Think tanks	Local institutions in developing countries	Scholarships	Improve well-being
Design technology	Vaccines Seeds	Tap scientific talent anywhere	In-house research Prizes	Connect to global Raise productivity

Each row denotes unique program logics, the last two columns spread across these as there is limited number of grantmaking practices and multiple ways each of them can connect with development outcomes.

(Table 1.1). Some act like think tanks and fund intramural research performed by staff or consultants, others act like granting councils and fund work performed by the research community. Collectively, such organizations pursue multiple approaches including funding researchers at home, abroad in developing countries, or collaboration between these two groups.

Habermann and Langthale (2010) distinguish among research "on" development as a social phenomenon done mainly by social sciences, humanities, and economics; "for" development supporting innovation in developing countries and oriented toward natural science and engineering; and policy-related work on strategy and practice of development cooperation. Their first category includes the long-standing tradition of "development studies," scholarship that seeks to understand the developing world, drawing on the traditions of sociology and anthropology. In contrast, their second category is more open, including researchers who do not necessarily specialize in the problems of the developing world, yet also is more restrictive, as it expects research will affect material conditions abroad. Their third category is yet more restrictive and casts the purpose of research as a cause–effect relation between donor interventions and outcomes (Rousseau 2006 and Nutley et al. 2007). According to Khagram et al. (2009), "successful" research outputs are accessible, credible, and actionable. In other words, research for the developing world should be easily communicated, accepted as valid, and inform decision-making.

This latter approach casts research as an input into official development assistance, akin to labor or capital. To the extent that the research agenda increasingly embraced a narrow focus on providing evidence on "what works," it excluded understanding of how the wider process of development unfolds. It also ignored the politics of knowledge: the potential for research to contest and reframe how societies understand themselves, the problems they face, and their potential solutions. Funders are encouraged to favor politically safe questions of technological innovation, limiting the opportunities to address more contentious questions regarding social norms or how power is distributed and used in society. Improving crops or vaccines holds the potential to provide more food or lessen the burden of disease, yet no amount of technological innovation can solve poverty if its conditions are rooted in larger social inequalities and deprivation (Edwards 2010). When research is devoid of politics, it ignores the constraints poor people face and their potential to affect change in their lives.

These diverse approaches and notions of research quality reflect the rise of empiricism and experimentation in the social sciences in the latter part of the twentieth century. Bastow et al. (2014) note that social science thinking and methods have evolved toward mathematicization, quantification, formalization, and theorization. These authors suggest this shift started with "physics envy" in the twentieth century, as economics and psychology sought to advance more rapidly by embracing consensual research priorities and codified knowledge in mathematics. The social sciences also experienced waves of rational choice and game theory in the 1990s, and of behavioral psychology more recently, covering cognitive limits, the effects of problem framing, and nudge effects (where the way in which information is presented influences how it is perceived and acted on).

Organizations vary with respect to the intended purpose and audience for the research they fund. Following Habermann and Langthale's (2010) typology, the purpose can range from understanding the natural world or society, to trying out new approaches or technologies, to assessing the outcomes of particular interventions. The audience can range from peers in academia, donor or partner governments promoting top-down development, or local people, civil society, social movements, or private enterprises engaged in bottom-up development. As funders choose among their goals, purpose, and audience, they set the cornerstones for the program theory that guides their grantmaking.

In practice, there are a limited number of funding instruments available. The tool of choice has become the project grant, although funders can and do offer a variety of awards, including scholarships or fellowships for talented individuals, block grants or core funding to particular research-performing organizations, or *ex post* prizes for research in particular areas or for answering a priority problem. The choice among these options relies on assumptions regarding the importance of the research process being connected to local conditions (Wagner 2008): whether to study local phenomena and reach local audiences (e.g. field-level agricultural production among farmers), or whether the research can take place anywhere and reach global audiences (e.g. vaccine development, design of low-cost products).

Funding organizations often embrace a combination of goals and approaches, seeking to simultaneously advance knowledge and build research capabilities required for future advances. The ability to pursue such aims requires a long-term vision that considers not just a few years and the immediate outputs of a particular project or program, but several years and the career advancement of young researchers and how research contributes to development outcomes for poor and disadvantaged members of society. This book reveals how the space to consider and pursue such longer-term goals was squeezed over time, as government expectations of public research turned toward more clearly defined and shorter-term results. At the same time, the idea of research for the developing world is increasingly intermingled with a rising demand for research on global challenges that affect both developing countries and advanced economies, such as infectious disease, food security, and climate adaptation (cf. Reid et al. 2010, Varmus et al. 2003).

Guston (2000) argues that "[t]he asymmetry of information between those who would conduct research and those who would govern it presents the central problem of science policy." The classic solution to such asymmetry is the principal–agent model. This model considers two rational actors: the principal who provides an incentive to the agent to conduct some work or provide a service on their behalf. In this simple situation, the principal does not have full information of what the agent is doing at all times. As a rational actor, the agent is expected to also pursue his or her own goals and interests in addition to doing the principal's bidding. The extent to which the agent acts on behalf of the principal, rather than for themselves, is a function of the incentives provided (e.g. payments) and the efforts invested to monitor the agent's activities.

This model has been expanded to cast research funders in the middle, between what government wants done and what researchers actually do (Braun 1993, Rip 1994, van der Meulen 1998, 2003). The research funder is a boundary organization that both responds to direction from government and provides incentives to researchers who compete for the resources offered (Figure 1.1). The funder is simultaneously an agent of the government and a principal to the research community. As Rip (1994) argues, funders "must legitimate next year's budget in terms of an attractive portfolio of projects to be funded, while the money must be disbursed in a way that is acceptable to the scientists." Braun (2003) describes the problem of governance as how to attract the curiosity of researchers to problems of research users. This includes the means by which policymakers get researchers to respond to policy demand, ensure they recruit qualified recipients (avoid adverse selection), and that these recipients apply themselves to the task (avoid moral hazard).

Research funders are thus intermediary organizations. Meyer and Kearnes (2013: 423) define them as entities that "structure expertise and policy imperatives... [and] selectively mobilise and reframe contemporary policy discourse and ideas of usability, applicability and impact so as to influence

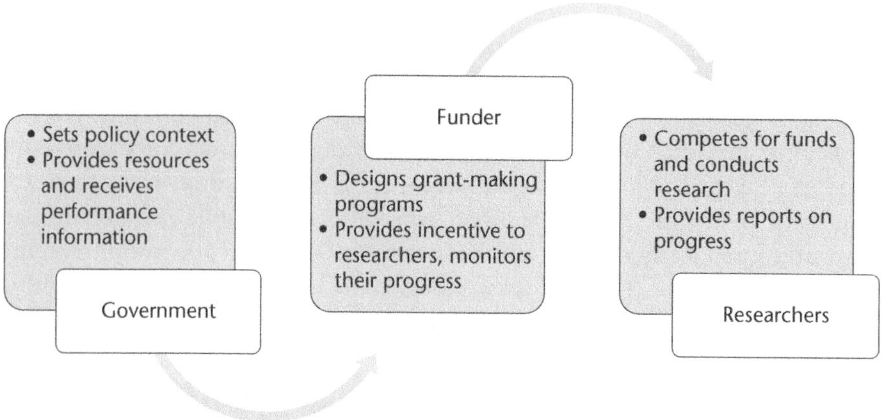

Figure 1.1. Principal–agent relations
Organizations that support publicly funded research are simultaneously an agent of home governments and a principal to researchers.

the conduct of researchers and research institutions." These authors identify three approaches to the study of such intermediaries: *documentary* (describing a shift toward distributed forms of governance), *contractual* (underpinned by principal–agent theory), and *performance* (behavior of intermediaries "getting things done"). These authors describe the contractual approach as drawing on the concept of rational choice, focused on "the delegation of political authority... and the particular mandates that enable intermediary organisations to operate simultaneously as principals and agents when acting as an interface between national governments and research communities."

Yet qualified researchers also choose among different funders when seeking support for their work. Shove (2003) and Grimpe (2011) consider the point of view of the researcher (agent) who manages different opportunities through sequential participation with different funders. Scientists can be assumed to select those grants for which they anticipate the highest "return." Over time, researchers string together separately funded projects to pursue their longer-term interests and professional career. Projects pull individual researchers into temporary, for-purpose networks with specific objectives. Individual researchers are akin to free agents that move between projects. When one project ends they enter into another, and may be part of multiple projects at any given time.

Researchers can be expected to ignore funding opportunities that stray too far from their interests or that do not further their careers. Funders thus compete for the limited time researchers have to prepare grant applications and project proposals. Qualified researchers can be expected to prefer opportunities that offer greater return on the effort invested in applying for funding.

In other words, publicly funded research is not exclusively a "buyer's market" in which researchers compete for scarce funding; it can also be a "seller's market" in which funders compete for scarce talent and ideas. Consequently, the funder must maintain some credibility within the research community to attract a pool of sufficiently qualified grant seekers. This is especially so in contexts where researchers have options to pursue funding from other organizations, such as domestic granting councils, philanthropic foundations, or international organizations. Any particular funder may be just one among a number of potential principals to the research community.

Between States and Markets

Despite its elegance, the principal–agent model ignores the wider governance of public research as well as the organizational routines within each funder. Polster (2003) describes such governance as "the courses of action in and through which research is conceived, produced, and transmitted to society." The OECD (2003) describes it as the *decision-making* processes that govern priority setting, funding allocation, and the management of research institutes, including how their performance is assessed. The OECD innovation strategy describes it as the *institutional arrangements* and *incentive structures* that determine how actors "interact in allocating and managing resources... to steer and give direction" (2010: 189, 191) to research and innovation. While these descriptions are somewhat abstract, Chapter 2 introduces the framework used to study the governance around, and routines inside, three organizations that fund research for the developing world. The remainder of this chapter discusses what research governance is, and how it is changing.

Any particular funder is itself an agent to multiple principals, and is exposed to a diverse range of expectations. Public funders in particular are embedded in a nested set of relationships. At one level, one can describe research governance in Australia, Canada, or the United Kingdom and how it contrasts to research governance in continental Europe or the United States. Yet there are also distinct relationships that enable or constrain the actions of each funder. Benner (2011) distinguishes among three levels: the macro goals for public research and its role in relation to the political and economic systems; the meso-level of selecting, monitoring, and evaluation of research grants; and the micro-level of negotiated practice within academic and research organizations. Edgerton (2009) similarly acknowledges the existence of multiple levels, stating there "is no stable entity called science which is governed, worried about, applauded, condemned, invested in, much less understood. Each small part of 'science' is governed by many institutions, and many policies."

Research governance is also a coordination problem, to ensure sufficient investment to produce a public good. Markets are expected to underinvest in research due to the indivisibility, uncertainty, and externalities associated with the creation of new knowledge (Arrow 1962). Some benefits accrue to those that copy or use such knowledge, rather than those who undertake and underwrite the research (Helpman 2004). Private firms in particular tend to invest in near-market research for novel products and services that can create new demand and enjoy temporary rents. There is little incentive to invest in basic or fundamental research that cannot be easily captured or utilized by its creator or sponsor. Public funding is necessary to correct this market failure, encouraging work that is valuable to society, but underprovided by the market.

Research governance traditionally centered on the academic community, with interaction among peers to determine membership in the scientific community, to identify priority problems, and to consolidate accepted knowledge. Polanyi's (1962) "republic of science" describes scientists as working in isolation from markets and society, a self-organizing community in which members optimize their time and effort based on the results published by others. Science is coordinated through perceived merit—including considerations of plausibility, accuracy, importance, and originality—rather than through the market principles of price, consumer surplus, and efficiency. This self-organizing research governance offers only an indirect promise of public benefit, focusing instead on how a given work is valued among peers.

State interests also form part of research governance, with public funding tied to the expectation of outcomes valued by government. Stretching back to before the eighteenth century, royal patronage of scientists formed part of the competition among nations for international prestige, such as the UK prizes for new military or navigational technologies. In the twentieth century, Slaughter and Rhoades (1996) describe the United States as funding "Cold War science" under a Keynesian state, justified by a narrative of winning battles against communism, polio, and cancer. The country subsequently shifted toward a "competitiveness agenda" under the neoliberal state, justified by a narrative of increasing the number of jobs and growing the country's share of global markets. Although the country does fund curiosity-driven research, the majority of public research funds are directed through mission-oriented agencies such as the National Aeronautics and Space Administration (NASA), National Institutes of Health, and Departments of Defense and of Energy.

Australia, Canada, and the United Kingdom all experienced greater pressure to rationalize public spending after the 1970s. Before this time, a vibrant research community was a *sine qua non* for social progress, valued for generating fundamental discoveries and for contributing to the national missions, such as exploration, public health, and national defense. After the 1970s, policy increasingly embraced the rhetoric of market principles for organizing public research, justifying investments based on their expected return. Granting councils began to consider user involvement, policy relevance, and potential for commercialization, alongside the traditional criteria of peer review and academic credentials. There was greater attention to "demand pull" based on the societal relevance of research, over "science push" based on researchers' autonomy in setting their agenda.

Inspired by the new public management, governments moved away from direct bureaucratic control toward more indirect "steering" through setting research priorities and evaluating outcomes. Governments became more proactive in guiding their investments and demanding to know more about the effectiveness and efficiency of the research they were funding. Policymakers questioned whether the research they supported was relevant to current public issues, and demanded new forms of evidence to inform their decisions (UNESCO 2010). Researchers—and the organizations that supported them—were pressed to identify how their work benefited others (Boden et al. 2006, Jansen 2007, Schubert 2009, Stephan 2012). Whitley (2011) describes changes in the relative authority of different groups including government, funding agencies, research administrators, individual researchers and teams, national and international scientific elites, and commercial and other external interests. Wagner (2008) argues that the research process became more networked as individuals increasingly collaborate to share funding, data, tasks, and infrastructure. Policy goals and the allocation of funding became increasingly negotiated among policymakers, researchers, and potential "consumers." Control over the research agenda moved away from the scientific community and expert opinion (endogenous) toward the realm of public policy and government decision (exogenous).

Public research funders responded in various ways, adopting targeted programs aligned to government priorities and competitive allocation of funds, as well as additional selection criteria for research proposals and more evaluation of project results. Targeted programs earmark funding to priority areas of perceived public interest, including explicit objectives to develop new technology and contribute to economic growth. Such programs tend to use time-limited project grants for work on specific problems. Consequently, funders scaled back on core funding, or institutional block grants, available for research-performing organizations to allocate internally among their own departments and projects.

Competition for project grants requires research-performing organizations to be at arm's length from government, opening opportunities for new entrants into the research funding "market" and avoiding capture by established actors. Meanwhile a move to concentrate funding encouraged more intense research, in fewer areas, by a smaller number of increasingly specialized units (Polster 2003, Benner 2011). A rise in competitive bidding reduced the researcher's time horizon and heightened the importance of performance assessment (Whitley and Gläser 2007). The time within which research is expected to lead to interesting results has shortened, and the opportunities for financial support for idiosyncratic projects has declined.

Funders expanded their use of *ex ante* evaluation of research proposals and the *ex post* evaluation of project results. Traditionally peer review of academic quality was the sole selection criterion for deciding which proposals receive funding. Yet increasingly the notions of relevance and usefulness became more prominent in such decisions. In other words, the criterion of external validity rose in importance. Funders focused on policy questions driving the research agenda, rather than the researcher's disciplinary background or preferred method (Ravallion and Gelb 2010). Funders also moved to limit the portion of overall costs they were willing to support, requiring recipients to secure additional funding from other sources. This condition of co-funding was a market test, demonstrating that others valued the proposed work and were willing to invest in it.

In terms of evaluation, funders have adopted increasingly elaborate systems for performance assessment, subjecting their grants to greater scrutiny. Productivity is assessed in terms of the quantity of publications and patents produced, as well as their quality in terms of citations or licenses. There is also interest in measuring impact or outcomes, whether in terms of the monetary value created by patents, licenses, and start-up enterprises, or detailed assessments of how research findings are adopted by practitioners and inform the thinking and actions of policymakers.

This new governance is not without its critics, who fear research funding has veered toward seeking profit instead of truth. Demeritt (2000: 323) laments the shift "from a metaphorical market of ideas . . . to an actual market system," while Shove and Redclift (2001: 388) argue that "academics now have to 'sell' research ideas to policy communities and respond to non-academic competition, whilst maintaining conventional academic credentials."

Recent calls to demonstrate value for money gloss over potentially incommensurable ways of understanding research and its utility to society. Research is not only a production process, assessed according to the quantity of publications or selling price of patents. It is also a process of discovery, assessed according to the evidence of progress on problems. Ultimately, society is more concerned about finding a cure for cancer, rather than the number of articles written about it. Rip (2003) suggests that the literature is already moving away from a narrow focus on static efficiency and effectiveness, toward a more dynamic interest in the appropriateness of past actions and improving performance over time.

Meyer and Kearnes (2013: 423) observe an increased attention in academia to the policy instruments employed by science intermediaries, such as funding formulae, which these authors see as affecting the "institutional contexts of scientific practice," including the incentives that shape the behavior of researchers. Extending the arguments put forward by these authors, these incentives even shape the career decisions of young professionals, for example choosing to specialize in lab-based genomic research focused on developing new crops versus field-based extension work focused on the practices of farmers in rural areas. States have used competitive resource allocation among universities and public research organizations to push them toward research related to public policy goals and commercializing their findings. Such "steering" of research purpose implies a move away from disciplinary goals and core problems, toward research that contributes toward "solving" societal problems.

Key Points

There is no one accepted definition of research for the developing world. Instead, different funding organizations adopted distinct approaches and modified them over time. To understand why this is so, it is important to move beyond the principal–agent model and assess what was happening in the wider research governance which influenced these decisions and the organizational routines within each funder. Australia, Canada, and the United Kingdom witnessed a shift in research funding toward a narrower agenda predicated on "solving" problems, raising revenues, and reducing costs. Researchers no longer have unquestioned authority to allocate public funds and govern their own affairs. The governance of publicly funded research moved from a self-organized "republic of science," to market-inspired goals negotiated among policymakers, stakeholders, and research "consumers." Researchers—and the funding organizations that support them—must demonstrate the value of their work, not only in terms of scientific excellence in the eyes of peers, but in terms of its cost-effectiveness and its impact in areas relevant to those beyond academia.

This raises a fundamental question regarding the *value* of publicly funded research. How is research valued? By whom? And what is it expected to achieve? The answers to such questions form the first principles underlying why science is considered useful to society. Often unstated and implicit, the extent to which research policy and practice endorse one form of value over another has profound consequences. At the level of research funders, it affects how their performance is assessed: what constitutes "success" for a funding program, which lines of inquiry and which recipients are funded. At the level of individual researchers, teams, and centers, it exercises a powerful influence on research careers, determining which actions are rewarded, and shaping how researchers invest their time and effort. The idea of "research for the developing world" is to apply science and innovation to benefit disadvantaged people and resource-constrained places. Yet between this lofty aspiration and the mundane details of grantmaking, diverse funding programs embrace different first principles. The history of funders in Australia, Canada, and the United Kingdom is marked by a tension among supporting the interests of research communities at home or abroad, the interest of home governments in pursuing their foreign policy and trade relations, and the interests of host countries abroad in furthering their national development plans. Leadership requires designing programs that secure the support of multiple stakeholders by at least partially satisfying the different values each associates with public research.

Given the shifts in research governance at home, funders can be expected to have strengthened their upward accountability to home governments, weakening somewhat their downward accountability toward host countries and research communities. The criteria by which funders are judged—and on which they base their decisions—is expected to turn toward the utility of research for influential stakeholders at home, and away from its relevance and contribution to the host societies abroad. Research for the developing world originated with a vision of empowering host societies: building their capability to create and adapt knowledge in order to address the needs of their citizens and shape their own future. Yet as home governments came to expect more direct benefits from public research spending, they favored research that informs decision making on how to invest foreign aid dollars or how to address shared global challenges.

This chapter has introduced the ideas of research for the developing world, and the changing governance of public research in Australia, Canada, and the United Kingdom. Chapter 2 introduces the framework used to study the governance around, and the routines inside, three organizations that fund research for the developing world. The subsequent chapters examine each of these organizations, identifying distinct periods of time when the funder pursued a particular approach to its work. Understanding how and why these approaches evolved when they did provides insight into the extent to which such work was subjected to the changing governance noted in this chapter.

2

Research Funders

Adapting to Government Expectations

This chapter introduces the framework used to examine the governance context for public research, and the response by three organizations that fund research for the developing world. Chapter 1 described how the context of research governance evolved in recent decades, exposing funders to new expectations on what research is meant to achieve, coming from a changing set of stakeholders. Yet research funding organizations are not passive. Leadership within these funders selects which expectations to respond to, and which to ignore. These choices influence how the funders craft various program offerings, which aim to maintain credibility with both their government sponsors and potential grant seekers in the research community.

Research governance is examined as a performance regime which includes expectations emanating from multiple sources, such as parliament, ministers, line departments, central agencies, beneficiaries, and public opinion (Talbot 2010). At any given moment, the viability of a public organization depends on achieving a connection between what the organization does and what such entities consider to be good performance. In essence, there is not a single government voice telling public organizations what to do, instead they have to contend with multiple principals shaping various dimensions of the policy space within which the organization operates. Yet performance regimes are not static, and the notions of what constitutes good performance do change over time.

Funders are adaptive organizations that build upon past experience and selectively decide how to respond to changing expectations. Research funders periodically renew their priorities and programs, and evolve certain patterns in how they engage with the research community and support research activities. In this way, research for development (R4D) funders learn by testing and refining different program theories (how they understand their actions contribute to international development). Successful experiences are codified into the grantmaking practices the funder uses to support research: who is eligible for funding, how to support them, and how research is used.

Performance Regimes

Dismayed at the diversity of approaches to performance management, Talbot (2010) argues for a coming together of theories. He posits that such a unified framework could involve three parts: *models* that identify both results and the factors that enable them, attention to *regimes* of power holders and the tools they utilize to shape performance of public organizations, and the public *values* that guide these power holders and public servants. His concept of "performance regime" is the ensemble of such formal and informal influences that direct public sector service delivery, through formal and informal cooperation and competition (Talbot 2008). This concept can be tailored to the context of the public entity under study, whether a research funder or a health ministry. These two entities are subject both to common and unique expectations. In the same country they are both subject to performance tools emanating from central agencies, yet are also accountable to distinct ministers and different sets of stakeholders. Such a regime is akin to the institutional setting (cf. Ostrom 2005), but emphasizes the model of performance held by influential actors and how their understanding is grounded in public values.

Talbot draws attention to the first principles underpinning a study of performance, the often unstated assumptions regarding the nature of reality (ontology), how one can know this reality (epistemology), and the techniques for knowing (methodology). He argues that many studies of performance start from weak or distorted theoretical assumptions about the behavior and motivations of individuals and organizations. He identifies four key problems including defining the unit of analysis and its boundaries, determining what is included (and excluded) from the concept of performance, choosing techniques to measure it (qualitatively, quantitatively, client satisfaction), and identifying the political implications of pursuing multiple values simultaneously. As noted in Chapter 1, certain areas of public policy are subject to multiple competing goals, including research for the developing world.

Talbot's performance regime thus combines the institutional context of actors and the powers they possess to steer public organizations, with performance interventions or the actions these actors undertake to influence the performance of public organizations. Talbot (2010: 83) identifies this as a realist approach, based in historical institutionalism that can be used to analyze changing governance of performance over time. He sees performance as both "brute facts" and socially constructed meanings attached to such facts.

The dimensions of performance are epistemologically real, as are the positions, attitudes, and beliefs held by real groups and individuals. Talbot cites Moore's triad of *public value* (1995) as delivering public services, achieving social outcomes, and maintaining trust and legitimacy; as well as Fried's triad of *ethics* (1976), including responsiveness to public demand (democratic ethic), compliance with rules (legal ethic), and economy in the use of resources (work ethic). His argument is that the sum of such varied influences shapes or steers performance for specific organizations.

Talbot draws on resource-dependence theory (Pfeffer and Salanick 1978), which sees organizations as successful if they can gather resources from their external environment, meeting competing demands from external stakeholders in exchange for the supply of resources. He also cites resource-based theories of the firm that concentrate on the internal capabilities, capacities, and resources of the organization (Barney and Clark 2007). With its emphasis on position relative to diverse power holders and stakeholders, the concept of a performance regime embodies insights from organizational studies. For example, Baum (1996) argues for understanding an organization's niche, benchmarking it against comparator firms, identifying how its services differ from what is offered by others. Poister et al. (2010) argue that organizational performance is a matter of fit with the surrounding context and operating environment, and requires periodic repositioning to maintain such a fit.

Performance regime thus acknowledges the institutional landscape within which a public organization finds itself. At its simplest, this means identifying where an organization fits within the bureaucracy, including its reliance on other entities for information, resources, and legitimacy. A map of the performance regime begins with the principal–agent model, tracing the formal lines of authority from the funder upwards into their home government and downwards into the research community. Next the map identifies power holders and stakeholders—in the public and private sector, at home and abroad—that might influence performance, yet stops short of uncovering their behavior, motivations, and expectations. In practice, public organizations are more responsive to actors such as the cabinet office and treasury, and less so to line departments outside their portfolio or distant from their mandate. As research for the developing world bridges the domains of public research, development cooperation, and foreign policy, it is useful to understand the structure, rationale, and performance within each of these policy domains.

The top part of Table 2.1 lists the indicators used to analyze performance regime. *Structure* refers to the legal entities that occupy the policy domains and how they are organized, such as research-granting councils, the foreign office, and aid agencies. *Rationale* refers to the narrative used to justify spending in these areas, including each entity's goals and scope of action, such as national

Table 2.1. Framework used in case studies

Context	Performance regime	Structure	Legal and organizational structure of public research funding and of foreign aid
		Rationale	Narrative used to justify funding, including national research priorities and the thematic and geographic aid priorities
		Performance	Mechanisms for allocating research grants and aid projects (intended outcomes and tools to assess each)
		Stakeholders	Additional expectations of funder's performance and the mechanisms used to enforce them (e.g. central agencies)
Agency	Program theory	Position	Changes in the funder's organizational structure, staffing, budget, leadership, or reporting relations
		Theory of change	What the funder sought to achieve, including the focus of its grantmaking programs
		Evidence	Information cited to demonstrate the funder's performance
	Grantmaking practice	Selection	Criteria and process for choosing recipients and funding proposals (e.g. location, nationality, excellence, relevance)
		Role	Daily tasks of staff, their interactions with recipients, and contribution to the research process
		Portfolio	Description of the grants made by the funder, including the recipients and types of support offered
		Implications	Incentives provided to the scientific community, and what the funder expected of its recipients

research priorities or the thematic and geographic focus within foreign aid. This is the context for defining *performance*, including the mechanisms used to allocate funding, the intended outcomes, and the tools used for assessment. Performance criteria will differ between public research and foreign policy, yet research for the developing world must satisfy both.

Beyond these policy domains, other *stakeholders* also hold expectations and possess mechanisms to enforce them, such as the governing party and the central agencies, including the cabinet office or treasury. These bodies shape the broader policy agenda, issue directives, and ultimately control the public purse strings. At the same time, the research community in each country has a more or less organized "science lobby" that actively courts government to influence research policy. Public entities must maintain their credibility with various actors who hold their own perspectives on performance. Funders can be expected to adopt programs that resonate with the multiple expectations of influential actors—within and beyond the domains of public research and foreign policy—including statements regarding the perceived research strengths of the home country.

Mapping power holders and stakeholders and their expectations permit a more detailed description of the governance context. This information provides insights into what drives changes in governance and whether this is due to shifts in resource availability, public management, or research management. These drivers are introduced below and will be revisited in the three comparative case studies in Chapter 3–5. These case studies explore the links between changes in the governance context for strategic planning and organizational response for performance improvements (Poister et al. 2010). The case studies are based on a combination of archival research, document review, and original interviews conducted in 2012 in Australia, Canada, and the United Kingdom. Quotes from respondents are from these original interviews.

The importance of *resources available* is self-evident: funders cease to exist without public money for their programs. The rise and fall of budgets influences the scale of such programs. Waves of budget growth permit funders the opportunity to expand their work, while waves of austerity require them to be more focused. Less evident are the conditions placed upon access to such funding—both the expectations placed on the funder when it receives additional money and the scrutiny it receives during periods of austerity. Such conditions can cascade down to potential grantees and force the funder to alter its selection and evaluation criteria. For example, programs can limit grants to a certain percentage of overall project costs or require that grantees interact with particular stakeholders, such as local communities, policymakers, or the private sector.

Public management is understood here as the ideas on the purpose, role, and operation of government. Public research funders are embedded within government and respond to waves of ideas on how they should organize themselves, including the functions of planning, evaluation, and performance management. At times, funders were left to simply pursue their own mandate, while at other times they were expected to make a contribution within a "whole-of-government" agenda. Such ideas shape the opportunities to support research for the developing world, and how funders relate to other parts of government, including the cabinet, the foreign ministry, and central agencies.

Research policy encompasses the decision-making processes over priority setting, the allocation of funds, and the management of research institutes and the assessment of their performance (OECD 2003). As described in Chapter 1, the pressure to rationalize public expenditures has prompted governments to become more proactive in directing their investments to areas expected to generate higher returns. Governments want to know more about the effectiveness and efficiency of the research they fund. These pressures led to changes in the policy and programs for publicly funded research, reshaping the ideas of "good practice" in supporting research for the developing world.

Adaptive Organizations

The performance regime provides the governance context within which research funders continually renegotiate how to pursue their mandate. Yet outside influences do not automatically translate into new directions. To gain traction and affect the organization's behavior, these influences must be taken up inside and inform internal decisions. Only then do influences begin to affect which problems warrant investment and the types of support offered to recipients. This section draws on ideas from strategic planning and program evaluation to reveal how funders adapt their program theory and reorient their grantmaking practices over time.

Organizations exercise their agency—the ability to act or intervene—when mediating the various expectations placed upon them. They do not passively respond to the whims of others. Whereas a legislative mandate forms a point of departure, management elaborates and over time modifies its approach toward implementing this mandate. Corporate strategies, strategic plans, and annual reports provide an initial articulation of this thinking. Strategic planning is a "disciplined effort to produce fundamental decisions and actions that shape and guide what an organization (or other entity) is, what it does, and why it does it" (Bryson 2004: 26). The concept of corporate strategy has evolved over time through a sequence of ideas, including: managing by objectives, creating synergies among complementary lines of business, maximizing shareholder value, and identifying core competencies (Faulker and Campbell 2003). A recent definition describes strategic planning "as a process for clarifying mandates and goals, scanning the environment for threats and opportunities, identifying strategic issues and ways of dealing with them, developing outcome measures and how to track progress" (KPMG 2008).

Mintzberg (2007) differentiates among four ways of understanding strategy: as a plan to guide an organization's future action, its position compared to others, its perspective on its role and purpose, and the pattern of organizational routines that emerged from past experience. Strategy as position reflects concerns of "niche" and "fitness," finding and maintaining a viable space in the operating environment, remaining competitive within the industry, and supported by public policy (Poister et al. 2010). By examining the governance context, the first part of the framework addresses this position. The second part of the framework employed here builds on Mintzberg's concepts of strategy as perspective and pattern.

Within the field of evaluation, *program theory* is the proposed causal explanation of how change occurs, and how the organization's actions are understood to contribute to that change (Rogers 2000). It involves assumptions regarding how the organization's activities contribute to real-world results. Funnel and Rogers (2011: xix) define program theory as "an explicit theory or model of how an intervention . . . contributes to a chain of intermediate results and finally to the intended or observed outcomes." These authors identify four general theories about how change occurs—reasoned action, empowerment, diffusion, and socio-ecological networks—each of which addresses different causal mechanisms. *Reasoned action* focuses on how human behavior is shaped by beliefs and attitudes regarding the consequences of that same behavior (e.g. health and safety training). *Empowerment* focuses on how the people affected by a particular problem can organize and act to address that problem (e.g. community development projects). *Diffusion* focuses on how ideas and innovations are invented, shared, adopted, or rejected among people (e.g. the spread of agricultural techniques). *Networks* focus how relationships among actors can enhance or constrain their actions (e.g. promoting policy change through political coalitions). Each of these theories can address different levels where change is expected to occur whether within an individual, organization, policy, or community. Each theory of change embodies particular assumptions, values, and ideologies.

Based on these four general theories of change, Funnel and Rogers (2011) identify five general categories of interventions, each with a distinct underlining logic. *Information* programs seek outcomes by educating a client through advice and understanding that encourages her or him to adopt the desired change. *Carrot-and-stick* programs seek outcomes by providing various incentives and sanctions intended to facilitate the desired change. *Case management* programs are tailor-made and "work with each case in a way that recognizes that . . . there are likely to be many and varied factors, many individualized intermediate outcomes, and many different processes for getting there" (2011: 367). *Capacity-building* programs seek outcomes by empowering clients to enhance their skills and ability over time so they are able to exercise greater control over their lives, while the *direct delivery* programs seek outcomes by providing a product or service. Overall, research for the developing world is rooted in information program theory: the belief that new knowledge and technology will change the opportunities for international development (Arrow 1962, World Bank 1998, Helpman 2004, Molenaar et al. 2009). Yet, as shown in subsequent chapters, organizations can simultaneously embody multiple program theories and grantmaking practices, as well as shift between different ones over time.

Program evaluation accepts and examines the distinction between what an organization intends to do—its explicit strategy or program theory—and what it actually does, or the implementation of that theory. Where Funnel and Rogers refer to theory of change and interventions, Chen (2005) distinguishes between a change model and an action model. The former includes the goals and outcomes, and the determinants understood to cause the problem the organization seeks to address, and identifies the interventions employed by the organization to change those determinants. In contrast, Chen's action model is the delivery protocols and plans for arranging the organization and ensuring a supportive environment.

In program evaluation, the absence of an expected outcome may be due to failure of strategy or implementation. The former is related to how one expects the world to work, while the latter is related to how one organizes to bring about that change. Thus it is possible to correctly implement a program theory that fails due to incorrect assumptions regarding how interventions actually work, and it is possible to have appropriate interventions that are incorrectly implemented. Chen (2005: 247) describes this distinction as the sound implementation of faulty causality (conceptual model failure) versus the faulty implementation of sound causality (action theory failure).

Chapters 3–5 are not concerned with the validity of the program theory per se, but identify when and why funders changed their understanding of research for the developing world. Indeed, corporate strategies seldom describe program theory in detail sufficient to serve as a basis for program evaluation. For this book, it is sufficient to identify notional program theories that guided grantmaking at different times, including when and why these shifts occurred. These are moments when the organization changed its "strategy as perspective," one means by which organizations respond to new pressures in the surrounding governance context. In contrast, an organization's "strategy as pattern" is embodied within the grantmaking practices, the everyday operations and routines that stem in part from past experience.

In the case studies in Chapters 3–5, program theory is analyzed using the indicators of position, theory of change, and evidence used in assessing performance (Table 2.1). *Position* describes how the funder organized itself, noting when there were significant changes in staffing, budget, leadership, organizational structure, or reporting relationships. The sum of these attributes speaks to where the funder fitted into the performance regime, and suggests the relative influence of external actors in prompting such changes. This serves to identify when there was continuity or when the funder was undergoing a period of transformation, highlighting moments of disjuncture that warrant further attention.

Theory of change is revealed through statements of what the funder sought to achieve and its choice of programs, which in turn showed how the funder opted to address certain problems over others. If available, data gathered for this indicator capture the criteria the organization used to select, elaborate, and approve different funding envelopes or programs. On occasion, this is stated explicitly in written documents, but is more often uncovered through interviews or deduced from program choice. Finally, *evidence* refers to the information cited by the funder to demonstrate its performance. This indicator notes the arguments employed at a corporate level to justify public spending, as well as the type of information the funder collects in determining the extent to which its programs are successful.

Attention to *grantmaking practice* is warranted for two reasons. First, while a research funder might pursue multiple program theories simultaneously—using different funding envelopes—the range of grantmaking practices is more limited. Second, organizational pattern can be more persistent than strategic perspective, as the grantmaking practices that guide staff may endure despite changes in corporate strategy and its embedded program theory. Public research funders are not exactly analogous to competitive firms, and *research strategy* is distinct from corporate strategy. The two overlap to the extent that research strategy involves the high-level choice regarding which problems to work on, and an explicit or implied calculation of expected return from investing in each. Yet research strategy is embedded in the organizational routines as a heuristic search process, "the procedures used to identify and screen research projects" (Nelson and Winter 1977: 52).

Grantmaking practices are "strategy as pattern." They serve as informal heuristics stemming as much from operational experience as from the formal program theory crafted by management. Paarlberg and Bielefeld (2009) argue that staff rely on simple heuristics that provide guidance in identifying priority, boundaries, timing, and exit—in other words rules of thumb regarding what is important, what is within and beyond program limits, when to act, and when to stop. Such rules-in-practice (cf. Ostrom 2005) are given life through the norms created by staff in carrying out their daily work of selecting proposals, setting funding procedures, monitoring current grants, and evaluating their results.

Grantmaking practice emerges from organizational learning and can circulate back into program theory. Subsequent generations of corporate strategy also formalize what was learned, rather than merely responding to stakeholder expectations. In other words, organizations do not necessarily reinvent themselves to match what the performance regime judges to be politically feasible. They also incorporate learned experience into future efforts to improve operations. This understanding of grantmaking practice echoes Nelson and Winter's (1977, 1982) description of how markets select among competing innovations and reinforce the position of certain standards over time. The result is that practices, routines, and innovations are influenced in part by past success and failure: some are ignored while others are picked up and "locked in" over time. Building on this insight, the literature on the economics of innovation (cf. Lundvall 1988) argues that past learning is embodied in the daily routines of staff.[1] Grantmaking practice is thus evolutionary, as a

[1] One such innovation is the use of a "milestone" approach which ties grant payments to different deliverables or progress markers during the project. Milestones provide evidence on

research funder's past experience shapes its approach to research for the developing world.

Research funding programs also evolve through interaction with the scientific community. Each program creates a funding envelope, articulating a thematic focus and desired outcomes, yet the substantive content comes from the proposals submitted. Programs are co-created as the funders' ambitions are mediated by the response from grantseekers who apply for support (Shove 2003). Research funding programs can thus grow and unfold in unpredictable ways, as each project carries with it the recipient's interests and history of prior research. This opens opportunities for program implementation to differ from program theory, as some intended actions are unrealized and some realized actions are unintended (Mintzberg 2007).

In the case studies in Chapter 3–5, grantmaking practice is analyzed using the indicators of selection, role, portfolio, and implications (Table 2.1). The overall purpose is to look beyond program theory in the abstract; to examine how funders implemented program theory in practice and how they used the resources available. In this sense, grantmaking practice is tailored to the work performed by research funders, and could easily be relabeled "organizational routines" in keeping with the literature on the economics of innovation. *Selection* refers to the criteria and process used to choose recipients and funding proposals. This indicator collects information on whether access to funding is restricted to particular countries (eligibility) and the criteria by which funding proposals are judged, such as: the qualifications and expertise of the proponent; the feasibility, originality, and relevance of the proposed work; engagement with stakeholders in the research process; and the work's potential contribution to knowledge or development outcomes. This indicator also notes how a funder gathers project proposals, whether through competitive calls, unsolicited submissions, or encouraging talented researchers to apply.

Role focuses on the real-life tasks of staff, rather than what the funding organization perceives as its contribution to the research process. This indicator draws on job descriptions and hearing former members of staff recount their personal experiences. A researcher's impression depends more on their specific experience of interaction with an individual program officer or coordinator than on their impression of a funding organization in general. The dynamic balance between government and the scientific community is reflected in how members of staff allocate their time. Beyond monitoring the project progress, staff make an intellectual contribution through such tasks as engaging recipients on research design and methods, connecting

how the research is progressing and, if necessary, offer an opportunity to redesign or reschedule future milestones to respond to any difficulties encountered. This approach requires staff with the expertise needed to engage recipients in the substance of their work.

them to peers working on similar problems elsewhere, and ensuring that the funder's programs built upon the state-of-the-art in different fields of knowledge. Thus, rather than starting with corporate strategy and looking at how it was enacted by staff, it is valuable to examine what staff do and identify what guides these efforts.

Portfolio refers to the actual grants made by the funder, including the types of support offered and the profile of recipients. Grant databases and annual reports provide information on the location and type of institutions that received funding (e.g. universities, government, for-profits, and not-for-profits whether located in the home country, in an advanced economy, or in a developing country). Finally, *implications* describes what the funder expected of its recipients, and consequently provides incentives for certain types of work, and to certain segments of the research community. As will be seen in subsequent chapters, funders can fail to attract the attention of prospective recipients if there is a mismatch between its programs, and the career aspirations or other incentives shaping the research community.

This chapter has introduced the framework used to analyze three research funding organizations, one each from the United Kingdom, Canada, and Australia. All three support research for the developing world, but evolved different program theories and grantmaking practices over time, in part due to changes in the governance context. Talbot's performance regime builds upon the principal–agent model to describe the ensemble of expectations emanating from power holders and stakeholders, and their tools and mechanisms for shaping public performance. Yet a look inside is necessary to identify which of these influences gained traction within each organization.

3

United Kingdom

Between Haldane and Rothschild

Among the three case studies covered in this book, the United Kingdom has the longest history of supporting research in the developing world. Early milestones include the founding of the Asiatic Society in 1784 and the Imperial Institute in 1887. Long before the modern era of foreign aid began after the Second World War, support for research was a well-established part of colonial administration, fragmented among different government departments. The Overseas Development Administration (ODA) thus inherited a tradition of funding research, which it divided into different thematic divisions. In this century, the new Department for International Development (DFID) consolidated this funding into a single unit within its policy division. Throughout these organizational changes, research had to compete for space and budget within an agency that was also responsible for bilateral, multilateral, and humanitarian assistance.

This chapter identifies distinct periods when research for the developing world was subjected to different expectations and adopted different goals (Figure 3.1). Initially, the performance regime was characterized by self-governance of research funding, under which scientific communities allocated funding among peers. The program theory guiding research funding was focused on maintaining a base of UK science specialized in the problems of tropical climates. This inspired grantmaking around core support to highly qualified people and established centers within the scientific community at home, part of which resided within government laboratories. In the next period, starting in the 1970s, the governance context encouraged a division between those who performed research and those who commissioned it. This period saw government exit service delivery, spinning off its scientific units to the academic or private sector. Program theory focused on purchasing knowledge and outcomes of interest to the aid agency. This gave rise to a

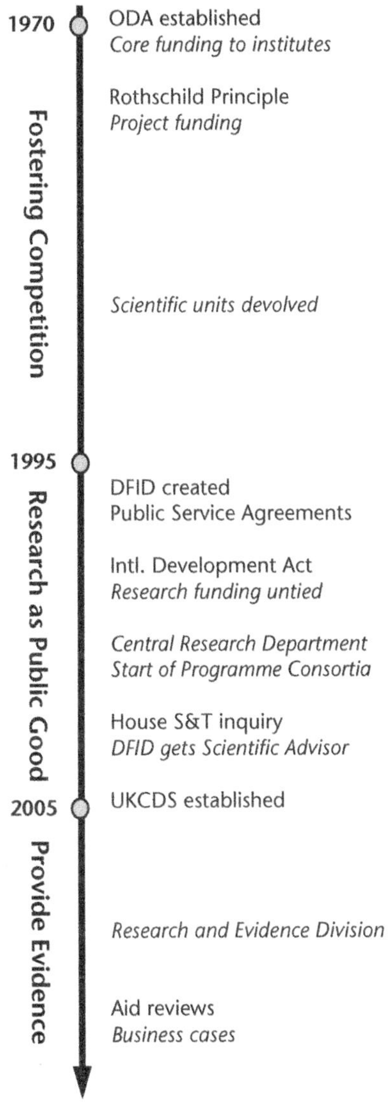

Figure 3.1. Timeline of UK case study

quasi-market pattern of project funding under which researchers would bid for the opportunity to contribute to the aid agency's work programs.

During the subsequent period, beginning in the 2000s, the aid agency received an increasing level of resources and a legislated mandate to contribute to global poverty reduction. Program theory saw research as a form of public good, placed at the service of furthering a global development agenda negotiated with other donors. Grantmaking practice evolved to include greater support to recipients located abroad and a move to larger projects, networks, and consortia of grantees. During the following period, the governance context re-emphasized ties with UK science, including notions of scientific excellence, rising scrutiny of foreign aid, and downward pressure on operating costs. Program theory embraced the potential for technology to change the lives of poor women and men, as well as the potential for research to inform an evidence-based approach to policy. Correspondingly, grantmaking expanded to include partnerships with the UK research councils, continued rise in average project size, and renewed consideration of how research informs the "value of money" of aid investments.

Origins

Research for the developing world emerged out of the political reality of the British Empire. UK science expanded in the eighteenth and nineteenth centuries as the Industrial Revolution reshaped the economy at home, and Britain coordinated a loose network of colonies abroad. Researchers roamed around the empire to study local phenomena different than what was found at home. Colonial and overseas administrators—driven by the goal of producing resources for trade—saw value in geology, land surveys, medicine, and agriculture to better understand and exploit the holdings they were responsible for. In short, research helped Britain understand and run the world, supported by an array of scientific institutions at home and abroad.

The Haldane reports in 1905 and 1918 mark a key point in UK science policy. As Secretary of State for War, and later Lord Chancellor, Richard Haldane chaired parliamentary committees that shaped the research funding landscape. The first report led to the creation of the University Grants Committee, providing block grants to institutions of higher education. The second report led to the UK research councils, providing scholarships and project funding for individual researchers. This second report (Cd 9230) established a distinction between funding allocated by scientists (to further the frontiers of knowledge) and funding allocated by government (for work that responded to the needs of each department).

Haldane was thus responsible for introducing a distinction between basic and applied research, and providing different funding streams for each. In this way, Haldane hoped to address a lag in UK military technology revealed by the First World War. Inspired by the then-new science of aviation—which integrated both basic and applied science—he sought to prepare the country for future challenges. Over time, the first part of this idea was reinterpreted as a "Haldane principle" that the research community should collectively determine its own priorities and allocate public funding. To this day, the Haldane principle is seen as a right to self-governance in the sciences, invoked to defend against the threat of government interference. This interpretation is not entirely accurate of Haldane's recommendations (Edgerton 2009). Indeed, research for the developing world was influenced more by the second part of Haldane's idea which led to government departments obtaining a budget line for applied research.

Between 1919 and 1930, the colonial office funded "poorer Colonies and Protectorates in conducting the necessary researches." Overseen by a Colonial Research Committee, the primary focus was the study and exploitation of local minerals, agriculture, animal health, forestry, and fisheries. Colonial science policy first coalesced in the early 1920s as the British government pondered the fate of scientific institutes in former German colonies in Africa (Worboys 1996). The Colonial Development Act 1929 provided grants and loans for the promotion of scientific research, complementing the Rockefeller Foundation funding in the 1920s to expand the London School of Hygiene and Tropical Medicine. In 1938, Lord Hailey's "African Survey" called for investing in research, drawing on British institutions which were seen as having better-qualified personnel and "the conditions, facilities and atmosphere necessary for good research work" (Jefferies 1964: 20). The Colonial Development and Welfare Act (1940) included a call for £50 million over ten years for development, and a separate amount of £5 million for research. By establishing this dedicated budget line, the Act recognized research as a distinct activity from building roads or infrastructure. This research fund was subsequently doubled to £1 million per year in 1946 and made an ongoing line item in the budget with no expiry. Jefferies (1964: 23) notes the Act embodied a conviction that research much be conceived on a long-term basis, noting: "The initiating of a project frequently involves a commitment for years ahead, and can only be undertaken if there is certainty that the necessary funds will be available and not subject to the hazards of a periodical re-submission to Parliament."

Hence the governance context privileged natural science inquiry to optimize the use of natural resources abroad, drawing on the scientific community at home. Britain established local institutions abroad to provide knowledge needed to plan and exploit local resources, and cultivated world-class research centers at home knowledgeable about the places and problems in tropical climates.

After the Second World War, the governance context sought the independence of former colonies and gained new faith in mission-oriented science. Britain and other war-weary economies had utilized their overseas colonies to draw in resources and benefits from world trade, yet the colonies were now more of a burden than a bounty. It was more cost-effective to let the colonies run their own affairs. At the same time, the war had injected optimism in the potential for public research. New technologies, such as radar, had emerged from government funding and concentrated effort, a model that would inspire research policy for decades.

As Britain negotiated the independence of its former colonies, scientific infrastructure abroad was akin to the children of a couple filing for divorce. The product of an earlier era, the soon-to-be independent countries had an array of local scientific establishments, ranging from departments of agriculture and health, to universities and field stations. With the newfound faith in science, there were great expectations that these establishments would be a motor for development: informing local government with needed knowledge and providing local industries with useful technologies. Britain could not simply abandon this infrastructure, as it relied on outside funding and skilled personnel. Thus Britain initially accepted an ongoing responsibility for research abroad, until the local economy could take over.

Between 1940 and 1960, Britain allocated £24 million to research at home and abroad intended to benefit the developing world. Funds were allocated through six different committees drawing in members from across multiple government departments. Together the committees formed the Colonial Research Council which provided financial support for local scientific institutions abroad. It also supported scientific units at home, including the Commonwealth Agricultural Bureaux, the London School of Hygiene and Tropical Medicine, and government labs such as the Transport Research Laboratory. These units, specialized in the problems of tropical climates, were seen as a unique, "world-class" service that was not available abroad.

The next decade saw a number of organizational changes. The council replaced the word "colonial" in its name, to become the Overseas Research Council. Its updated mandate was "to advise on . . . policy in respect of scientific research undertaken in or for overseas territories . . . of methods of making the results of research available in these territories; and of assistance to the scientific services of those territories" (Jefferies 1964: 40). The council initially provided budget support for the operating costs of local institutes abroad, as well as travel grants that enabled visits by expatriate specialists to work and train abroad. The former loose, cross-government structure was replaced with a formal Department of Technical Cooperation, bringing together expertise on colonial development and incorporating a number of previously independent research centers. In 1964, this department became the Ministry of Overseas Development, recognizable as Britain's foreign aid agency.

In summary, the initial period was characterized by self-governance under which scientific communities allocated funding among peers. Program theory focused on maintaining a base of UK science specialized in the problems of tropical climates. This inspired grantmaking around core support to highly qualified people and established centers at home within the UK, part of which resided within government laboratories.

Fostering Competition

In the 1970s, the governance context for public research began to shift toward fostering competition among researchers. Edward Heath's Conservative government (1970–4) created a central policy review team in the Cabinet Office as an internal think tank to aid government problem solving. Lord Victor Rothschild was appointed to lead this team and introduced the largest shift in UK research policy since Haldane. Rothschild's framework called for customer–contractor relationships between those that funded and performed research. Under his vision: "Departments, as customers, define their requirements; contractors advise on the feasibility of meeting them and undertake the work; and the arrangements between them must be such as to ensure that the objectives remain attainable within reasonable cost" (Cmnd 5046, 1972).

Rothschild's principle of customer–contractor relations became the new cornerstone of UK research policy. Government was now seen as a purchaser of knowledge services within a marketplace, in which there were assumed to be a large number of potential service providers. Government was no longer expected to be a mere patron of research, but an "intelligent consumer" of it: able to absorb available knowledge and independently determine the need for new research. Yet the Rothschild principle faced three issues during implementation. First, the research "market" for specialized fields—such as trypanosomiasis and locust control—was oligopolistic, with a small number of well-connected researchers at one or two institutes. Second, few departments had the technical expertise required to review and synthesize existing knowledge, much less design a call for proposals and conduct merit review. Third, departments faced the dilemma of what to do with the scientists on staff and research centers dependent on government funding.

The first two issues were addressed by establishing teams of advisors within each department on the scientific aspects of government policy. These advisors were to act as honest brokers, taking in ideas from the outside, to define competitive bids based on departmental objectives. Advisors consulted the research community on the feasibility of meeting particular requirements, yet excluded that community from government's priority setting and funding decisions. The third issue proved more difficult. Departments faced a practical reality of needing to provide for the short-term survival of their scientific units while reducing their medium-term reliance on government funding. In practice, calls for proposals need to provide some support to preferred providers. Such was the challenge that research for the developing world would soon face.

Yet foreign aid was initially protected as government looked first at defense and health. After merging into the Foreign and Commonwealth Office, Britain's foreign aid agency was renamed the Overseas Development

Administration (ODA). The ODA housed a number of scientific units and provided core funding for many more. It even began to prepare an annual report on its research activities, noting that "British scientists have a long history of achievement in helping to tackle the problems of the tropical and semitropical areas," and describing research as the "adaptation of existing technologies to the circumstances of countries which are tropical and underdeveloped" (ODM 1974). Research funding grew fourfold over the decade, from under £4 million to almost £14 million per year. The bulk of this funding was dedicated to grants for research projects carried out on a contract basis by individual researchers or teams and the recurrent costs of centers in Britain which gave scientific and technical help to the developing countries. ODA also provided support for international research cooperation and research in developing countries. ODA initially provided core funding to maintain research institutes abroad, yet soon switched to project funding "to solve specific problems... outside the financial or technical capacity of local programmes" (ODA 1980). Local governments were expected to assume responsibility for the ongoing operating costs.

By the mid-1970s, ODA acknowledged the Rothschild principle, but implemented it half-heartedly. ODA argued that it "... interprets to its research 'contractors' the needs of its overseas 'customers' and commissions work on their behalf" (ODM 1975). In other words, ODA saw itself as a proxy customer, representing the demands of developing countries, which were limited in their ability to fund research or influence the UK research community. Project ideas were assessed according to "scientific soundness..., the degree to which they met the Ministry's criteria, and their claims for financial support" (ODM 1975). ODA began to emphasize the potential for research to inform practice abroad: "the results should filter down to those who really need to know—the farmer in the field, the workers at the bench and the doctors and nurses in the bush" (ODM 1977).

Yet the presence of a Labour-majority government (1974–9) temporarily reduced the pressure to implement Rothschild. ODA continued to deal incrementally with the array of funding relations it had inherited at home and abroad, with a large number of scientists relying on ODA directly as government employees or indirectly through research grants.

Neoliberal Values Ascendant

The United Kingdom then entered a period of reforms under Margaret Thatcher's Conservative government (1979–87) which revived the Rothschild principle. The House of Commons (1983) noted that "scientific research... should be subject to 'customer–contractor' relationships, whereby work is commissioned by a paying customer." The result was a "marketization of research" with changes in the form of public ownership, its organization, and governance (Boden et al. 2004). In the words of one respondent, "there was a sword of Damocles hanging over social sciences in Britain."[1] Thatcher's government felt public research had a "provider mentality" in pursuing its own curiosity, oblivious to whether or not it had any public impact. Government expected every public institution to be aware of its costs and able to demonstrate public benefit. As the reforms curtailed research performed with government, a greater portion of public research was performed within universities.

The Conservative government soon called for scrutiny reports on ODA's scientific units. In 1980, the research budget exceeded £15 million per year and the in-house scientific units employed more than 1,000 scientists and support staff. As a result of the reports, the Directorate of Overseas Surveys—which provided mapping services to developing countries—lost two-thirds of its staff and began to commission aerial surveys from private companies rather than conducting them in-house. Similarly, two of ODA's units were merged to form the Tropical Development and Research Institute. The House of Commons complained that "though purporting to deal with efficiency, [the reports] largely ignored benefits and were concerned almost exclusively with costs . . . the 'Rothschild principle' is of only limited applicability to the kind of work [these units] do" (House of Commons 1983). Yet the complaint fell on deaf ears. Indeed, a subsequent wave of reforms starting in 1988 would see government move a number of functions out of the bureaucracy into quasi-independent "executive agencies" to be run as corporations. This Next Steps Initiative essentially split the role of providing advice and implementing policy, establishing market-inspired arrangements between ministries and these executive agencies.

ODA needed to demonstrate that it was serious about the government's concerns, including the usefulness of outputs and a commitment to efficiency. It adopted an "emphasis . . . on research likely to be of practical use in a reasonable period of time, and . . . of direct relevance to the poorer sectors of poorer countries" (ODA 1988). More significantly, ODA began to divest itself of its scientific units, particularly those related to agriculture and the natural environment. To ease the transition, ODA needed to find a way of supporting its former scientific units while also presenting the image of consumer–contractor relations with the scientific community. The challenge was to rationalize funding to see these organizations move to new ownership.

[1] Quotes from respondents are from original interviews conducted by the author in 2012.

In the words of one respondent, "the size of investment was determined by how much do these institutions require to survive."

The response was five thematic work programs which laid out priorities toward which research grants were supposed to contribute. In the words of one respondent, these programs were "based on a logframe: we would define purpose and goals, and we would then contract out; the competing bodies would come back with objectives, activities and resources." The largest was the Renewable Natural Resources Research Strategy—affectionately known as the "yellow brick"—which lasted for fifteen years. In short, whereas ODA had previously been a fairly responsive funder, allowing recipients to pursue their own goals, it became more proactive, expecting recipients to contribute to a program of its own design.

In essence, ODA altered its relationship with the scientific community. Having already shifted from core to project funding abroad, it now similarly revised its offer to the scientific community at home, requiring them to fit their interests within a larger thematic strategy. Reflecting this shift, ODA stopped describing its research portfolio as "support to British scientific establishments" in favor of "R&D programmes... managed and carried out by centres in the UK" (ODA 1992). Grantmaking moved to a combination of competitively awarded projects and progressive independence of organizations reliant on ODA.

The End of an Era

Reforms to UK research policy accelerated further under John Major's Conservative government (1987–97). The *Realising Our Potential* White Paper called for public research money to be directed toward contributing to wealth creation and quality of life. This imperative was even applied to the UK research councils, requiring them to reformulate their missions toward these goals and toward responding to "users", including "industrial or service sectors, private and public, as well as central and local Government" (Cm 2250, 1993). Two of the research councils were merged to create the Biotechnology and Biological Sciences Research Council (BBSRC), and the Economic and Social Research Council (ESRC) began to relate part of its budget to national priorities in order to satisfy its political masters and retain some freedom to hold more open grant competitions.

With respect to ministries, *Realising Our Potential* reaffirmed and strengthened the customer–contractor principle. Departments were to be intelligent customers: determining their own needs and commissioning work from suppliers who competed to meet the government's specifications. Departments were "expected to mount competitive tenders wherever practicable, and to seek value for money" in order to achieve "the utility and quality of research needed" (Cm 2250, 1993).

The dual impact of the Next Steps Initiative and *Realising Our Potential* was keenly felt within ODA's natural resources program. In the early 1980s, a rich array of scientific units within and outside ODA could trace their legacy back to the colonial period. By 1990, many of them were consolidated under the Natural Resources Institute (NRI), an executive agency. NRI was expected to survive selling its research and consultancy services, chiefly to Britain's overseas aid, but also to the World Bank and the European Commission. NRI was required to charge prices that reflected the full cost of its services, rather than relying on ODA for indirect costs. In the words of Anthony Beattie (1994: 16), the director of NRI: "What is new in recent years is the involvement of ODA headquarters in setting the agenda and commissioning programmes of work—or projects—under quasi-contractual arrangements. We have moved... the service provider's discretion has been considerably curtailed—on the argument that client involvement will enhance effectiveness and efficiency."

The agricultural research community initially believed that "what it does will not fit easily or satisfactorily into the world of contractual relations and markets," and that sooner or later the pressure would go away "leaving researchers to go back to a golden age" (Beattie 1994: 20). Yet the government continued to see the market for research services as intrinsically similar to the market for other professional services. Six years after becoming an executive agency, the remnants of NRI were transferred to the University of Greenwich. While the NRI continues to exist today, it is a ghost of its former self, with just one-tenth the number of staff it had in the 1980s and little sign of its lineage back to the Imperial Institute.

The health research community fared somewhat better. The London and Liverpool Schools of Tropical Medicine were less vulnerable given their connection to higher education. Their employees were not civil servants and their back-office services relied on university administration. ODA entered into "concordats," or partnerships, with the Medical Research Council, which became an intermediary between ODA and the health research at home.

ODA began to encourage its recipients to take on a role in championing the adoption of their findings. It believed that "effective dissemination of research outputs is essential if research is to have any impact... In the past... dissemination to policymakers and practitioners has often been less effective" (ODA 1993). The focus on outcomes within work programs meant the "good" research practice saw researchers engaged in the field, as advisors or agents promoting particular policies or techniques, rather than the disinterested third parties largely outside of development practice. This also meant working through additional intermediaries, such as non-governmental organizations (NGOs) like Oxfam or ActionAid. The distinction between a research project and a development project was blurred as both were expected to achieve real-life change abroad. Looking back at UK research in development studies since 1980, Meier (1994: 466–7) lamented that basic research was being crowded out, as funding directed the research efforts toward shorter-term projects and the "quicker payoff" in which "standards of technical rigour have, at times, been ignored..., less concerned with high theory, relatively weak in quantitative and econometric techniques of analysis." Changes in the UK approach to research funding were beginning to alter what counted as research for the developing world.

In summary, during this period the governance context encouraged a division between those who performed research and those who commissioned it. This period saw government exit service delivery, spinning off its scientific units to the academic or private sector. Program theory purchased knowledge and outcomes of interest to the aid agency. This gave rise to a quasi-market pattern of project funding under which researchers would bid for the opportunity to contribute to the aid agency's work programs.

Under the old era, ODA provided core funding to maintain world-class science at home—some of which was inside government—and contribute to capacity abroad. Yet the waves of reform under Conservative governments shifted ODA toward project funding based on consumer–contractor relations. Work programs embraced government-defined objectives, in which ODA considered itself as a proxy client, purchasing services on behalf of developing countries. The roles of research funder and performer were divided, with ODA retaining the former and divesting itself of the latter. The work programs also included a covert lifeline to some of ODA's scientific units, to ease their transition into a new reality in which they needed to sell their services to survive. Many of them experienced mergers and privatization, and some simply ceased to exist. Meanwhile ODA needed to show that its research funding was applied and practical, and consequently began to press its recipients to play a role in getting "research into use."

Research as a Public Good

After seventeen years of Conservative rule under Thatcher and Major, anyone hoping for a return to the blind government patronage of the sciences would be disappointed. Market relations had been introduced to govern publicly funded research. Tony Blair's Labour government (1997–2005) would not turn back the clock, but instead saw further changes affecting research for the developing world. The first was to create DFID, separate from the foreign office and represented by a senior-level minister in the Cabinet. The second was to introduce new performance management tools and an "evidence-based" approach to policy. The third was to critique DFID's use of science, prompting the department to give research funding more prominence within its hierarchy. This section describes each of these changes in more detail.

Since 1979, the foreign aid program had been part of the Foreign and Commonwealth Office. Despite a brief period of independence under the Callaghan government (1976–9), the aid program had been subservient to foreign policy and commercial relations throughout much of its history. Yet the New Labour government quickly redefined the purpose of foreign aid as "the elimination of poverty and encouragement of economic growth which benefits the poor" (Cm 3789, 1997). The UK was an early advocate for, and adopter of, the Millennium Development Goals (MDGs), and entrenched its new aid policy into legislation. The International Development Act 2002 required that the Secretary of State be satisfied that development assistance was likely to contribute to a reduction in poverty. Such assistance was to further sustainable development in poorer countries or improve the welfare of their people. The Act also formally untied aid, removing any requirement to prefer UK companies or providers in the delivery of development programming.

DFID was also given a remit to examine all government policy affecting developing countries, including migration, defense, and trade. Thus the aid program went from being a stand-alone portfolio to being a key ministry with a sweeping role across government. With its new mandate, DFID was connected to a network of actors across Whitehall, including the Department of Trade and Industry, Department for Environment, Food and Rural Affairs (DEFRA), Office of Science and Technology, UK Research Councils, British Council, and the Chief Scientific Advisors.

DFID saw research as knowledge management: a means to "know what will work and what will not work" and a source of solutions that could be replicated elsewhere. The 1997 White Paper cited various examples of research impact, including: conditions necessary for microcredit, effectiveness in treating HIV, deploying low-cost water treatment, nutrient analysis of crops, controlling pests in rice and aquaculture, and new design for wood stoves (Cm 3789, 1997). The elimination of poverty and protection of the environment was seen to require improved access to knowledge and technologies by poor people. DFID would also adapt existing knowledge to the particular circumstances of developing countries and, where necessary, invest in developing new technology. Finally, research was also expected to "find local solutions to local problems" through better understanding of social, economic, political, and physical environments (Cm 3789, 1997).

Yet DFID senior management also feared research funding had been captured by the research community at home. One respondent recounts that Secretary of State Clare Short "was fed up with meeting little old men in white coats who thanked her for forty years of research on the hind leg of a mosquito."

Research became prominent within DFID: research was no longer the poorer cousin to bilateral aid. The bar was raised again with the release of a second White Paper focused on the impacts of globalization. It identified "research that benefits the poor" as a global public good which was underfunded. Most research and development capacity was located in developed countries and oriented to their needs. This is most clearly illustrated in drug development, where the problems of rich consumers (such as male impotence) attracts substantial investment, while the problems of poor consumers (such as tropical diseases) are largely ignored or "neglected." To address this market failure, the Blair government committed to "help focus more of the UK and global research effort on the needs of the poor" and "strengthen the capability of developing countries to produce, adapt and use knowledge, whether produced locally or internationally" (Cm 5000, 2000). The International Development Act 2002 untied aid, include research funding, allowing DFID to go anywhere to obtain the knowledge it needed without preference for UK researchers. Development assistance was expected to be untied, country-owned, and demand-led: characteristics that encouraged greater participation from developing countries and continued to focus attention on the "uptake" of research into policy and practice.

Research for the developing world had been given a new mandate and heightened expectations. In the words of one respondent, "DFID decided it would service the international development agenda... It drove the agenda around development objectives rather than making the best use of existing capacity" at home. Staff began reimagining DFID's approach to research funding, inspired in part by the Blair government's introduction of new tools for performance management and "evidence-based" policy. A cornerstone of this approach was the *Modernising Government* White Paper. Where the Conservatives had sought to emulate a market, Labour sought the "use of evidence and research so that we understand better the problems we are trying to address... [and] pilot schemes to encourage innovations and test whether they work" (Cm 4310, 1999).

UK policymaking experienced a positivist shift, with greater expectations that research would lead to improved social policy, particularly in health, education, and policing (Sparrow 2011). To simplify somewhat, the previous test for government policy and programs had been: was it affordable and did government consider it the right thing to do? Under an evidence-based approach, this test became: what is known about the problem, how was the proposed solution supposed to work, and how would government know whether it did work? Assumptions that were previously accepted as common sense were now open to questioning. The importance placed on the experience of public servants diminished, as the evidence-based approach demanded support in the form of baseline studies, empirical data, and evaluation.

In short, there was a new demand for public research.

A Contract with the Treasury

Blair's government also vowed to continuously improve value for money in service delivery. Echoing the language used by Rothschild, the *Modernising Government* White Paper cautioned that "public services can be organized too much around the structure of the providers rather than the users" (Cm 4310, 1999). To address the perceived bias, Blair's government brought in new tools for performance management. First there were Public Service Agreements (PSAs), or four-year contracts between the Treasury and line departments defining the service that the government "purchased" through the budget process. Second there were subsequent Comprehensive Spending Reviews through which Treasury assessed the extent to which line departments delivered on this contract, in order to set a new agreement and budget for the following four years. Thus spending reviews provided a periodic opportunity to refine the performance framework against which the line department would report against. Where the Conservative government had introduced contractual relations between a line department and its executive agencies, the Labour government extended this practice to the relations between Treasury and line departments.

DFID quickly adopted the MDGs as the basis for its PSA, committing to reducing poverty and improving health in developing countries. This was a courageous move for two reasons. First, there was a mismatch in timetables. While the MDG timetable aimed for results by 2015, the Treasury used annual and four-year cycles for budgeting and performance reporting. Second, the department could not guarantee these outcomes, but merely contribute toward them as a member of the international community.

Yet the PSA gave the illusion of certainty, implying that government was purchasing a particular outcome, such as longer life expectancy in Tanzania. The subsequent spending reviews inevitably revealed a "failure" to achieve some of these targets, as they were disconnected from what the department could actually control. The National Audit Office cautioned that DFID staff "may not know exactly what impact their efforts are having given the wide range of other agencies and external political, economic and social factors involved" (UK 2002). The Comprehensive Spending Reviews also allowed the Treasury to introduce cross-government directives to control operating costs: DFID soon faced the triple challenge of managing a growing aid budget, while decreasing its staff and internal costs, and decentralizing to offices outside of London.

With respect to research funding, the Labour government built upon Rothschild's idea of the intelligent consumer. The UK comptroller and auditor general asserted that all government departments were expected "to be clear about their strategic research aims and establish coherent systems for procuring research—including its commissioning, quality assurance, and use" (UK 2003). In particular, the comptroller argued that those responsible for research had to ensure its quality and relevance, and that findings were used to improve service delivery and to inform policy. Furthermore, departments were expected to have a clear understanding of future demand and supply of research—pertinent questions and the capability of potential providers—and to consult research users to identify and prioritize their requirements. Meanwhile in academia, the UK Research Assessment Exercise had been established by the Thatcher administration in 1986 and was now encouraging researchers to move on rapidly to new research projects, effectively discouraging longer-term dissemination of their work (Burawoy 2011, Surr et al. 2002).

DFID began to examine its approach in light of these new expectations. A knowledge policy unit was established in 1998 to learn from the research being funded, yet the day-to-day management remained dispersed across the policy division, including separate teams for economic and social research, health and population, education, engineering, renewable natural resources, and social development. Each of these teams had evolved their own "strategy, with distinct procedures . . . including separate guidance to applicants, reporting procedures . . . how to set research priorities . . . how to disseminate research findings; how to assess impact, and so on" (Surr et al. 2002: 34). An evaluation of research funding found that when a project failed it was due to inadequate depth and rigor in proposals, insufficient attention to connecting with potential users, and lack of effort spent in collaboration and capacity (DFID 2000a).

The department adopted a "science innovation strategy", yet it mostly described the status quo, rather than laying out a vision for the future. It noted that funding was mostly allocated through competitions targeted to meet specific policy needs, yet at times DFID responded to researcher interest through peer review involving internal and external assessors (DFID 2000b). The annual research budget reached £147 million in 2001–2, equivalent to over 4 percent of the UK budget for official development assistance. At the time, the largest beneficiaries were universities (accounting for 70 percent of all recipients), followed by not-for-profits (20 percent), and others (3 percent), including foreign governments (Surr et al. 2002). While DFID expressed a desire to increase private-sector involvement, for-profits represented just 3 percent of its recipients.

DFID decided to improve its research management skills, understood as its ability to define a research policy and strategy, identify projects, monitor budgets, and assess research impact (Surr et al. 2002). Research for the developing world was defined as: (1) correcting for market failure by providing incentives or otherwise stimulating demand for research that addresses problems of the poor; (2) providing evidence on the effectiveness and efficiency of donor and host government interventions; and (3) empowering poor countries to decide their own path, and to use modernization via knowledge to boost productivity (Surr et al. 2002). To rationalize internal costs, DFID also wanted to fund fewer, larger-value projects—involving networks of organizations—and partner with other research funders, such as the UK research councils and the European Union (EU). DFID decided to consolidate its existing research programs into a single research group:

> headed by a senior civil servant who would be responsible for the overall strategic management of research and for representing DFID in Whitehall and the EU and other international fora... Advisors would be both in research teams and within policy themes (as well as linked with country programmes via their advisory networks). This should keep research informed by DFID's priorities and vice versa, and improve the relevance of research and its effective dissemination and promotion. (Surr et al. 2002: 10)

The Central Research Department (CRD) was established in 2003 within the policy division. It began with just seven full-time employees led by Paul Spray who, despite a rich career within the foreign aid program, identified himself more as a development generalist than a research specialist. The MDGs also imparted new ideas on aid effectiveness: development assistance was expected to be untied, country-owned, and demand-led. These characteristics encouraged DFID to place increased emphasis on the participation of developing countries in its research funding, and continued to focus attention on the "uptake" of research into policy and practice.

Science Strikes Back

DFID's use of science soon became the subject of an inquiry under the House Committee on Science and Technology. Parliament, encouraged by the government's Chief Scientific Advisor, was concerned that DFID was disconnected from the government departments responsible for science, under-resourced to fully participate in research partnerships, and in dire need to invest in scientific staff (Sivadasan et al. 2003).

At one level, the inquiry was concerned about DFID's ability to act as an intelligent customer. In the words of one respondent, "there was really no apparatus for assimilating, dealing with, and disseminating results of the research that was done." This situation had been aggravated by the move toward fewer, larger projects. DFID had begun to fund "research programme consortia", or networks comprised of four-to-six institutions, some of which were located in developing countries. This type of grantmaking moved more funds in each project, but also shifted research management partially to the recipients. DFID would interact more with the lead managers within each consortium, who in turn coordinated the researchers involved. Staff had limited interaction with individual researchers, which was feared to erode DFID's ability to use the results of the research it funded (House of Commons 2004). In the words of one respondent, the relationship with research community had "moved gradually from working-on-top-of-you, to working-with-you, and then let's-give-you-money to do research."

At another level, the inquiry sought to reverse a perceived move away from supporting researchers at home in the UK. The inquiry report introduced the term *development sciences* to refer to "the full spectrum of social and natural sciences, engineering and technology undertaken with the purpose of informing, supporting or promoting international development" (House of Commons 2004: 10). Development sciences were seen as distinct from development studies. Witnesses argued that the UK had strong experience in agricultural, biotechnology, and medical research. David King, the government's Chief Scientific Advisor, cautioned that "DFID's untying of research may well compromise the sustainability of the UK research base operating in areas of particular relevance to the developing world." In its report, the select committee argued that the "erosion of the UK research base in development sciences is now endangering the future ability of the UK to sustain this leadership role" (House of Commons 2004: 4). Fueled by discontent over previous shifts in grantmaking, a strong science lobby emerged to argue for the participation of the domestic research community within foreign aid, arguing that science:

> make[s] an invaluable contribution to development by, reducing disease burdens and food insecurity; facilitating communications; enabling monitoring of global and national environments to minimise conflicts and give warning of natural disasters, and developing new ways of using water, energy and other natural resources... [and] engender a culture of inquiry, openness and respect for evidence. (House of Commons 2004: 9)

Although the bulk of the inquiry focused on research management within DFID, it also made other recommendations. First was to give greater prominence to capacity building. The inquiry report argues that "the UK has an obligation to support capacity building in science and technology for development" (House of Commons 2004: 45) in developing countries, including human resources, physical infrastructure, and stronger research and education systems. Second was to appoint a Chief Scientific Advisor, following a 2002 recommendation in the government's "Investing in Innovation" strategy that called for such a position in all departments that used or commissioned significant amounts of research.

DFID responded with an increase in research funding. The aid budget was growing rapidly, particularly in the run up to the UK hosting the 2005 G8 meeting in Gleneagles with its focus on aid to Africa. The country's official development assistance had reached £4.1 billion by 2004–5, and was projected to reach £6.5 billion within three years. The House of Commons committee argued that there should be a "commensurate increase in the availability of funding for development sciences R&D in the UK, in order to strengthen the evidence base available for international development policy-making, and to safeguard the UK's ability to maintain a leadership role in the field" (House of Commons 2004: 82).

As for a chief scientific advisor, the title was initially added to the job description of the director of the CRD. Now wearing these two hats, Paul Spray prepared the *Research Funding Framework 2005–2007*. By the end of this period, DFID expected to dedicate at least £100 million per year to research, and the framework described how to direct this new spending. Two-thirds was dedicated to four priority themes: sustainable agriculture, "killer diseases" (HIV, malaria, and tuberculosis), state fragility and governance, and climate change. These themes mapped closely to the various interests within DFID and were intended to ensure that everyone—DFID management and the UK research community alike—felt they had a stake in them. The remaining one-third of funding was spread across other MDG-related research, as well as smaller policy-oriented projects (£100,000 to £300,000 each) which provided a window for responding to ideas proposed by the research community (DFID 2004).

Research began to enjoy a rising profile within DFID. Despite the minor portion of DFID spending invested, research projects contributed many of the examples highlighted in the department's annual report to Parliament. This was in part because research projects were more directly tied to results, compared to budget support in partner countries. Meanwhile Secretary of State Hilary Benn was keen that DFID research be seen as credible in the eyes of the UK research community, not least owing to the fact that his brother was an active member in the Royal Society of Chemistry. By 2006, the CRD staff grew to thirty people, divided between program managers responsible for administrative and financial aspects of funded projects, and research advisors responsible for program development, monitoring, and evaluation. They would prepare concise descriptions of an under-researched area that served as the basis for competitive tenders. Projects were selected using a two-stage process with an internal review for identifying promising concept notes, followed by external peer review of the subsequent, more detailed proposals.

In summary, during this period the governance context invested the aid agency with an increasing level of resources and a legislated mandate to contribute to global poverty reduction. The program theory guiding funding decisions saw research as a form of public good, placed at the service of furthering a global development agenda negotiated with other donors. The grantmaking practice that evolved saw an increase in support to recipients located outside the UK and a move to larger projects, networks, or "consortia" of grantees. The Labour government adopted the rhetoric of an evidence-based approach to policy, heightening expectations that research would demonstrate and enhance government performance. DFID saw research as a global public good, part of the UK contribution toward the MDGs. Yet subsequent spending reviews required that the department control its operating costs: to manage a growing budget with fewer staff.

Research funding switched from individual projects with single recipients, toward much larger-value research consortia involving multiple recipients. Consequently much of the responsibility for shaping a research program was effectively transferred to recipients. This move attracted new criticism regarding DFID's use of science. Whereas ODA research advisors previously fostered competition among potential providers—establishing market-inspired relationships between government and researchers—DFID was now expected to have a coherent approach to its research funding that contributed to development, informed DFID practice, and engaged actors in UK research policy. The performance regime surrounding the department is depicted in Figure 3.2

The Promise of Technology and Evidence

The year 2005 marked a peak in public support for development. The UK chose to focus the G8 summit on development in Africa. Many donor countries were increasing their aid budgets, and civil society campaigned to "make poverty history." The world was seen to have the resources, and now the political will, to eliminate absolute poverty and achieve the MDG agenda. This optimism cascaded over into DFID, which had established itself as the cutting-edge of the public service. It drew young, career-minded professionals away from traditionally more popular departments, including the Treasury and the Foreign Office. Research enjoyed pride of place within the department, responsible for a portion of the aid budget.

Research for the developing world was entering a new period. DFID recruited its first full-time Chief Scientific Advisor, Gordon Conway, former

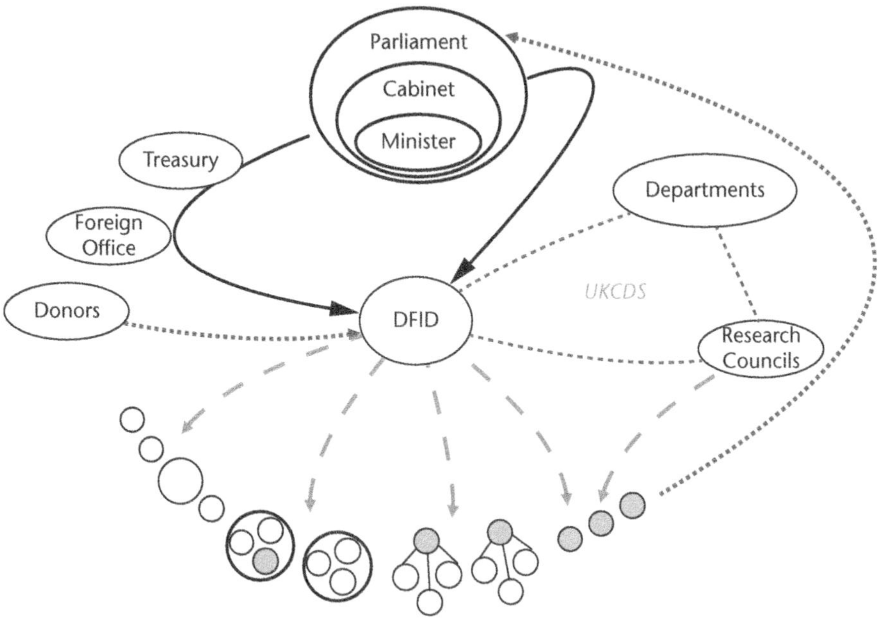

Figure 3.2. Performance regime surrounding DFID

Solid lines represent formal lines of authority, dotted lines describe the flow of program ideas, and dashed lines show funding relationships. The upper portion represents governance context; the lower portion describes grantmaking, with shaded circles representing UK recipients. From left to right: support to recipients abroad, international initiatives with multiple participants, consortia led by UK institutions, and support to UK recipients.

president of the Rockefeller Foundation and a fellow of the Royal Society who had pioneered the science of integrated pest management. Responding to the House of Commons committee inquiry, his tenure saw DFID take a greater interest in so-called platform technologies and expand its partnerships with the UK research councils. These steps re-established ties with the natural sciences in the UK, embracing the promise of technology to create new opportunities for poor people abroad. Yet DFID also expected research to inform the department to become more effective and efficient in its bilateral, multilateral, and humanitarian aid. Government continued to press departments to control their operating costs, limiting the amount of time staff could invest in research management and monitoring.

Toward the end of the decade, DFID's program theory for research would shift away from an approach framed by development studies, and toward a way of thinking based more on clinical medicine. David Cameron's Conservative-Liberal coalition government (2010–15) arrived in power just as the developed world faced its worst financial crisis since the 1930s Great Depression. This marked the beginning of austerity budgets and saw the PSAs replaced with new tools for performance management. Foreign aid was initially "ring fenced" and protected from budget cuts, yet this heightened the scrutiny to which DFID spending was subjected. Research would be increasingly seen as providing evidence on which forms of spending offered the best "value for money."

Partnering With the Councils

The Blair government's third White Paper on development policy promised to double DFID funding for research. Responding to the House of Commons committee inquiry, the White Paper argued that DFID would "exploit science to fight poverty", such as the potential for upstream natural sciences and technological advances. Research promised to lead to "a new generation of drugs, vaccines and treatment methods . . . new technologies for water treatment and purification . . . and adapting to the impact of climate change" (Cm 6876, 2006). The White Paper also reiterated an expectation that research would provide developing countries with access to international expertise and encourage local researchers to address the needs of the poorest members of their societies.

Researchers were not expected to work in isolation, but to link with a variety of partners that could help ensure the uptake of research into practice, including community groups, the media, and the private sector. Recipients were not only expected to be highly qualified researchers, but also adept networkers, entrepreneurs, and innovators.

The government's Chief Scientific Advisor, David King, convened a "Development Science Working Group" to reflect on how the government might better coordinate UK support to medical, agricultural, environmental, and other areas of research. At one point, this group considered a new research council dedicated to development sciences. Yet this option would have redirected funding from DFID and the existing research councils, without necessarily improving coherence among the various offerings of these funders.

The government instead opted to create a UK Collaborative on Development Sciences (UKCDS) to "maximise the impact of UK research on international development." Its initial members included DFID, Wellcome Trust, the line departments for health and for innovation, and the research councils for the natural environment, biosciences, medical research, and economic and social research. The UKCDS had a modest staff of roughly five people, considered employees of the bioscience research council (BBSRC) but working out of the offices of Wellcome Trust, a private charity dedicated to medical research. UKCDS sought to help its members identify future research needs, improve coordination, and share good practice. While it did not have any formal powers, UKCDS was expected to both enhance DFID's links with other research funders, and ensure the UK research councils supported opportunities for work on international development.

DFID began to issue joint calls for proposals with a greater number of the UK research councils. Such partnerships were a win-win for DFID: it was perceived to be commissioning high-quality science, and doing so by buying into the existing peer review process, rather than setting up and running such competitions itself. Consequently, part of DFID's portfolio moved toward more upstream research, including plant genomics and human vaccines. The pool of potential grantees grew from the former development studies community interested in poor countries abroad, to take in a wide community with skills in lab-based sciences at home that could be applied abroad. In the words of one respondent, it widened the field to "anyone who can slice in a salt-tolerant gene." Yet a new tension emerged: proposals with the best science did not necessarily have the greatest relevance to development.

The councils were already struggling to balance the criteria of research quality and impact. Each of the councils had its own program theory for research, but faced a common performance regime. In 2006, all the councils were asked "to make funding decisions based on assessments of research excellence and the potential economic impact" (Holmes and Harris 2010: 395). Consequently the councils had embarked on an "excellence with impact" agenda, which emphasized demonstrating impact, engagement with research users, and support for people in knowledge brokering roles. Hence the opportunity to work with DFID was attractive: it would provide an example of demand from a government department, and DFID funding would match or exceed those offered by the councils. Yet the councils' program theory continued to privilege quality ahead of impact, while DFID expected research to be relevant and have practical application. The Secretary of State argued that DFID was not interested in funding research per se, but in its benefit for developing countries.

Somehow the peer review process had to reconcile the criteria of quality and impact. Early competitions used parallel review committees, one focused on the scientific quality of proposals and the other on their relevance to development. The project ideas that were ranked highly by both committees were invited to submit full proposals. Yet the result was perceived as somewhat disappointing to both sides, projects midway between the comfort zones of basic and applied science preferred by the councils and DFID. This move also re-established the prominence of UK researchers in DFID funding. To be eligible for council funding, project ideas needed to include a UK researcher. Furthermore, developing-country colleagues were at a disadvantage, lacking experience in presenting their ideas for consideration in UK peer review.

Additional differences between DFID and the councils surfaced after the selection process. The councils were accustomed to relying on academic incentives of tenure and university careers to encourage recipients to get on with their research, yet DFID was accustomed to playing an active role in monitoring progress of the funded work. In some instances, the grantees were asked to revisit their project design in order to retrofit logical frameworks, milestones, and deliverables. Furthermore, recipients were expected to provide regular updates on their work and respond to periodic requests for information coming from DFID.

Funding Global Science and Informing Aid

The promise of upstream science and new technology was also present elsewhere in DFID's research portfolio, with new support to a variety of international alliances and product development partnerships. These partnerships combined funding from the public and private sectors to identify, refine, and take to market medicines and other technologies for poor countries. They were intended to address the "market failure" created by the low financial demand exercised by poor people, which meant that certain technologies were not profitable for the private sector to invest in.

Product development partnerships were seen as a means to coordinate across government, academia, companies, and civil society to underwrite the R&D costs and facilitate the discovery and diffusion of new technologies. Such partnerships operated as virtual non-profit R&D organizations, outsourcing activities to academic or private firms and providing technical oversight and research management (Grace 2010). Product development partnerships also sought in-kind contributions from private firms in the form of staff time, use of laboratories and production facilities, and access to proprietary information, such as candidate molecules for new drugs. Examples included the International AIDS Vaccine Initiative (IAVI), Global Alliance for Vaccines and Immunisation (GAVI), and Global Alliance for Livestock Veterinary Medicines (GALVmed).

Two factors encouraged DFID to adopt this approach to grantmaking. The first was the beliefs and convictions of DFID's Chief Scientific Advisor. Gordon Conway championed these initiatives based on his experience with the Rockefeller Foundation, which had been an early supporter of product development partnerships inspired in part by delays in public research through the United Nations. The second factor was the opportunity to minimize operating costs by moving large amounts of funding in single grants. Thus the DFID research portfolio now included a greater diversity of approaches, with research program consortia, collaboration with the research councils, and product development partnerships adding to the more traditional research projects with single recipients or contributions to multilateral programs, such as the Consultative Group on International Agricultural Research (CGIAR) or World Health Organization (WHO).

Meanwhile, under the Blair and Brown governments, Whitehall expected that public research funding would provide an input into an evidence-based approach to policymaking. The Cabinet Office defined evidence as "expert knowledge, published research, existing statistics, stakeholder consultations, previous policy evaluations, the Internet, outcomes from consultations, costings of policy options, output from economic and statistical modelling" (Davies and Nutley 2002: 4). Much of the public sector adopted a new concern for gathering evidence to substantiate policy objectives, instruments, and monitoring.

Clinical medicine was held up as an ideal for this approach. Clinical medicine starts with a clear outcome which allows practitioners to establish a hierarchy among different methods. For example, if the desired outcome is reduced mortality or disease, the mechanism is a drug or vaccine candidate. Randomized experimentation is a means of establishing validity, or "truth," followed by observational studies and professional consensus. Within government, this clinical medicine philosophy was increasingly applied more widely within health policy, as well as other areas of social policy, including justice and education. Yet, similar to international development, these sectors simultaneously seek multiple outcomes, often negating the possibility of establishing a clear hierarchy among methods and types of knowledge that counts as "evidence" (Davies and Nutley 2002).

Yet the performance regime in the UK required evidence to underpin all decisions. For example, the policy process required some form of evidence as to the extent of a particular problem or the effectiveness of some form of intervention. There had to be some proof before the problem was accepted as deserving to be on the government agenda, or before an intervention was accepted as deserving of public funding. In other words, policy goal X was important, or policy instrument Y worked, because of evidence Z. Consequentially, experience-based knowledge or expert opinion counted for much less than they had in the past. The emphasis was very much on the instrumental use of empirical evidence to inform practice, rather than the conceptual use of theoretical knowledge to frame policy (Nutley et al. 2007).

The twin promises of technology and evidence were integrated into the DFID *Research Strategy 2008–2013* (2008). DFID expected to spend up to £1 billion on research within this five-year period, thus the stakes were high and there was opportunity to move beyond the department's previous directions. The Director General of Research and Policy, Andrew Steer, described DFID priorities as a product of "where would research have the greatest potential impact on changing the way one tackles poverty? New priorities set by the minister. What are other research funders doing? [And] what is the opportunity cost of research in one area versus another?" (House of Lords 2010: 75).

Following a substantial consultation with research communities at home and abroad, the strategy included some substantial continuity. It defined research for the developing world as a means to "make faster progress in fighting poverty and achieving the MDGs" and called for continued support to health and agriculture. These two themes continued to account for the largest shares of the portfolio, at £50 million and £40 million respectively in 2007–8. Next in size was research on economic growth and on fragile states—which accounted for £10 million and £12 million respectively—which could trace their lineage back to the old work programs. The strategy also laid out new investment in the areas of research communications, climate change, and future post-2015 challenges. Collectively these themes accounted for £16 million in 2007–8.

The focus on research communications responded to demand for evidence-informed practice. The strategy argued that it was "more likely that people will act on evidence that is built up over many years, in different contexts, once this has been communicated effectively." Thus part of the value of research was seen to lie in bridging this last mile, to reach a potential audience that could "use research to bring about real change" (DFID 2008: 10). Accordingly, the strategy called for investing up to 30 percent of the research budget into making research "available, accessible, and useable." Recipients and DFID were both responsible for research communication. Funds were earmarked within each grant for recipients to share their findings, while DFID increased its own spending on research communication and synthesis. In the short term, DFID's approach was framed by the experience of development practitioners (based on a belief that each country's development experience was unique), yet it increasingly adopted the philosophy of clinical medicine (based on a belief in universal facts about what worked and what did not).

DFID's new strategy outlined four intended results: policy knowledge for developing countries, the international community, and DFID; evidence to inform decision making about international development; technologies developed and used in developing countries; and capabilities to do and use research. DFID sought a proactive role in shaping the research agenda, asserting that its staff would "take the lead intellectually in delivering high-quality research that shapes ideas, policy, and practice" (DFID 2008: 37). Research would focus on DFID partner countries in Africa and South Asia, responding to local demand and improving the capability of these countries to carry out research. Yet in practice, it would be difficult for the London-based research staff to feed into spending by local country programs or tap into local knowledge of host society research needs and potential recipients.

Gordon Brown's Labour government (2007–10) released yet another White Paper on international development, establishing the DFID priorities as economic growth, climate change, and conflict. Foreign aid was to be directed "based on the principles of country income, population size and confidence that resources will be used effectively" (Cm 7656, 2009). DFID continued to be squeezed on operating costs, with a promise to "deliver an additional £155 million of value-for-money savings by 2010–11." These savings were to be found in part by "improving value for money in the research budget." Echoing the optimism over the promise of technology and evidence, the White Paper argued for focusing research on "best bets ... innovations with the greatest potential to lift poor people out of poverty." The examples cited included drought-resistant maize and vitamin-enriched crops. Meanwhile DFID research was also expected "to ensure that decision makers have the best evidence of what works" (Cm 7656, 2009).

In 2009, Chris Whitty was recruited to DFID to occupy the now recombined post of Chief Scientific Advisor and Head of Research. This included both a corporate role to facilitate the use of science throughout DFID, as well as direct oversight of the staff responsible for the research funding decisions. This post was just two levels from the top of DFID management, reporting to the Director General of Policy and Research, which in turn reported to the Permanent Secretary. Whereas the past directors of DFID research were career public servants, Whitty was trained as a medical doctor and would continue to keep a foot in academia, teaching part-time at the London School of Hygiene and Tropical Medicine. He had the gravitas of coming from the other side of the fence, being part of the medical research community and seeing research management from that point of view. To meet the expectation of informing DFID policy and operations, the CRD was soon renamed the Research and Evidence Division (RED). Under the new division, research was not only for reducing poverty, but for "doing more with available funds ... [to] avoid developing expensive ideas that do not work" (DFID 2009: 1).

The division began to fund systematic reviews on questions facing DFID operation across the department. The method of systematic review compiles a synthesis of past research findings by: asking a precise question, establishing an explicit protocol for how to identify and include previous studies, and conducting a meta-analysis of the data from these studies. A systematic review assesses the rigor of previous studies, and excludes from the meta-analysis those studies that are considered to have poor-quality designs. Systematic reviews originated in clinical medicine, as a means to look at the effectiveness of a particular drug or intervention, with the aim of informing practice and better targeting future research effort. The RED collected a series of questions from across DFID, which were then tendered to the research community to apply for. It also worked with donor agencies in Australia, the United States, and Canada on additional calls.

The use of systematic reviews was controversial. Drug effectiveness could be established by a controlled context and causation rooted in biochemistry and human physiology. Yet changes in poverty happen in an uncontrolled context due to multiple causal mechanisms stemming from the interaction of economics, politics, and the actions of donors, partner governments, and poor people themselves. Some of the questions identified for a systematic review were fairly general in nature, such as "what factors limit the use of cleaner cookstoves?" This made it difficult to identify which past studies were appropriate to include in the meta-analysis. Conversely, the focus on high-quality studies led to reviews that included a very small number of findings or that excluded studies that were seen as pertinent by development practitioners (Hagen-Zanker et al. 2012). As the reviews were conducted by outsiders, they tended to lack the nuance needed to tailor their presentation to the practical needs of DFID staff. Furthermore, adapting Sparrow's argument on evidence-based policing (2011), a systematic review selects a tiny fraction of scientific methods applicable to international development and narrows the range of solutions available.

DFID continued to move toward targeted research, becoming less responsive to researcher interest. Prior to the 1990s, ODA projects had been primarily determined by the research community, while under RED the research themes—and increasingly the research questions—were determined primarily by government. Yet a more nuanced balance of Rothschild's and Haldane's visions was emerging in UK research policy. A House of Lords inquiry into public research argued that "plurality and diversity . . . allows multiple opportunities for the best research to be funded." Those responsible for research funding were to exercise careful judgment about how to deploy "limited funds between competing priorities so that the pursuit of knowledge and its translation into practical applications meet the needs of society" (2010: paras 22 and 1).

Echoing earlier concerns, witnesses to the inquiry expressed doubts over whether government departments knew "who to ask or what to ask," and argued that targeted funding risked producing poorer quality or even mediocre research (House of Lords 2010: paras 44 and 52). Applying this concern to DFID, one respondent lamented, "the way [researchers] are being funded is turning everyone into a short-term consultant and analyst." Having worked hard to establish its scientific credibility, this was not a desirable image for DFID. Despite continued pressure to control operating costs, research management required skilled people. The RED soon grew to over a hundred employees and began to give evidence to parliamentary inquiries in the areas of health and food security.

DFID was well positioned to respond to an emerging concern with global challenges, common to UK and developing countries. In 2009, the government's Chief Scientific Advisor, now Sir John Bebbington, argued that the twin forces of climate and demographic change would provoke a "perfect storm" of food, water, and energy scarcity within twenty years. The scale and urgency of these problems was seen to require greater collaboration across government and with other countries. The House of Lords argued that highly competitive funding systems discouraged such collaboration, instead rewarding individual pursuits and providing an incentive to keep research progress private until peer-reviewed publication. The inquiry further lamented that "research councils do not reward or facilitate interdisciplinary or groundbreaking work [and] departmental priorities outweighed cross-Government priorities" (House of Lords 2010: para 38).

Research Under Austerity

David Cameron's Conservative-Liberal government (2010–15) inherited the consequences of the 2008 financial crisis that rocked North America and Europe. The G20 response had seen the UK and other countries introduce two years of stimulus spending. By 2010, reduced revenue from a slowed economy had forced government finances into deficit with national debt increasing by 50 percent, to over £760 billion. The new government crafted an austerity budget, introducing tax hikes and cutting departmental spending by up to 25 percent. It also replaced the PSA with a new requirement for departments to prepare "business plans." Spending proposals were subjected to a new set of tools developed by HM Treasury, framed around a "five case model" of concise arguments outlining how the proposals contributed to government strategy, optimized value for money, and were commercially viable, financially affordable, and achievable (UK 2011).

The international development budget was protected, or ring fenced, and further increased as the new government maintained a commitment to spend 0.7 percent of gross national income toward official development assistance by 2013. Yet this continued growth in foreign aid meant that DFID would be subjected to intense scrutiny. Transparency and value for money were the priorities for DFID under its new Secretary of State, Andrew Mitchell, with an Independent Commission for Aid Impact (ICAI) reporting directly to Parliament on the effectiveness of various aid programs. The government also quickly launched "root and branch" reviews of bilateral and multilateral aid. The bilateral review saw DFID end its aid to sixteen countries, including China and Russia, and refocus on twenty-seven other countries, primarily in South Asia and eastern Africa. The multilateral review identified agencies DFID would stop funding or place under special measures. It prioritized support for the World Bank, regional development banks, UNICEF, the GAVI alliance, and the Global Fund to fight AIDS, Tuberculosis and Malaria (DFID 2011a).

Value for money became the prominent watchword within the department. In releasing the reviews, the Secretary of State argued they represented a "determination to deliver the greatest possible return on investment, both for the world's poorest people and for the British taxpayer" (DFID 2011a). The DFID business plan for 2011–15 asserts that it "will no longer support projects that are failing to perform . . . spend as much money on marketing and communications . . . [or] provide substantial aid to countries that do not need it" (DFID 2011b: 5). DFID re-emphasized the use of results-based management and quantitative commitments, including numbers of children to be enrolled in school and women to receive access to family planning. In such cases, value for money meant achieving these targets at a minimal cost. Yet DFID also wanted to help protect livelihoods from the effects of climate change and make countries safer from violent conflict. Such goals were not so easily measured or verified. They lacked a counterfactual of how conditions might otherwise evolve without UK intervention, and it was difficult to distinguish DFID's contribution from the efforts of others.

The purpose of RED was to commission research on key questions in development. It was expected to develop new technologies (such as new drugs, vaccines, or drought-tolerant crops), find better and more cost-effective ways of delivering aid, and help DFID and partner countries make the best policy choices. The latter goals assumed an internal demand for research. Every DFID project was expected to be justified through statements summarizing evidence on the need for the intervention, as well as evidence on its potential or real impact (House of Lords 2012). By 2012, RED had an annual budget of £235 million, up from £130 million in 2008, and expected to reach £320 million by 2014 (House of Commons 2012). Up to one-third of this budget was to be directed to ensuring that "research evidence from any source gets to the policy makers and end users who need it" (DFID 2009: 1).

RED staff had a role in synthesizing evidence from a variety of sources, assessing its quality, and communicating the findings. The division's work now involved producing four types of "evidence products," including systematic reviews contracted out to universities, in-house evidence papers providing DFID's own perspective of the state of the science, classical literature reviews, and rapid reviews intended to respond to urgent policy needs (House of Commons 2012). Chris Whitty described himself as having three roles: ensuring that the evidence base was strong and reached users across DFID, contributing to the professional development of staff, and strengthening DFID's peer review and "proper mechanisms for commissioning research rather than a slightly ad hoc process" (House of Lords 2012: volume 2, 139). Yet Whitty also cautioned that uncertainty continued to exist. It was often impossible to answer a minister's question or provide a definitive recommendation "either because the studies are not there or because they have not been done to a high enough quality" (House of Commons 2012: Report HC377i, page Ev38, reply to Q99 in oral evidence given on 25 June 2012).

DFID had strengthened its engagement with academics, despite some clear challenges. The incentives for academics were to compete for Haldane-style funding from the research councils, and to publish in order to enhance their university's standing in the Research Assessment Exercise. Despite the rise in demand for academic input from evidence-based agenda, government departments continued with Rothschild-style contracts focused on their own needs. The potential to participate in, and contribute to, policymaking held some attraction, but many academics were reluctant to chase after government contracts at the cost of progressing in their own careers.

DFID sought to break this impasse in three ways. First was through senior research fellowships offering established academics an opportunity to work within the department for a limited time (DFID 2009). Second, some DFID posts were modified to permit staff to hold both academic and public service responsibilities. Chris Whitty and his deputy continued to hold their university jobs, albeit with reduced teaching and research responsibilities. This meant that staff would not have to forego their standing in the world of academia while contributing to DFID. Third, Whitty convened an informal Research Advisory Group (iRAG) of outside academics, chaired by the Vice-Chancellor of Cambridge University, to provide ongoing independent advice on the current and future relevance of DFID's research agenda.

In summary, during this period the performance regime re-emphasized ties with UK science, including notions of scientific excellence, and witnessed rising scrutiny of foreign aid, including downward pressure on operating costs. The program theory guiding funding decisions embraced the potential for generating technologies to change the lives of poor women and men, as well as the potential for research to inform an evidence-based approach to policy. Correspondingly, grantmaking expanded to include partnerships with the UK research councils, continued rise in average project size, and renewed consideration of how research informs the value for money of growing aid investments (Figure 3.3).

Key Points

UK research policy was subject to a tug-of-war between the Haldane principle (under which the research community is essentially self-governed) and the Rothschild principle (under which research is for hire). Haldane divided

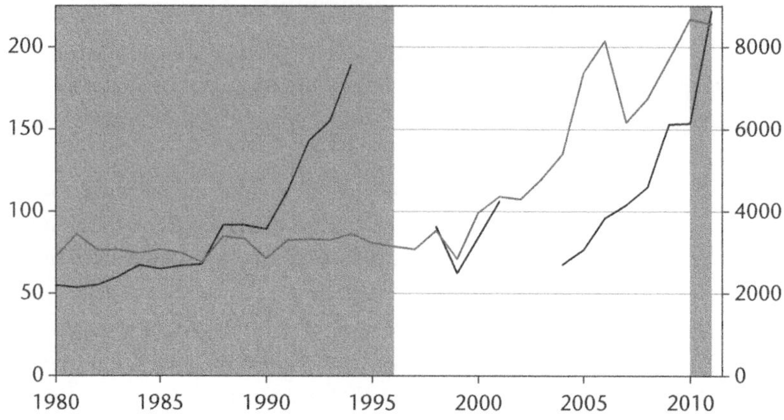

Figure 3.3. United Kingdom's R4D spending since 1980

ODA/DFID grants to research in dark (left axis) compared to UK's official development assistance (right axis). All amounts are expressed as million GBP adjusted to 2011. Gaps represent times when research spending was not reported separately. The shaded years represent time when the Conservative party was in power.

ODA Report on Research, DFID Annual Reports and OECD statistics

research commissioned by departments for a specific purpose from research funded by councils for more general use. Lord Rothschild saw applied research as having "a practical application as its objective," best governed by the principle of "the customer says what he wants; the contractor does it (if he can) and the customer pays" (Cmnd 5049: 1972, para 6). After 1979, Conservative governments pursued an agenda to make the public service more economical, efficient, and effective. Reforms saw the government's scientific units spun off into quasi-independent entities. These agencies were expected to fend for themselves, with their access to public funds governed by a customer–contractor relationship. Pressure mounted for competitive tendering of public funding, and for the measurement and audit of outcomes utilizing performance indicators.

Research for the developing world has deep historical roots in the United Kingdom. The current arrangements with DFID trace their lineage back to the early twentieth century, predating the era of foreign aid. Upon its creation, the ODA inherited a legacy of funding relations from the previous Colonial Research Council, including scientific units within government, world-class centers at home, and a host of institutes abroad. The initial focus was on maintaining the UK science base and reducing the dependency of institutes abroad by switching its offer from core funding to project funding. With the advent of the Rothschild principle, ODA established an arm's-length relationship with the scientific units previously part of government. ODA kept its research funding fragmented among policy divisions responsible for agriculture, health, economics, etc. The adoption of work programs after 1993 saw a more deliberate attempt to set the research agenda and foster competition within the research community.

Following the creation of DFID in 1997, research was subject to mounting critique from inside and outside the department. In response, a CRD was established to strengthen DFID's ability to manage its research funding. Research benefited from an increasing foreign aid budget, yet struggled with the Treasury's efforts to control operating costs. Funding moved from "retail to wholesale," away from small grants with individual research teams, and toward larger grants with either consortia of recipients or international alliances. The International Development Act in 2002 untied foreign aid, and saw an increase in research funding to recipients abroad. Later in the decade, DFID sought to re-establish its scientific credibility, working more closely with the research councils to promote the promise of new technology, and positioning itself as the provider of evidence upon which to base foreign aid investments. This latter role became particularly pronounced in the follow-up to the Labour push for evidence-based policy and the Conservative focus on value for money during times of austerity.

The periods described in this chapter closely match Bastow et al.'s (2014) identification of three eras of UK governance. These periods include a pre-1980 government science characterized by Weberian bureaucracy with in-house scientific expertise; pre-2000 new public management with the creation of quasi-markets by outsourcing government science and emphasizing evidence-based policy; and the current digital-era governance privileging quantitative approaches and focusing on real-time impacts. The second era included dividing "purchasers" from "providers," making providers compete with each other, and using performance contracts instead of relying merely on public service ethos.

The governance context can be described in terms of resource availability, public management, and research governance.

In terms of the *resources available*, the UK initially supported the costs of local research facilities abroad and world-class centers of excellence at home. By mid-century, the UK government sought to reduce overall costs by encouraging the governments of the newly independent countries to fund local research. Meanwhile, the move from core funding to competitive work programs was a means of rationalizing government expenditure on UK recipients. The rise of official development assistance this century saw a disproportionate increase in research funding. Yet the New Labour discipline of spending reviews saw strict controls on the resources available for staffing and internal costs, encouraging a move from "retail to wholesale" funding: supporting larger projects, networks or "consortia" of grantees, and co-funding with the UK research-granting councils. Recent austerity budgets saw research as providing evidence that informed the design of aid investments.

In terms of *public management*, Haldane established that line departments should have a budget line for research, which ODA initially used to maintain the UK research centers specialized in the problems of tropical climates. The market-inspired thinking of Rothschild and Thatcher eventually led to a split between those who performed research and those who commissioned it. ODA exited service delivery entirely, spinning off its scientific units to the academic or private sector. Following the creation of DFID, research was seen as a public good contributing to the international agenda beyond the UK. Research for the developing world benefited from an outside "science lobby" as domestic researchers were primary beneficiaries of ODA grantmaking until the untying of aid. The shift away from domestic research providers provoked an attack on DFID's use of science, leading to the creation of a Chief Scientific Advisor, the first of whom brought in a focus on platform technologies, such as ICTs and genomics. His successor imparted a model inspired by clinical medicine, resonating with an evidence-based approach to policy championed by Blair. The result was a shift to seeing research as an internal service to demonstrate the value for money of foreign aid.

In terms of *research policy*, the research community invented a "Haldane principle" of self-governance under which government was merely a benign benefactor. Later, Rothschild's ideal of "customer–contractor" expected government to be an intelligent consumer, specifying exactly what it needed from the research community. Research shifted from responding to the interests of the research community to instead encouraging work on the interests of government. The UK research community was initially seen as a close ally worthy of support, but was later recast as a consultant to be managed through contractual relations. These two forms of governance coexist in a dynamic tension between what government wants done, and what researchers are interested in doing. Even when ODA adopted competitive funding mechanisms, the relationship with the research community was not entirely arm's length. Government officials would turn to the research community in crafting the terms of reference. Meanwhile, researchers are judged more on their publication record than on their participation in government funding opportunities.

The agency of ODA and DFID is seen in how these organizations responded to a changing context through the evolution of the program theory used to guide funding decisions and grantmaking practices.

In terms of program theory, ODA initially focused on the science base at home, maintaining highly qualified people and established centers within the UK research community. Later the work programs offered competitive funding for projects to further outcomes of interest to the aid agency. DFID initially shifted away from the domestic research community in favor of the global development agenda negotiated with other donors. More recently, DFID embraced perspectives based on the promise of technology and a clinical approach which sees research as providing evidence as to what is needed and what works. Both of these perspectives opened up funding to recipients beyond those that self-identified as working on international development. Yet new perspectives did not completely displace older ones; instead there has been a layering of grantmaking logics over time. For example, DFID continued to provide core funding to the Overseas Development Institute (ODI) despite long abandoning a perspective of maintaining the UK science base. A growing research budget provided space for multiple program theories to coexist and thrive.

Drawing on Funnel and Rogers' (2011) concepts of program theory, the UK approach to research was often based on a diffusion theory of change, initially underpinned by a direct delivery archetype. ODA inherited a set of scientific units at home that saw government responsible for conducting research. In the 1980s and 1990s, the importance of this archetype eroded with the slow move to competitively awarded work programs and the eventual phasing out of direct delivery during the Next Steps Initiative. With the establishment of DFID and substantial budget growth, research funding oscillated between diffusion and reasoned-action theories of change, which interpreted research as technical innovation and evidenced-based policy. In both cases, research funding was underpinned by a carrot-and-stick archetype, correcting a market failure by providing researchers with a financial incentive to do work that benefited developing countries.

In terms of grantmaking practices, ODA initially provided core support to highly specialized senior researchers and research centers, based on historic relationships with institutes at home and abroad. Slowly ODA sought to rationalize these relationships, initially shifting from core funding to project funding for institutes abroad, which were increasingly expected to provide their own operating costs. A similar shift occurred in the relationship with the domestic research community, with the work programs moving UK institutes from core funding to project funding based on competitive calls for proposals. The work programs saw the overall pool of recipients contract, as some entities merged and others ceased to exist. The staff role of a "research advisor" evolved from a subject-matter expert engaging with the external research community, toward an internal role providing technical support within DFID. Meanwhile the recipients of UK funding needed to satisfy an increasing number of expectations, including scientific quality, relevance to developing countries, and getting "research into use." Beyond generating new knowledge and technologies, projects were expected to actually deliver development, demonstrating their contribution to outcomes such as raised incomes and improved well-being.

4

Canada

Hopper's Vision of Empowerment

Even as Canada established its donor agency in 1968, prominent individuals envisioned a separate organization specialized in research. Canada's International Development Research Centre (IDRC) would come to adopt the grantmaking practices of a philanthropic foundation, with a substantial role for its program officers to interact with recipients. As IDRC staff focused their gaze on the developing world, management cultivated a network of allies within Ottawa, periodically repositioning or restructuring IDRC to adjust to a changing performance regime.

Such research was subjected to three distinct periods of performance expectations and goals (Figure 4.1). At first, IDRC was afforded a substantial degree of autonomy. Program theory was based on *capacity building*: strengthening research communities in developing countries to address their own problems. Grantmaking provided direct project funding to southern recipients, loosely linked to the themes of information, health, agricultural, or social science. A second period, starting in 1991, witnessed waves of budget cuts in the federal government that heightened demands to control operating costs and to demonstrate the utility of research. Program theory emphasized *policy influence*: research as an input into local efforts to address poverty abroad, requiring recipients to connect with audiences able to influence such issues. IDRC restructured itself and adopted a set of Board-approved program strategies which influenced project selection. A third period, starting in the early 2000s, emphasized alignment with the priorities of Canada's foreign policy. Programming was increasingly tied to government funding decisions, or committed to programs partially funded by the Canadian International Development Agency (CIDA) and donors outside Canada. Program theory valued research for its actual contribution to changed policy and practice in the developing world, with an increasing array of expectations placed upon its recipients. Grantmaking embraced competitive calls for

Figure 4.1. Timeline of Canada case study

proposals alongside the older practices of responding to unsolicited proposals and proactive project development by IDRC staff.

Origins

In contrast to the United Kingdom, Canada opted to create a distinct for-purpose organization to fund research for the developing world. The idea originated in the 1960s. At home, Lester B. Pearson's Liberal government (1963–8) rewrote the social contract with the introduction of universal health care and the Canada Pension Plan. Abroad, Canada established itself as an independent actor in foreign policy, championing the concept of peacekeeping following the Suez crisis and avoiding involvement in the Vietnam War. Canadian pride hit a peak in 1967, with the centennial celebrations and hosting of the World Exposition in Montreal. The time was ripe for bold thinking about the country's role in the world.

CIDA was established in 1968, building upon the External Aid Office within the Department of External Affairs which had coordinated Canada's participation in the Colombo Plan. Maurice Strong was appointed Director General of the External Aid Office in 1966. Coming from industry, he questioned the lack of a research branch, which in his experience worked to identify new products and improve production. When Strong met Barbara Ward, author of the book *Spaceship Earth*, the two began to conceive of a foundation or think tank, a Canadian equivalent to the Brookings Institute or the Hudson Institute (Stockdale 1995). Ward enticed Pearson to support the idea, who announced the government's intention to do so in June 1967. With the blessing of Cabinet, Strong convened a steering committee of deputy ministers to refine the idea further (Seward 1974).[1] The committee retained A.F. Wynne Plumptre, a former Executive Director with the World Bank, to prepare a feasibility study of an organization "for the promotion of research directed towards developing countries" (1968: 1).

Plumptre (1968) interviewed various officials in Canada and abroad, and found substantial support for the idea of applying and adapting new technology to the problems of developing countries. He found less enthusiasm for the alternatives of reviewing the results of past programs to improve future aid, or acting as a databank to coordinate international research efforts. Plumptre also discouraged gathering operations into a single location, cautioning that "useful research . . . will take place in the developing countries themselves . . . where the results of the research will have to be applied." He argued that the Canadian government should provide a "substantial and reasonably assured" flow of funds that simultaneously responded to the needs of developing countries and "had application to Canadian experience and Canadian problems" (1968: 5).

Following the transition to Prime Minister Pierre Trudeau, a new Secretary of State, Mitchell Sharp, proposed that Cabinet approve an independent corporation, focused on the problems of underdeveloped countries, drawing on Canadian expertise and experience (Canada 1968). The Cabinet memo

[1] Strong also drew on the UK experience by including Geoffrey Oldham (University of Sussex) in this work. Oldham would continue to contribute to IDRC's work throughout its first decade.

described an "action . . . [and] solution-oriented" organization leading to "policy options and their presentation in usable form to the decision-makers." Reflecting the tenor of the times, the organization was expected to make a uniquely Canadian contribution to the world, reflecting the "country's experience of bilingualism, biculturalism, multi-racialism and federalism."

Simultaneously, in 1968 World Bank President Robert McNamara invited Pearson to chair a commission reviewing the effectiveness of the previous twenty years of development assistance. The resulting report—*Partners in Development*—noted a sense of aid fatigue: "international support for development is . . . flagging . . . its feasibility, even its very purpose is in question. The climate surrounding foreign aid is heavy with disillusion and distrust" (Pearson et al. 1969: 4). Among the many concerns raised,[2] the commission called for greater assistance to research, arguing that "a large effort is needed to absorb, adapt, and develop scientific and technical knowledge in developing countries" (Pearson et al. 1969: 21, 202–7).

As the Pearson commission report was going to press, back home the Trudeau's Liberal government (1968–79) introduced legislation into the House of Commons for debate. Based on frustrated attempts to fund research through CIDA, Strong ensured the bill granted a degree of political independence, as a Crown corporation with its own Board of Governors. While the Board would be appointed by federal government, ten of its twenty-one members could be non-Canadians, ensuring the voice of developing countries in its governance. In January 1970, Sharp moved the bill to a second reading, describing its role to "assist the developing countries to build their own scientific and technological capabilities so that they will [be] . . . contributors in their own right to the solution of their own problems" (Seward 1974: 25). The bill was passed unanimously and, with Royal Assent in May 1970, IDRC was born.

Under the Act, IDRC was "to initiate, encourage, support and conduct research into the problems of the developing regions of the world." It was granted a four-part mandate to: (a) enlist the talents of natural and social scientists and technologists in Canada and other countries; (b) assist the developing regions to build up the research capabilities, the innovative skills, and the institutions required to solve their problems; (c) encourage generally the coordination of international development research; and (d) foster cooperation in research on development problems between the developed and developing regions for their mutual benefit (Canada 1970: s4.1). The challenge ahead was to put this broad mandate into practice.

[2] The report critiqued the use of tied aid, foresaw the problem of external debt among developing countries, and called for "structural adjustment" on behalf of industrialized countries to absorb an increase in imports from developing countries (Smillie 2011).

That job fell to the Board of Governors, particularly the Chairman and President. Indeed, the Act describes "IDRC" as the Board, with the power to appoint such employees as they felt necessary (Canada 1970: s3 and s14). Pearson became the first chairman,[3] providing him with an opportunity to pursue his Commission's recommendations. As a former head of state and Nobel laureate, he provided the political gravitas necessary to ensure the new IDRC was taken seriously. In contrast, following another of Plumptre's insights, the first IDRC President would command respect within the world of research, rather than politics. Strong recruited David Hopper for the job, a Canadian engaged in India's "Green Revolution" to boost agricultural productivity. Hopper had a background in agricultural economics from McGill and Cornell Universities, and had worked with both the Ford and Rockefeller Foundations. Strong had been impressed when he met Hopper in 1967 and sought to emulate the foundation model in the new Centre.

The legacy of preparing the IDRC Act gave Pearson and Hopper a "smorgasbord of ideas" (Seward 1974: 28), a diverse variety of perspectives on research for the developing world upon which to model the new Centre. Yet it would prove to be Hopper's interpretation that would have a lasting influence on the IDRC's philosophy and operations.

Capacity Building

Behind the scenes, ahead of the first meeting of the Board of Governors, Pearson advocated for IDRC to become a think tank that mobilized Canadian expertise. Given the positive reputation of the ODI in the United Kingdom, there were some who thought that IDRC should become the "ODI on the Rideau" River. Yet Pearson was quickly eclipsed by an alliance between Strong and Hopper. As the IDRC Board of Governors convened for the first time in October 1970, Canada was in crisis as the Front de libération du Québec (FLQ) had resorted to kidnapping and murder in their demands for the people of Quebec to have greater autonomy over their own affairs. Under the protection of bodyguards and beginning to experience ill health, Pearson was less strenuous in defending his vision for IDRC. Even as the IDRC Act was being drafted a year earlier, Strong had stated his own vision "to help developing countries to acquire their own problem-solving capabilities" (Stockdale 1995: 168). Meanwhile, Hopper—after years of working alongside Indian scientists and farmers—had a deep conviction that lasting change depended on supporting the people of developing countries to take control of their own development.

[3] The terms used here reflect the language of the IDRC Act, which referred to "chairman" until 2008 when the Act was amended to "chairperson."

This conviction permeated Hopper's inaugural speech to the Board, in which he argued for a conscious choice: emphasizing the second part of the mandate (building research capabilities abroad) by adopting a particular approach to the first part (enlisting the talents of scientists abroad). He saw IDRC's role as "expanding the horizons of indigenous research workers by giving them improved facilities and greater opportunities to collaborate closely with associates elsewhere in the world engaged in similar problems" (IDRC 1970). His vision was based on the conviction that "they, not we, are the best judges of what is relevant to their circumstances" and aspired to grantmaking that would "leave the direct management of our support in the hands of our partners."[4] This speech became the cornerstone of IDRC's program theory, serving as the de facto corporate strategy for the next twenty years. In it, Hopper foreshadowed aspects of the organization that would emerge, including a focus on rural people, addressing problems common to multiple countries, and locating a significant part of IDRC operations outside of Canada.

The young IDRC enjoyed a legislated mandate and high-level champions in the world of politics and research. Given Hopper's direction, IDRC focused on funding research performed by organizations in developing countries, rather than engaging in its own work or funding Canadians. Canadian scientists might find their way into IDRC projects, but the tendency was to place a developing-country researcher as the principal investigator. Under Hopper's guidance, and that of the management team he assembled, emphasis was placed on addressing problems that affected more than one country. Rather than bilateral programming, IDRC's perspective was regional, and it established offices in Asia, Africa, and Latin America.[5]

Management organized IDRC into four program divisions corresponding to agriculture, health, information, and social sciences. Early projects were rooted in one of these four divisions and tended to focus on enhancing a single commodity, crop, or economic activity, typically within a single scientific discipline. For example, the first decade included projects to develop new crop varieties, hand pumps, biogas digesters, cooking stoves, and pit latrines, as well as economic studies of how poor people made their living, such as through informal trade or as rickshaw drivers (IDRC 2000). The result was a balance of being proactive in the pursuit of thematic priorities, yet responsive

[4] Hopper (1979) would later reflect upon his experience at IDRC and concede that at certain times it was necessary simply to tap the best minds to quickly address a pressing need, rather than wait years building up new local capability to address development problems.

[5] Within the first five years, IDRC established regional offices in Singapore, Bogota, Dakar, Beirut, and Nairobi. Security concerns prompted IDRC to leave Beirut and Bogota, relocating these offices to Cairo (1975) and Montevideo (1989) respectively. IDRC also opened an office in New Delhi in 1983.

to the particular circumstances in developing countries and the ideas of particular researchers.

Under the Act, IDRC was not "an agent of Her Majesty" (Canada 1970: s18.1) and its employees were not public servants. A significant portion was not even Canadian, as management actively recruited program officers based on their experience and expertise, regardless of nationality. Today it is difficult to imagine how program officers plied their trade in an age before fax machines, computers, and Internet. The role of a program officer was very much to seek out project ideas, scouting developing countries to identify their needs, and spotting talented people and organizations that could address them. Staff would regularly work with prospective recipients on their project proposals, elaborating ideas to the stage where they could be taken to the Board of Governors for approval.

As Hopper had directed, most projects looked beyond the national level, to foster collaboration among researchers located in different countries; this helped to overcome the isolation from peers, resources, and literature that then plagued scientists working in developing countries. In the words of one employee, program officers acted as "wandering minstrels," painstakingly building networks by sharing what they had seen, and who they had met as they travelled from one location to another (Muirhead and Harpelle 2010: 96). During the course of a project, program officers would regularly travel to visit recipients in the field—to monitor how the project was progressing, offer mentoring in research techniques and access to academic literature not available locally, and to broker contact with peers abroad.

Relations With Ottawa

Financial and administrative autonomy from the rest of the federal government allowed IDRC management the freedom to design the Centre as they saw fit. Yet by the late 1970s, central agencies challenged this autonomy in an attempt to reassert control. IDRC's annual budget had grown rapidly, from $2.5 million to $36.9 million during the seven years between 1971 and 1978. As IDRC's budget grew and the initial euphoria of its creation wore off, ministers began to ask what Canada was getting in return for its investment. In considering the allocation of external aid in 1977, Cabinet made two requests: calling on the Treasury Board Secretariat (TBS) to conduct an evaluation of IDRC activities, and calling on the Privy Council Office to clarify IDRC's relationship with CIDA and the Minister of State for Science and Technology (IDRC 1977).

The Treasury Board evaluation was largely positive in its assessment of IDRC programming. Nonetheless, it was critical of the somewhat ad hoc manner in which the Centre had evolved. In response, IDRC established an Office of Planning and Evaluation, which soon began an annual process of "Program and Policy Reviews" to satisfy the TBS requirement for three-year operational plans. Meanwhile, the Privy Council Office began a process to reschedule Crown corporations, and include them under provisions of the Financial Administration Act. Close contact between IDRC management and Privy Council officials allowed IDRC to argue successfully for preserving its autonomy in order to receive funds from non-Canadian sources and to engage developing countries independently of the federal government. IDRC would be covered by the Financial Administration Act, but given certain exemptions, comparable to the Canadian Broadcasting Corporation and Bank of Canada.

The challenge to its status revealed a need for IDRC to pay as much attention to concerns within official Ottawa as it did to the needs of developing countries. At home, the optimism over Canada's role in the world had been replaced by concern over the price of oil and the emerging phenomenon of economic stagflation. One of IDRC's original champions, Pearson, had passed away and Hopper left in 1978 to accept a senior position within the World Bank. IDRC management, particularly Strong who was now the chairman, realized it was not enough to be well regarded outside of Canada; IDRC needed a domestic constituency within Canada and allies within the government.

This task formed part of the mandate for Ivan Head, who arrived as IDRC's new President in 1978. Trained as a lawyer and having previously served as Trudeau's foreign policy advisor, Head was the mirror opposite of Hopper: someone from the world of politics rather than the world of science. Nonetheless, Head was experienced in navigating official Ottawa and knew the importance of positioning IDRC not as wholly independent, but as useful to government. He would publicly speak of IDRC as an expression of Canadian foreign policy, rather than an instrument of it. While the program officer might be focused on IDRC's relationship with researchers in developing countries, management and the Board needed to be attentive to IDRC's relationship with the Canadian government.

IDRC was under the portfolio of the Minister of State for External Affairs, and formally the Centre connected to the machinery of government at two levels: the chairman was accountable to the minister; and IDRC officials interacted with their counterparts in the department responsible for development assistance. In practice, IDRC maintained a wider range of ties with CIDA, the Department of Finance, and central agencies, at the levels of deputy ministers, assistant deputy ministers, and director generals with geographic responsibility for parts of the developing world. Management invested time in a deliberate attempt to cultivate "friends of IDRC," an influential network that knew of and appreciated the Centre's work. It was also a practical means of gathering insights into the government's decision-making and policy processes, purposefully fact-checking what came through official channels. Much of this lobbying on behalf of IDRC was invisible to its staff: it tended to ebb in good years, but increase to a fever pitch on occasions when IDRC felt threatened.

In the late 1970s, IDRC repositioned itself as Canada's response to an international agenda. In 1979, the United Nations convened a Conference on Science and Technology for Development (UNCSTD). These were heady times as the rise of oil wealth in parts of the developing world fueled the rise of the Non-Aligned Movement and talk of a New International Economic Order. For the Canadian government, IDRC was a ready-made platform for Canada going into the conference, and was more palatable than the alternative of establishing a new multilateral agency or fund under the UN system. IDRC jumped at the chance to assert itself as such, convening a preparatory meeting in Toronto (Gordon 1979) and working closely with External Affairs to prepare positions and briefings, acting as the department's brain trust on such issues.

A new pattern had emerged. IDRC could not take its existence for granted merely because of its founding legislation. It needed to constantly renew its ties to official Ottawa and reposition itself as contributing to the priorities of the day. The government provided funding that allowed IDRC to support researchers abroad, and in return the Centre was attentive to the exigencies of foreign policy.

Throughout the 1970s and 1980s, IDRC proved its usefulness to the Department of External Affairs in sustaining critical social science inside countries experiencing dictatorship. In Chile, Argentina, and Uruguay, IDRC supported organizations that allowed economists and political scientists to continue doing their work at home. Alternatively, in Uganda IDRC provided an "underground railway for intellectuals" to escape persecution and work in other countries (Muirhead and Harpelle 2010: 76). IDRC's arms-length status was useful for government, allowing it the means to engage in situations where it did not or could not take an official position. The most prominent instance would occur on South Africa in the late 1980s when, with the blessing of the Prime Minister, IDRC assisted the African National Congress and Mass Democratic Movement to prepare the policies needed for a post-Apartheid era.

With its own position in Canada's foreign policy family, IDRC was somewhat insulated from the periodic shift in CIDA's priorities. It was even more isolated from Canada's science policy. IDRC would occasionally reach out to the Minister of State for Science and Technology, and later Industry Canada, but these relationships were of little consequence in determining IDRC's fortunes.

Canadian universities resented that IDRC did not dedicate more of its resources to Canadian researchers. In response, Ivan Head's tenure saw

IDRC's agricultural division station five program officers within Canadian universities, and the Centre adopted a "cooperative program" in 1981 specifically aimed at encouraging collaboration between Canadian researchers and peers in developing countries (Muirhead and Harpelle 2010: 113 and 119). Whereas IDRC in the 1970s had spent under 2 percent of its funding at Canadian universities, in later years Canadian institutions were involved in as much as one-fifth of IDRC projects. Nonetheless, IDRC management and Board continued sending the bulk of the Centre's resources abroad, encouraging Canadian scientists to seek support for their work through the tri-councils for natural, social, and medical research.

Serving a New Master

The arrival of Prime Minister Brian Mulroney's Progressive Conservative government (1984–93) presented IDRC with a new challenge. While the passage of the IDRC Act had enjoyed unanimous support in Parliament in 1970, IDRC was closely associated with Liberal leadership, particularly Pearson and Trudeau. Indeed IDRC's budget had doubled under Trudeau's second government (1980–4), from $40 million to over $80 million. The challenge was to position IDRC as an organization the new government would identify with and support.

That opportunity came with a review of Canada's foreign aid, chaired by William Winegard. A former President of Guelph University, Winegard had been an IDRC governor in the late 1970s, prior to becoming a Conservative Member of Parliament in 1984. Unsurprisingly the committee report endorsed IDRC's raison d'être. Titled *For Whose Benefit*, the report noted that IDRC helped developing countries overcome dependency on "technology conceived and produced outside their borders and without reference to their needs" (Canada 1987: 77). While critical of a number of aspects of the foreign aid program, the report simply encouraged IDRC to do more "to ensure the practical application of its research," suggesting staff exchanges with CIDA and greater use IDRC research in CIDA projects (1987: 20).[6]

A more ringing endorsement came the following year as the Office of the Auditor General (OAG) included IDRC in a special report focused on well-performing organizations:

> IDRC is considered worldwide to be one of the best organizations of its kind. Its high performance is based on a number of elements: people who are competent,

[6] The desire for greater synergy between IDRC and CIDA arose in later reviews, up to the 2007 OECD-DAC Peer Review of Canada.

> committed and value-driven; continuity of leadership; a clear and strong sense of mission and purpose; a strong client focus; autonomy and flexibility at all levels; risk-taking and innovation; freedom from political and central agency interference; tailor-made internal regulations and reporting requirements; and continual self-scrutiny of strategies and activities. (Canada 1988)

Thus IDRC thrived in the first years of the Conservative government, and by 1988 reached a budget that exceeded $110 million per year. Continued growth nonetheless strained the organization, which had retained the same structure and strategy for almost two decades, despite tripling the size of budget and staff. Each of the four divisions operated more or less independently of each other, seeking out and proposing projects based on their individual merit, with little sense of how they might complement each other or contribute to corporate goals.

In 1985, IDRC management and the Board endorsed a mission and set of objectives through the seventh *Policy and Program Review*: "to support research of direct relevance to and demonstrable potential for Third World development, with relative emphasis on poverty problems; and . . . to assist developing countries to build and maintain indigenous research . . . capacity . . . mainly in terms of human resources" (IDRC 1985: 13). On the surface, these objectives were quite broad, describing the status quo rather than suggesting a change in direction. Nonetheless, a careful reading of this document shows that IDRC was struggling with some fundamental questions:

> In the early years of IDRC, strategic planning was characterised by a commonly shared philosophy based on a generous mandate allowing considerable freedom to explore, innovate and create . . . it is now timely to evolve further and to develop clearer strategic policy guidelines, beginning with more formal statements of broad Centre objectives. (1985: 1)

In particular, the 1985 *Policy and Program Review* reveals greater emphasis on demonstrating how projects were expected to contribute to development outcomes. The document states bluntly that the "'burden of proof' for all proposals lies with the proponents, who should explain the socio-economic context and implication of each activity, including how the potential outputs could contribute to the Centre's mission" (1985: 32). IDRC began to layer new expectations on its recipients. Beyond conducting sound science that respected disciplinary norms, recipients needed to show alignment with IDRC's programs, as well as define and reach an audience for their work. In 1986, Head convened management to further re-examine the mandate and function, highlighting new concerns for interdisciplinarity in research design and the utilization of research results. IDRC divisions were encouraged to identify the results of their work and to consider research as a means to achieve development, rather than an end in its own right.

Management also struggled with the question of geographic balance in IDRC programming. Lower-income countries with higher levels of poverty were arguably in greater need of support, but had a relatively meager base of local researchers and organizations with which to engage. So-called emerging economies, such as India and Brazil, had rising incomes, rising inequality, and an increasingly rich array of research talent. Given IDRC's tendency to be attentive to local researchers, the voices from the latter threatened to drown out the former and, given IDRC's limited budget, it was tempting to work where such talent already existed rather than build it from scratch. As had become IDRC's practice, the policy decision was not cast as a choice between two extremes, but a question of balance.[7] At the time, management and the Board decided that in principle IDRC could fund work in any developing country, yet proposals from more advanced economies would receive proportionately greater scrutiny and be eligible for less comprehensive support.

In summary, during this first period, the performance regime afforded IDRC a substantial degree of autonomy. Central agencies occasionally sought to reassert control over the Crown corporation, but IDRC defended its niche within foreign aid by cultivating a network of allies in the bureaucracy. Program theory emphasized capacity building: strengthening research communities in developing countries to address their own problems. Grantmaking provided direct project funding to southern recipients, loosely linked to the themes of information, health, agricultural, or social science.

Budget Cuts

Keith Bezanson was appointed as the IDRC President in 1991, inheriting a Centre that had changed little over time. Over two decades, the parliamentary appropriation for IDRC had grown from $5 million to $114 million per year, while the number of staff had expanded to over 600 (IDRC 1991b; Beemans 1999). Yet IDRC retained thematic divisions that would have been easily recognizable to Hopper or any of the original IDRC governors. In contrast, the coming decade would be a turbulent period that would see IDRC's status threatened once again and its budget slashed on two occasions. The combination of these shocks, along with changing ideas on how to organize science, provoked a substantial restructuring of IDRC.

Whereas Head had come from the world of politics, Bezanson came from the public service. Having worked for CIDA for most his career, he served as

[7] Hopper (1973) had set this pattern with an essay identifying eleven policy issues on which IDRC needed to choose a path incorporating competing goals, such as: support research at home *and* abroad, on topics identified by proponents *and* those selected by IDRC staff.

Canada's ambassador to Bolivia and Peru in the mid-1980s, before joining the Inter-American Development Bank. He knew about development and foreign policy, and came to IDRC with definitive views that the Centre had grown too complacent: confident in its own inherent value, but with little sense of how it connected to the rest of government (Muirhead and Harpelle 2010: 208).

With the approach of IDRC's twentieth anniversary, Bezanson led the drafting of a new strategy, finally replacing Hopper's inaugural speech. Bezanson recast the IDRC mandate as "empowerment through knowledge": encouraging the creation, adaptation, and ownership of the knowledge that people of developing countries judge to be of the greatest relevance to their own prosperity, security and equity. While the strategy retained the essence of Hopper's vision, Bezanson was convinced that the idea of development had fundamentally changed with the end of the Cold War and the rise of globalization.

In particular, Bezanson was determined to sharpen IDRC's programs and reduce operational expenses. He was shocked that IDRC was spending close to 40 percent of its budget on operating expenses and staffing, and immediately set a target ratio of 70:30 between programming and operational expenses. First, each program officer was to boost the value of programming they handled, encouraging southern institutions to manage the day-to-day technical and financial management of projects. Second, Bezanson convinced the Board of Governors to reduce the staff by 20 percent. He even sent the new strategy to Paul Tellier, Clerk of the Privy Council, along with a handwritten note promising this reduction (Stockdale 1995).

Such steps made Bezanson unpopular among staff, yet his reforms were intended to help IDRC adapt to a changing performance regime. Canada's foreign aid budget had grown at 7 percent per year throughout much of the 1980s, much above the rate of growth of the national economy. By the 1990s, the national debt was a rising concern and the decade ahead saw reductions in government spending in order to balance the books. The government also faced new pressures with the collapse of the Soviet Union. The 1991 federal budget scaled back the growth of aid to 3 percent and embedded aid within an International Assistance Envelope (IAE) which allowed for spending development assistance money in Eastern Europe. Facing slower growth and new pressures, it was only a matter of time before there were implications for IDRC. The first impact came in April 1991 when the government decided to take away $7 million of IDRC's budget to help Canada address famine in Africa. In nominal terms, this returned the parliamentary funding for IDRC back to its 1988 level, making a reduction in spending inevitable.

By the end of the fiscal year, the number of IDRC staff went from 592 to 486 persons. Bezanson encouraged IDRC to seek out opportunities to do contract research on behalf of other organizations, as well as co-funding from other donors in IDRC projects. Referred to in-house as "resource expansion," the intent was to diversify IDRC's sources of revenue: to compensate for the reduction of parliamentary funding by hosting big ideas that would leverage funding from outside sources. Pierre Beemans, then an IDRC vice-president, (1999) would later note that "rather than cut our programs to fit our budget cloth, we decided to try to attract other funding agencies to invest in our activities or to join with us in jointly-managed ones." Within a few years, Bezanson would boast that "about a fifth of all IDRC projects now involve at least one other funding agency. In addition, most Centre projects provide for contributions in cash or kind from recipient institutions" (IDRC 1994: 35). IDRC would argue that its status as a Crown corporation was justified in order to receive such funds.

A key example was IDRC hosting a "Micronutrient Initiative," started in 1992, to address deficiencies in vitamin A, iron, and iodine in the diets of people in developing countries. The initiative attracted support from the World Bank and would be the first time that the government provided a special-purpose appropriation to IDRC, essentially earmarking funding to this specific initiative rather than providing core support to the IDRC Board. The Micronutrient Initiative would eventually leave IDRC in 2002 as a stand-alone legal entity. Another example was the "essential health interventions" project under which IDRC, World Bank, and CIDA set out to test the assertion in the 1993 *World Development Report* that a small increment of funding could dramatically reduce mortality through better targeting of health care to the local burden of disease. Over the decade, pilot results in two districts of Tanzania, including a 40 percent decline in child deaths, provided the proof of concept that attracted support from the UK charity Comic Relief to scale up the efforts across the country.

Embracing Rio

No sooner had IDRC begun to adjust to a smaller budget, than its status as a Crown corporation was once again threatened. Since the late 1980s, the Mulroney government had been reviewing Crown corporations, in an effort to reduce government spending and "letting market forces take the initiative to enhance Canada's competitiveness" (Canada 1991: 76). The effect was to eliminate many Crown corporations altogether through privatization, merging their operations into line departments, or simply reducing government funding to them. The federal budget in 1992 announced the elimination of forty-six government entities. Small and less visible to Canadian citizens, IDRC was originally considered for inclusion in this list (Muirhead and Harpelle 2010: 209).

Last minute efforts by Hugh Segal, then Mulroney's Chief of Staff, modified the budget's reference to IDRC (Stockdale 1995). Instead of eliminating the Centre, the government now intended to "introduce legislation to change IDRC's legal status to that of a departmental corporation... [to] bring its administrative regime into conformity with that of the rest of the public service, while maintaining the Centre's distinctive research function and its international board" (Canada 1992a: 128). Pierre Beemans would subsequently recall the lack of domestic outcry "gave us a vivid idea of how alienated IDRC had become from its Canadian roots," and management once again learned the need to "cultivate senior decision-makers in DFAIT, CIDA, PMO/PCO, [and] Finance" (1999).

The threat to IDRC's status was short-lived and the promised legislation was never introduced. Instead IDRC was granted a new lease of life in June 1992, just months after the February budget.

As world leaders convened in Rio de Janeiro for the United Nations Conference on Environment and Development (UNCED), the relationship between developing countries and industrialized ones was once again in the forefront of international relations. The model of IDRC, investing in local researchers to address their problems, was a good fit with the emerging discourse of North–South cooperation. More importantly, one of IDRC's original champions, Maurice Strong, chaired the conference and had numerous opportunities to engage the Canadian delegation and Mulroney himself (Muirhead and Harpelle 2010: 228).

Whether through policy fit or personal lobbying, the Prime Minister announced that IDRC's mandate would be broadened "to emphasize sustainable development issues... [and] help to ensure a quick start on implementation of the UNCED Agenda 21 program" (Canada 1992b: 17).

Furthermore, the Prime Minister committed to provide $115 million annually in core support to the organization, noting that this would total more than $1 billion over the next ten years. Bezanson grabbed hold of the Prime Minister's endorsement, and within a month IDRC released a volume describing how its current and future work contributed to this "expanded" mandate.

As Agenda 21 was an unwieldy 600-page document, it was easy to link existing IDRC projects to its various entry points. Nor was such a match accidental. IDRC had hosted the Brundtland Commission's consultations in the mid-1980s, and became the repository of the Commission's archives following the publication of *Our Common Future* (World Commission on Environment and Development 1987). The year 1992 would nonetheless be the turning point in which IDRC embraced "sustainable and equitable development" as the principle underpinning all its work. IDRC continued its disciplinary divisions, yet a new three-year corporate program framework emphasized how projects contributed to sustainable development, under the themes of biodiversity, food, technology, policies, and information. The long-standing focus on agriculture and rural development began to evolve toward environmental and natural resource management. Meanwhile, IDRC began to offer training and support in environmental economics in Southeast Asia, and championed the new field of environmental health by tracing the cause of mercury contamination through the food chain in the Amazon.

Yet within two years, Mulroney's promise of sustained funding for IDRC disappeared. The election of Jean Chrétien's Liberal government (1993–2003) saw the federal government conduct a sweeping "program review" to reduce spending across the public service. Between 1995 and 1997, the IAE was scheduled to reduce from \$2.6 billion to \$2.1 billion per year, equivalent to a 21 percent cut (Canada 1995). In nominal terms, the parliamentary appropriation for IDRC shrank from \$112 million to \$96 million per year. In real terms, the combination of cuts during the 1990s reduced the appropriation by 35 percent (IDRC 1995a). As much of IDRC's funding in any given year went to pay expenses on existing projects, the Centre cut its 1995 allocation budget for new projects by 30 percent.

By the summer of 1995, Bezanson led management through an exercise that John Hardie (the Director of Planning) would later describe as simultaneously downsizing, restructuring, and reorienting thinking to new philosophy (Muirhead and Harpelle 2010: 259). A smaller budget meant a further need to reduce expenses: the number of IDRC staff would shrink to 427 by the end of the fiscal year, and to 347 by 1998. The health sciences division disappeared almost entirely: reduced to a single project on health care in Tanzania and a modest set of projects on human-environmental health. After twenty-five years, the old disciplinary divisions were collapsed into a single "programs branch."

Program officers were assigned to time-limited teams, or "program initiatives." The Board of Governors would no longer approve individual projects. Instead the Board approved program-level strategy for each initiative, and delegated authority to IDRC management to approve projects in line with those strategies. Programs were challenged to "define a research problematique and... address it over a given time period (3–5 years); establish networks among recipient institutions... [and] bring in external funding" (IDRC 1995b). In return, each program would undergo an external evaluation at the end of this lifespan, the results of which would inform the Board's decision whether to renew, modify, or close the program.

This structure of program initiatives responded to changing ideas about research management, particularly "mode 2" science. IDRC's original structure was perceived as what Gibbons et al. (1994) refer to as "mode 1": researchers working in isolation producing disciplinary knowledge on problems defined in academia. In contrast, the new program initiatives were expected to support participation of poor people and policymakers in jointly solving interdisciplinary problems identified in society (Slaymaker et al. 1998). The program initiatives also responded to a changing performance regime. Staff noted that "[t]he competition for funds is rising," requiring managers to "ensure utilization of research results and use evidence of impact to convince the public and decision-makers of the value of research efforts" (Daniels and Dottridge 1993: 206). Management subsequently cautioned that "[i]n a period of scarcer resources, science has had to become more accountable. Inputs and outputs [a]re to be measured and science supply was to be integrated with market demand" (Slaymaker et al. 1998: 10).

The program initiatives were IDRC's new way of doing business. While IDRC continued to fund research projects, the ambition for what these projects were expected to achieve had grown. Referred to as "capacity building," IDRC described the results of its work as assisting developing-country researchers in "designing and monitoring projects, interdisciplinarity and research utilization, linkages with peers and scientific networks to access new ideas and methods, [to gain] greater confidence and experience, [and] enhanced profile and credibility" (IDRC 1996: 18). Yet when IDRC adopted a second corporate program framework in 1996, research capacity came second to a new emphasis on "policies and technologies that enhance the lives of people in the developing regions." Research for the developing world was expected to lead "directly to sustainable improvement in the quality of human existence, or... improved understanding of factors that affect development" (Slaymaker et al. 1998: 6).

New Leadership, New Ambition

In 1996, Bezanson's term as IDRC President was renewed for a single year, fueling rumors that the government intended to close the Centre. Sensing an opportunity, the University of British Columbia (UBC) proposed to host a "virtual center" not unlike Pearson's vision—it would essentially replace IDRC by refocusing on mobilizing existing expertise within Canada. Led by UBC President David Strangway, the proposal was supported by former IDRC President Ivan Head who by then was based at the university. Maurice Strong once again emerged to neutralize this threat to IDRC, this time from his position leading a task force examining how Canada connected to the world. The task force report argued that intellectual capacity, rather than size of the economy, increasingly determined a country's stature on the international stage. The report described IDRC as a strategic asset for Canada, acting as a knowledge broker with emerging economies. In receiving the report, the new foreign minister Lloyd Axworthy rejected the UBC proposal and offered Bezanson an additional mandate (Muirhead and Harpelle 2010: 263–4). Yet the turbulence at IDRC had taken its toll, and Bezanson soon moved to the University of Sussex as director of its Institute of Development Studies (IDS).

Maureen O'Neil was appointed as IDRC President in April 1997. With a list of accomplishments that included President of the North-South Institute and Deputy Minister for Citizenship in the Ontario government, O'Neil combined an understanding of international development and knowledge of how to navigate the machinery of government. In June, she was joined by Gordon Smith, who was appointed Chairman of the IDRC Board. A former Deputy Minister of Foreign Affairs, Smith once again provided IDRC with the high-level gravitas that would convince government that a steady hand was in charge overseeing IDRC management.

Following the trauma of the program review years, the end of the decade was a period of renewed calm. The federal government started realizing surplus budgets once more. Over the next twelve years, the government would invest an additional $13 billion into Canadian research (Doern and Stoney 2009: 10–11). The expanding resources benefited the granting councils and funded new mechanisms including the Canadian Foundation for Innovation (for science infrastructure at universities), Genome Canada (for the genetic sciences), and Canadian Research Chairs (to attract Canadian talent to stay or return home). The new funding also enhanced the importance of university-based research in Canada, as the boom in spending largely bypassed government labs and science-based departments.

As the parliamentary appropriation for IDRC came from the foreign aid budget, the Centre did not directly benefit from increased science spending. Yet it indirectly enhanced the legitimacy of IDRC's work. Research was recognized as important for Canada's own development, therefore it followed that it should be important to the development of other countries as well. This message as soon reinforced by the World Bank, as President James Wolfensohn outlined a vision for changing the organization into a "knowledge bank." This echoed one of the original competing perspectives for IDRC at its founding, and became the theme of the 1998 edition of the flagship *World Development Report* under the title "knowledge for development" (World Bank 1998).

This more favorable performance regime gave O'Neil a new degree of freedom in preparing a five-year corporate strategy (2000–5). The program initiatives were regrouped under three areas: environmental and natural resource management, social and economic equity, and information and communication technologies for development (ICT4D). O'Neil also continued to shift IDRC toward influencing policy, rather than merely building capacity. The phrase "closing the loop" entered the corporate vocabulary, representing a conscious push to ensure that findings reached policymakers and other

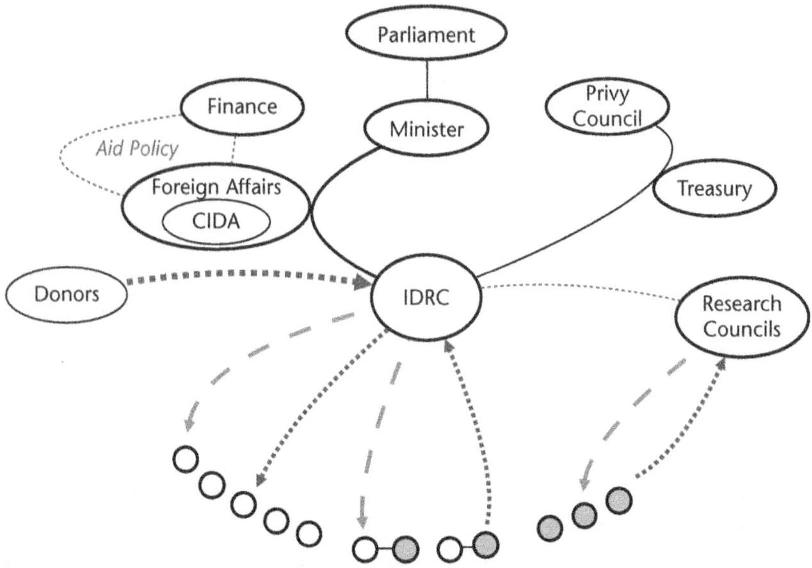

Figure 4.2. Performance regime surrounding IDRC

Solid lines represent formal lines of authority, dotted lines describe the flow of program ideas, and dashed lines show funding relationships. The upper portion represents governance context; the lower portion describes grantmaking, with shaded circles representing recipients in Canada. From left to right: support to recipients abroad, networks with multiple participants, and twinning Canada with south recipients.

audiences able to act on such findings. This goal was subsequently described rather bluntly as "IDRC wants to be able to demonstrate to those who influence or control our funding that we support research that produces useful development results" (IDRC 2002).

In summary, the second period witnessed waves of budget cuts in the federal government, heightening demands to control operating costs and to demonstrate the utility of research. Program theory began to emphasize policy influence, seeing research as an input into local efforts to address poverty abroad and expecting recipients to connect with an audience that would act on their findings. Following restructuring, IDRC continued to offer project funding, but required that these contributed to Board-approved program strategies. The emerging performance regime that was beginning to surround IDRC is depicted in Figure 4.2.

Eroding Core

The new century would once again transform the performance regime surrounding IDRC. After the turbulence of the 1990s, the arrival of Maureen

O'Neil and the launch of a five-year strategy was a new beginning. Coming out of the 2002 Monterrey conference on financing development, Canada committed to doubling its official development assistance, and soon established a timetable for doing so via annual 8 percent increments to its aid budget. The next federal budget committed that IDRC would receive a proportional 8 percent increase in its funding during each of the next two years (Canada 2003: 169), thus cutting through the old haggling with CIDA over what share of a growing aid budget would go to research. IDRC and central agencies had advocated for greater transparency in how funding decisions were made. Behind the scenes, the Department of Foreign Affairs and International Trade (DFAIT) and CIDA began work on a new management framework for the IAE.

IDRC's second five-year strategy began in 2005 with tidying the structure inherited from the previous ten years. IDRC retained the three program areas—ICT, environment, and socio-economics—each of which housed a small number of programs, now firmly entrenched as IDRC's preferred way of organizing its work. Despite the increasing budget, the overall number of programs reduced, in order to have larger teams with a global remit. A diverse array of corporate projects, explorations, and secretariats had evolved in the late 1990s and early 2000s as part of IDRC's push to diversify revenue. These were now converted into stand-alone legal entities, merged into regular programs, or transferred to institutions outside of IDRC. For example, a Model Forests' Secretariat moved to Natural Resources Canada, and an Institute for Connectivity in the Americas was integrated into the ICT4D program area.

Beyond such changes in organization, O'Neil continued to press a change in purpose, reinforcing the mantra of "research for policy influence." This goal was enshrined in the new strategy (IDRC 2004: para 62) and the work funded by IDRC programs was expected to inform policies that benefited poor women and men (Carden 2009). IDRC continued to view the world in terms of geographic regions, rather than focusing on particular countries. The earlier 2000–5 strategy had committed IDRC to spending half of its budget in Africa, and a quarter in each of Asia and the Americas. These notional targets continued to guide management as a rule-of-thumb, but IDRC stopped formal tracking and reporting on such. This was partially due to the difficulty of parsing project spending that involved multiple regions or that did not have an obvious geographic footprint, for example the benefits of new seeds could touch multiple regions regardless of where the research was conducted.

The 2005 budget introduced a new management framework for the IAE. The framework distinguished five categories, or "pools," of activities eligible for funding: development assistance to poorer countries, initiatives to enhance global peace and security, contributions to international financial institutions, responses to humanitarian crises, and support for development research (Canada 2005: 217). At one level, the framework simply affirmed the status quo, recognizing the distinct interests of CIDA, DFAIT, the Department of Finance, and IDRC. Yet at another level, beyond what was contained in the budget, the framework laid out a process for allocating the promised increases of funding in future years. No one minister would control the IAE, instead senior officials would facilitate a "competition of ideas," collecting and assessing proposals for how the incremental funds could be used. Government officials would then prepare options, or packages of proposals, for deputy ministers who would prepare a recommendation for Cabinet supported jointly by the three ministers responsible for international cooperation, foreign affairs, and finance.

De jure, IDRC held a weak position within this competition of ideas. The 2005 budget assigned a lead manager for each of the "pools," making DFAIT responsible for development research. IDRC was expected to submit its ideas through DFAIT, placing that department in the dual roles of both representing IDRC interests while also presenting arguments in favor of its own initiatives. On occasion, IDRC might be invited to attend part of a meeting to describe its proposals, but these engagements occurred among officials or assistant deputy ministers. IDRC was excluded from the final negotiation among deputy ministers.

Yet IDRC found ways to enhance its de facto position away from the negotiating table, by engaging with—and gaining support from—CIDA, DFAIT, and the Department of Finance. IDRC had constructive relations with all three organizations, aided by the fact that each was genuinely interested in different parts of IDRC's programming, whether health and environment, peace and conflict, or development economics. At the same time, IDRC requests for additional funding were modest and at a scale that did not necessarily compete with these organizations' own funding requests. This was an intentional tactic on behalf of IDRC management, which sought to maintain the Centre's parliamentary grant at roughly 4 percent of the envelope, pitching for incremental funding to expand existing programs. IDRC staff also interacted with Privy Council Office and Treasury Board officials. These central agencies did not have a vested interest in the allocation of new aid money, and often advocated in favor of including IDRC, up to the point of decision making. They also provided insights on how the allocation process was unfolding, clarifying the evolving criteria used to assess proposals.

The arrival of Stephen Harper's Conservative government (2006–) did not immediately alter this "competition of ideas" process. The new government was quick to dissociate itself from a short-lived international policy statement the previous Liberal administration had released in 2005. Yet the IAE framework persisted and IDRC was initially able to continue its strategy of modest requests for incremental funding. IDRC would trawl through its pipeline of proposed projects and identify items that resonated with what government was interested in funding. While the justification for the funding request was based on what each IAE partner promised to do in the short term (one-to-three years), the allocation of incremental resources was ongoing. In the words of one official, it was "forever money" that was added to the organization's reference level, which TBS used as a base for departmental spending in future years. Thus any funds allocated to IDRC amounted to an ongoing increase in its parliamentary appropriation. In the short term, IDRC obtained new resources for projects the Centre largely wanted to fund anyway. Thus the "competition of ideas" freed up existing resources. In the medium term, these new resources promised to become core funding available for the IDRC Board to allocate as it saw fit.

Aligning With Donors and Science

IDRC negotiated a new round of program-level partnerships with other donors, including on climate change adaptation in Africa with the UK government, and an initiative to support policy research think tanks with the William and Flora Hewlett Foundation.[8] Such partnerships represented a conscious move away from the indiscriminate "resource expansion" of the 1990s which had focused on time-limited project funding from any organization, toward ongoing program-level collaboration with like-minded organizations. The new practice focused on a select set of "donor partners," avoiding those that had proven difficult to work with, whether due to conditions placed on their funding or a tendency to micro-manage how IDRC used the funds. IDRC's intention was to enter into true partnerships with other funders, investing Centre funds in order to avoid being merely an implementing agency.

Within official Ottawa, such donor partnerships were a double-edged sword. On occasion, the Department of Finance suggested that since IDRC was successful at raising funds abroad, it did not require as much support from taxpayers. IDRC management responded that it was the ability to leverage Canadian funding that had allowed these partnerships to occur. More often than not, IDRC's ability to attract funding from outside Canada was positively received. After all, if UK taxpayers and private philanthropists entrusted their resources to IDRC, surely it was a good use of Canadian taxpayers' dollars.

The Conservative government's initial priorities for foreign policy emphasized Canada's NATO mission in Afghanistan, asserting Canada's sovereignty in the Arctic, and enhancing commercial and security relations in the

[8] The first example with DFID represented over $50 million over five years, while the second example eventually grew to $115 million when the Bill & Melinda Gates Foundation joined.

Americas. IDRC management seized upon the imperative to contribute to rebuilding Afghanistan, but conditions on the ground presented a challenge to IDRC's usual "hands-on" approach of working directly with local researchers. Security concerns restricted the ability of IDRC staff to visit the country, and much of the Afghan research community had already emigrated. IDRC eventually funded a handful of projects, including modest support to Kabul University to collaborate with other institutions of higher education throughout the Hindu-Kush mountain range. Yet these projects were led through the IDRC Regional Office in New Delhi, with no engagement in the cross-government task force, whether at DFAIT or the Privy Council Office. IDRC was better placed to contribute to the government's agenda on the Americas. Once again, the IDRC Regional Office in Montevideo played a vital role, keeping IDRC programming visible with Canada's ambassadors in the region and designing an initiative that encouraged think tanks in Latin America to critically assess how their countries were contributing to Haitian security and development. Yet such efforts were relatively modest, a symbolic nod toward government priorities. In the words of one IDRC official, "an investment of two percent of the budget to protect the remaining ninety-eight percent" of IDRC programs.

The change in government did encourage a shift in IDRC programming on science and technology policy. After a long absence from the field, IDRC created a new program area in 2005, motivated in part by renewed enthusiasm for advances in science to help achieve development goals (UN Millennium Project 2005) echoing the discourse of the 1970s. IDRC management sought to seize upon the former Prime Minister Paul Martin's promise to devote 5 percent of Canada's R&D to "a knowledge-based approach to develop assistance for less fortunate countries" (Canada 2004). Initially, IDRC expected this new program area to enhance the positive impact of new technologies, strengthen innovation and science policy in developing countries, and foster collaboration with Canada's research-granting councils. Yet under the Conservative government, the international tone of Canada's science policy turned from altruistic assistance to poorer countries, toward enhancing Canadian participation in international collaboration. In 2007, a new federal science and technology strategy identified four thematic priorities—including environment, natural resources, health, and ICTs—which closely matched IDRC's own priorities. Over the coming years, the government would express an expectation that public research funding would enhance the competitiveness of Canada's industry.

A substantial amount of the work funded under the new program area soon came to focus on international collaboration, including an initiative to twin southern researchers with Canadian Research Chairs and joint calls with the Canadian Institute for Health Research (CIHR) and the Social Sciences and

Humanities Research Council (SSHRC). In each case, the granting council funded the participation of Canadians while IDRC funded the participation by developing-country scientists. Whether by coincidence or following the shift in government priority, IDRC placed proportionately less emphasis on new technologies or S&T policy in other countries.

While the foreign aid budget increased after 2002, Canada's science budget had grown since 1997 and Canadian universities were increasingly enthusiastic about international collaboration. Joint calls with the research-granting councils was a mixture of self-interest and altruism. Such partnerships helped raise IDRC's profile within Canada, associating itself with the government's support for science. Launch events became opportunities for ministerial announcements that put IDRC in the spotlight, including one event held within the parliamentary precinct. IDRC was also motivated to share its experience with international research collaboration. IDRC explained its procedures for grant administration, including how it dealt with multiple recipients, in multiple countries, using multiple currencies. The reaction of one granting council official was "IDRC manages nightmare projects" due to the complexity involved. The granting councils were used to focusing on *ex ante* project selection and managing peer review processes, and were surprised to learn of the amount of attention IDRC invested to *ex post* evaluation and ongoing project monitoring.

An expanding budget for IDRC allowed health programming to thrive once again. The project on essential health interventions in Tanzania slowly expanded to a new program initiative working on the governance of health systems and financing health care. This work was initially housed under the social-economic program area, but soon grew beyond it as IDRC also began to tackle electronic information systems and the use of mobile devices in health care. In 2008, IDRC re-established health as a separate program area, no longer subsumed under social and economic policy.

Fitting into Government

Starting in 2007, the Conservative government launched a series of "strategic reviews" under which each year a number of departments were asked to assess the entirety of their existing programs. Each review was to identify at least 5 percent of department spending that was performing less well, or seen as a relatively lower priority. The initial intention was to identify opportunities to redesign programs and better align them with government priorities, yet over the subsequent four years, the reviews would come to focus more on simply reducing government spending. In this respect, IDRC was fortunate to be included in the first year of the strategic review, when the process still permitted departments to propose options for reinvesting the 5 percent of funding under examination.

DFAIT and CIDA were included in the first round when it launched in spring 2007. As an afterthought, the Privy Council Office added IDRC in early summer in order to look across the entirety of the IAE. Each of the three organizations conducted their own review, coordinating with others, but ultimately preparing their own individual submissions to the Treasury Board. IDRC was allowed to retain its funding, reallocating it to programming more closely aligned with government priorities. The quality of the IDRC submission no doubt helped, as did the opportunity for O'Neil to plead the Centre's case directly before Treasury Board ministers.[9]

The logic of the strategic review worked against the ongoing growth in the international assistance budget. Any savings identified among the IAE organizations needed to be replaced if Canada's was to meet its ongoing commitment to double foreign aid. Indeed, the "competition of ideas" process continued parallel to, and disconnected from, the strategic review. Yet ministers had begun to see the "competition of ideas" as captured by the bureaucracy: a collusion among officials on how to divide funding among themselves and their departments' interests. The strategic review previewed an interest at Cabinet level to get beyond merely allocating the incremental increases in funding to review instead the entirety of international assistance.

In 2008–9, the Cabinet established a new set of five thematic priorities for the envelope: stimulating economic growth, increasing food security, securing the future of children and youth, ensuring security and stability, and advancing democracy. CIDA was the lead agency for the first three priorities: responding to the twin crisis in global finance and food prices then rippling across the world. The banner of "children and youth" combined the agency's long-standing work in education and health. In contrast, DFAIT was the lead for the last two priorities, given the department's interest in global security and international relations. Whereas the previous Liberal government had emphasized "good governance," the Conservative government was interested in "democracy promotion." The 2008 Speech from the Throne contained a promise to establish a new agency for this purpose (Canada 2008). In setting these five thematic priorities, the Cabinet defined new criteria to assess spending proposals, including the extent to which they: aligned with the government's thematic and geographic priorities, placed Canada in a leadership position, built on proven approaches, were able to demonstrate clear and

[9] Originally the IDRC Chairman, Gordon Smith, was to make this presentation. Based in British Columbia, he was unable to attend the Treasury Board meeting when it was rescheduled due to other Parliamentary business.

measurable results, and fostered innovation by leveraging funding and efforts from beyond government.

Despite IDRC's affinity with innovation and partnership, the Department of Finance drove these criteria in two distinct ways. First, as an explicit challenge to CIDA and DFAIT to avoid proposals that simply sought more resources to do the same type of programming as in the past. The Cabinet was interested in using international assistance to do things that were new, different, and transformational. Second, the Department of Finance brought forward its own proposals for using foreign aid dollars as an incentive to encourage the private sector to develop new technologies and services, rather than grants to developing countries or contributions to international organizations.

An early example of this approach was the 2007 announcement of an advance market commitment in which Canada and other donor countries would offer a guaranteed price for a successful pneumococcal vaccine (Canada 2007: 265). The idea was to overcome the market failure caused by the high costs of research required to develop such a vaccine, which was not easily recovered from the required selling price should the product remain affordable to those who most needed it. Rather than underwrite the costs of research up front, which might or might not be successful, the advance market commitment sought to transfer this risk to pharmaceutical firms, guaranteeing a price that would suitably reimburse costs once a successful product was developed. The appeal of such an approach was the availability of information on the number of potential beneficiaries and estimated R&D costs, which permitted the calculation of the required price. Using similar logic, the Department of Finance subsequently championed a "pull mechanism"—later rebranded as AgResults—to encourage the private sector to develop and distribute agricultural technologies to boost harvest quality (such as reducing aflatoxins in groundnuts) or reduce post-harvest loss (such as grain storage bags). AgResults contemplated not only a prize for developing such products, but also a premium based on the numbers of farmers that adopted it (AusAID 2012a).

The Department of Finance also played the role of a central agency shaping funding decisions. On more than one occasion, the department simply bypassed the seemingly consensual "competition of ideas," to pre-commit IAE funding through the federal budget without consulting CIDA or DFAIT. For example, the 2008 budget dedicated an initial $50 million for a new Development Innovation Fund (DIF) "to create breakthrough discoveries with the potential to significantly improve the lives of millions in the developing world" (Canada 2008: 182–3). While the budget text mentions that this fund would be implemented by "partners in the research community working with IDRC", the announcement came as a surprise to IDRC, CIDA, and DFAIT alike. The idea had originated with Dr. Peter Singer at the University of Toronto, a recipient of the Bill & Melinda Gates Foundation. Singer proposed to establish a similar "grand challenges" initiative in Canada in the form of an independent foundation. The previous Liberal government had established a number of for-purpose organizations, including Genome Canada and the Canadian Foundation for Innovation. Yet the Conservatives had little appetite for creating new organizations, especially as the OAG had recently critiqued the lack of government oversight and the accountability of such foundations.

The DIF would finally become operational in 2010 as a five-year, $225 million initiative. Part of the intervening two years involved haggling among officials to strike a deal which transferred responsibility for the fund to the Minister of Foreign Affairs, away from the Minister of Finance who had championed the idea and whose electoral district included the University of Toronto. A new entity was established—Grand Challenges Canada—the funding for which was routed through IDRC. The Centre would be responsible for evaluation and reporting on the Fund, while CIHR would manage the peer review process toward selecting new projects. Both IDRC and CIHR would participate in the board of directors governing Grand Challenges Canada.

In hindsight, the announcement of the DIF in 2008 marked two distinct turning points. First, it confirmed that IDRC no longer held a monopoly over "development research." IDRC had to compete not just with other uses of the foreign aid budget, but also with other perspectives on research for the developing world. Second, IDRC could no longer argue for an increase in its core funding. IAE decisions were increasingly bound to discrete, time-limited initiatives. Moving forward, once an initiative expired—or "sunset"—its funding would no longer automatically remain in the entity's reference level, but was in principle "free" to be allocated anywhere in the envelope for any purpose. In the medium term, this was expected to increase the amount of the foreign aid budget ministers could allocate as they saw fit, rather than tying it up in department budgets.

Adjusting to Austerity

In mid-2008, David Malone took over as the IDRC President. A career diplomat, Malone's experience spanned decades and included postings as Canada's ambassador to the United Nations and to India. He admired IDRC's legacy of soft diplomacy, and how programming had created a network of influential people who thought well of Canada. Malone defined himself as a scholar, previously taking leave from government to manage the International Peace Academy in New York, and continuously writing books and articles on international relations. Fresh from the strategic review experience, the IDRC Board of Governors expected Malone to cultivate contacts in official Ottawa who appreciated IDRC as aligned and useful to the government's agenda. The OAG completed a special examination of the Centre in 2008, giving IDRC a clean bill of health, thus the challenge facing the new President was more about external relations than internal management.

In 2009, IDRC management decided to discontinue the program area dedicated to information and communication technologies for development (ICT4D). Having justified itself as overcoming the "digital divide," the recent explosion of Internet access and mobile phone use in developing countries had partially fulfilled this objective. What ICT4D required now was deeper investment in scaling-up, which was beyond IDRC's niche of incubating new ideas and pilot projects (Canada 1970: s2b). Some employees moved to the health or agricultural program to work on ICT applications, and a smaller team was retained in the science program to address issues related to open government, science, and education. Meanwhile the global crisis in food prices in 2008–9 prompted IDRC to shift back to agriculture, via a new partnership with CIDA to establish a competitive food security research fund for collaborative projects involving Canadian and developing-country scientists.

Apart from these shifts, the *Strategic Framework 2010–2015* (IDRC 2009) brought about incremental change in IDRC's structure and programming on the environment, health, and social and economic policy. The Board and management chose to persist with its practice of thematic programming, first choosing the problems to address, then finding prospective recipients with interesting ideas, which determined the geographic footprint of its programming. CIDA announced a new list of focus countries for Canada's bilateral aid in 2009. Yet IDRC did not see itself as bound to this list, as its projects involved and benefited multiple countries. In this regard, IDRC enjoyed the passive endorsement of senior government officials—including the CIDA President—who saw the list as governing CIDA spending and considered IDRC too small to warrant much attention.[10] At the working level, officials from CIDA and TBS were often less understanding, and the list played a role in shaping which countries were eligible for joint CIDA-IDRC partnerships, such as the new food security research fund. Meanwhile, DFAIT officials appreciated IDRC's presence in countries where CIDA was not present, which gave them something concrete to point to in terms of cooperation with Canada.

With the encouragement of the Board of Governors, IDRC restated its business model as a "grants-plus" approach: not only funding new opportunities for research, but engaging with its recipients throughout the research process as a mentor, and facilitating their access to both peers and policy

[10] IDRC managers spoke with these officials and obtained verbal commitments, but no public or written statements, that IDRC was exempt from the list.

audiences (IDRC 2009: para 42). Rather than a new direction or break with the past, "grants-plus" simply restated how IDRC already saw itself.

In practice, IDRC staff pursued multiple expressions of this model. At one extreme, many projects still resulted from talent-spotting by program officers seeking out or responding to promising developing-country researchers, working with them to refine their ideas through multiple iterations on project proposals. This approach placed the IDRC program officer as an engaged mentor working directly with southern scientists to boost their skills over time. At the other extreme were projects that resulted from competitive calls in which written proposals were assessed against explicit eligibility and selection criteria. Such competitions were often structured as a two-stage process: an initial call for short concept notes—describing the project idea—followed by an invitation for the more promising proponents to prepare full proposals.

Under such competitive mechanisms, engagement with IDRC staff was much more restricted so as ensure all proponents were treated equally and received the same information. The application process had to be explicitly described in the calls for proposals and any additional information provided in frequently asked questions (FAQs) posted on the Internet. Some IDRC staff initially resisted this approach, fearing it would give an advantage to more experienced applicants better able to express themselves in written English or French. At the same time, IDRC management initially expected competitive calls to be less labor-intensive and allow the Centre to optimize the balance between research grants and internal costs. The value of competitively allocated projects was commonly over twice that of talent-scouting projects (in excess of $1 million over five years versus $300,000 over three years). Assuming the costs of monitoring and administering a project were fixed, boosting the average value per project would control internal costs.

With experience, both staff and management learned that these assumptions were partially false. The selection criteria for competitively allocated projects could include consideration of the potential for training younger and developing-country scientists; drawing on senior researchers in the project to act as mentors, rather than assuming this was a task for IDRC staff. Indeed, in the 2000s IDRC had outsourced some competitive grant competitions to trusted organizations in developing countries in order to provide opportunities for young researchers and for new grantees beyond IDRC's regular network of contacts (IDRC 2006). Meanwhile competitive calls did not necessarily save on workload in the near-term, as there was a substantial workload in setting up the call and coordinating the peer review process. Furthermore, a million dollar project, that involved two or three recipient institutions, meant each institution received $300,000 to $500,000. Thus the push for fewer, larger projects did not necessarily translate into fewer, larger grants. To some extent, this negated the expected saving on administration costs.

Between 2008 and 2010, the government of Canada once again moved from surplus to deficit. The financial crisis of 2008–9 saw government revenues decrease and stimulus spending as Canada's part of the coordinated response among G20 countries. The 2010 federal budget announced that "future IAE spending levels will be capped at 2010–11 levels and will be assessed alongside all other government priorities on a year-by-year basis in the budget" (Canada 2010: 142). Having fulfilled the 2002 Monterrey commitment to double foreign aid to $5 billion, the government would stop the yearly practice of 8 percent increases. The careful wording of the budget also left the door open to future reductions in international assistance.

Management of the IAE was also evolving. Within official Ottawa, there was no longer any support for the five purposes—or "pools"—of IAE spending. Funding for crises was fixed at $200 million per year, and funding for international financial institutions was determined by the level of Canada's contributions to the World Bank, IMF, and regional development banks. Despite the historic record of IDRC accounting for 3–4 percent of Canada's foreign aid, there was no support for assigning a fixed share of the IAE to development research, and much less that this should go to any single organization. More generally, there was a tension between DFAIT and CIDA regarding the appropriate balance between spending on each other's thematic priorities, pitting "food security, economic growth, and children and youth" against "peace and security, and promoting democracy."

The process of allocating IAE funds was no longer a competition of ideas within government departments, but an allocation among "competing pressures" imposed from outside, such as commitments at leaders' summits or to international organizations. Through the 2010 budget, the Minister of Finance asserted control over his colleagues. Now part of the regular process of preparing the federal budget, IAE funding would no longer be decided between the Ministers of International Cooperation and of Foreign Affairs. De facto, CIDA and DFAIT lost their exclusive access to this funding and could no longer simply allocate it to proposals they themselves had developed without passing the scrutiny of finance officials.

The final year of the IAE increment was largely dedicated to initiatives related to the G8 and G20 summits, which Canada would host during the summer. At the World Economic Forum, the Prime Minister announced a major push to reduce maternal and child mortality, two of the MDGs that lagged behind on progress toward the 2015 targets. Despite a long process among government departments to identify and shape a variety of proposals for the summit, the push on maternal and child health—or the Muskoka Initiative—swept up much of the available funding for the year.

During preparations for the summit serious attention was given to the theme of "innovation for development." While DFAIT officials consulted IDRC, negotiations among G8 members eventually focused on two potential proposals, one to establish a program of research chairs in African universities, and another to create a network based on the African Institute of Mathematical Sciences (AIMS).

The AIMS proposal was championed by Neil Turok, a South African physicist living in Canada as Director of the Perimeter Institute for Theoretical Physics, an organization established with a donation from Mihal Lazaridis, co-founder of Research in Motion (Blackberry). Turok had established the first AIMS-Centre in Cape Town in 2003 to provide a training facility that enabled African students to pursue graduate-level training in mathematics. Housed within a single building, AIMS-Cape Town included classrooms, computer labs, and dormitories. Turok had drawn on his professional contacts to bring in renowned professors to give short courses. Given the success of this first AIMS-Centre, Turok proposed to create a pan-African network with similar centers in different parts of the continent. In 2008, Turok gave a passionate lecture as recipient of the TED (Technology, Entertainment, Design) prize based on the idea that the "next Einstein" could be an African who would produce future leaps in scientific understanding.

Through preparations for the G8 summit, DFAIT officials sought to entice financial support from other countries. When it became clear that others would not offer new funding pledges, the AIMS proposal dropped from the G8 agenda. Yet Turok's personal diplomacy with the Prime Minister resulted in a decision that Canada would make its own $20 million contribution toward establishing the next three AIMS centers, initially planned for Senegal, Ghana, and Ethiopia. One can speculate that the Prime Minister's decision resulted from Turok's ability to raise private funding from foundations and companies, the tangible targets in terms of numbers of potential students trained, and Turok's connection to Canada. Beyond living and working in Canada, Turok's parents had been part of the anti-Apartheid movement supported by the Mulroney government.

DFAIT officials turned to IDRC with a "take it or leave it" offer of being responsible for Canada's contribution to AIMS. Similar to the earlier DIF, the proposal was generated outside of government. It also enjoyed the support of a high-level champion who bypassed the machinery of government and the customary process of bottom-up policy development and budgeting. DIF and AIMS were both outside IDRC's accustomed grantmaking practice of engaging proponents in crafting their proposals. As ready-made initiatives, it was initially difficult to see how IDRC would add to it beyond providing a channel for Canada's funding. Yet both were now part of Canada's support for development research, and refusing a role in them would have made IDRC increasingly marginal to the government's agenda.

A greater share of IDRC's budget was now pre-committed to specific initiatives, whether through partnerships with foreign donors or those designed outside of IDRC and endorsed by the Government of Canada. Consequently, a smaller portion of IDRC's budget could be considered "core" funding, available for the Board of Governors to assign to programming conceived by IDRC staff. In the corridors, staff were concerned that IDRC was becoming more attentive to donors and the government, and less responsive to the voices of developing-country researchers. Furthermore, both AIMS and DIF were time-limited initiatives: once they expired there was no guarantee that IDRC would continue to receive the funding they represented. After a decade of growing budgets, IDRC faced the prospect of needing to contract in future years.

That future arrived quicker than anticipated. The Conservative government was struggling to reduce the deficit and remained critical of departmental program spending, prompting a one-time "strategic and operating review" launched in 2011. The review involved all departments and agencies and sought proposals for reducing their budgets by between 5 and 10 percent. Unlike 2007, this time the Minister of International Cooperation led a single, horizontal review of IAE spending. Officials from CIDA, DFAIT, the Department of Finance, TBS, Privy Council Office, and IDRC met throughout the summer and into the fall to assess different proposals and negotiate how to share the pain of budget cuts. The 2012 federal budget announced an overall reduction of 10 percent in Canada's international assistance, divided more or less proportionally across the IAE partners, slightly more for IDRC, and none to Canada's contributions to the international financial institutions (Canada 2012: 213 and 272).

IDRC closed two regional offices and one of its research programs. The regional office closures reflected an ongoing concern to boost the ratio of research grants versus internal costs. IDRC eliminated over seventy positions between headquarters and the regional offices. Singapore and Senegal represented the two most expensive office locations, thus the greatest amount of potential savings. While Singapore was no longer the developing country it was in the 1970s, both closures left IDRC struggling to reassess its field presence in Southeast Asia and in West Africa. Given the scale of the cuts, management also needed to scale back on programming and concentrated the pain in the Innovation for Inclusive Development program.[11] The program was typical of past IDRC work, something ahead of the curve, that other funders had not (yet) adopted. Yet the program was a victim of the new

[11] Approved by the Board of Governors in summer 2011, the program proposed to identify and scale up examples of grassroots—or frugal—innovation where poor people resorted to inventive means of addressing their needs, such as converting used cooking oil into fuel for taxis (*Economist* 2010).

performance regime that emphasized alignment with government priorities of food security, economic growth, and security.

The model that had served IDRC well in the past was based on the assumption that the parliamentary appropriation was core funding available for the Board to allocate as it saw fit. Yet the IAE allocation process had begun to undermine this model, as access to new funding was restricted to specific, time-limited initiatives tied to government priorities. Indeed, the IDRC Act was modified in 2012 to reduce the size of the Board to up to fourteen members. As a greater share of IDRC's budget was earmarked to specific government initiatives or donor partnerships, it squeezed the resources available to pursue original programming that did not align with the priorities of others. As one respondent lamented, "IDRC is mostly ignored, sometimes resented, and seldom appreciated...there is almost a conscious policy of eroding the Board's independence in taking decisions."

In summary, starting in the early 2000s the performance regime emphasized alignment with the priorities of Canada's foreign policy. The role of the IDRC Board eroded as programming decisions were increasingly tied to government funding decisions or committed to programs partially funded by CIDA and donors outside Canada. The program theory that guided R4D funding valued research for its actual contribution to changed policy and practice in the developing world, with an increasing array of expectations placed upon its recipients. Grantmaking saw competitive calls for proposals join the older practices based on proactive project development by IDRC staff and responding to unsolicited proposals and partnerships.

Key Points

IDRC largely preserved both Maurice Strong's vision of an independent research funder, as well as David Hopper's vision of an organization dedicated to supporting the ideas of researchers in the developing world. Both these traits became part of the organization's DNA: staff and management embodied these commitments. Yet Strong and Hopper were more than intellectual contributors to the IDRC mission and mandate. They proved to be the first in a line of high-level thought and opinion leaders that protected and nurtured the Centre over time, and rallied to IDRC's defense whenever it was threatened. Individual champions played a substantial role in how Canada defined and funded research relating to the developing world over time. IDRC management would cultivate and periodically renew its network of allies among the federal bureaucracy, across foreign policy, and inside central agencies. Meanwhile contact with Canada's research policy was less substantial and less critical to IDRC's fortunes.

Yet the federal government was never entirely at ease with IDRC's independence, and periodically moved to curtail its freedom. While the IDRC Act established the Centre at arm's length from government, central agencies imposed the disciplines of planning and evaluation, as well as ministerial responsibility for portfolio management. DFAIT, CIDA, and central agencies might not have controlled IDRC governance, but they did influence the process through which the Centre obtained its funding. Over time, IDRC appeased these actors by positioning itself as an expression of Canada's foreign policy and contributing to the policy priorities of the day. For the most part, such positioning could be symbolic, a veneer of responsiveness covering a deeper program theory and grantmaking practices that proved largely persistent in type of recipients and average grant size.

Budget cuts in the 1990s triggered a substantial restructuring, intended in part to demonstrate that IDRC's work contributed to development results. Interdisciplinarity, research utilization, and policy influence became watchwords as IDRC redesigned and renewed its program framework. This century, a growing foreign aid budget initially allowed IDRC to expand those programs that aligned with government priorities or that leveraged outside funding through donor partnerships. Yet such conditional access to new funding slowly eroded IDRC's autonomy, as outside actors came to play a larger role in designing programs and selecting projects.

In terms of the *resources available*, IDRC's budget rose for two decades, but fell in the 1990s with the government's efforts to reduce the deficit (Figure 4.3).[12] Bezanson sought to reduce IDRC's reliance on government funding by securing project co-funding from other sources. The subsequent rise of IDRC's budget this century was largely due to special-purpose allocations and demonstrating the Centre's alignment to IAE priorities, including the joint food security fund with CIDA. Thus while IDRC was able to save itself from some of the pain of budget cuts and shared in the benefits of a rising aid budget, in both cases new resources came with conditions, rather than core funding for IDRC's regular business model .

In terms of *public management*, IDRC aspired to emulate the philanthropic foundations in the United States, including their independence from government and political mandates. Yet as a Crown corporation largely dependent on an appropriation from Parliament, government periodically attempted to reassert control over IDRC. Survival relied on cultivating allies within the bureaucracy and demonstrating alignment with government priorities, including two rounds of strategic review. IDRC was responsive to both

[12] A push to diversify sources of revenue softened the reduction in Parliamentary appropriation in the 1990s. The allocation dedicated to the Micronutrient Initiative (1997–2002) hides the low point and slow increase in IDRC "core" funding.

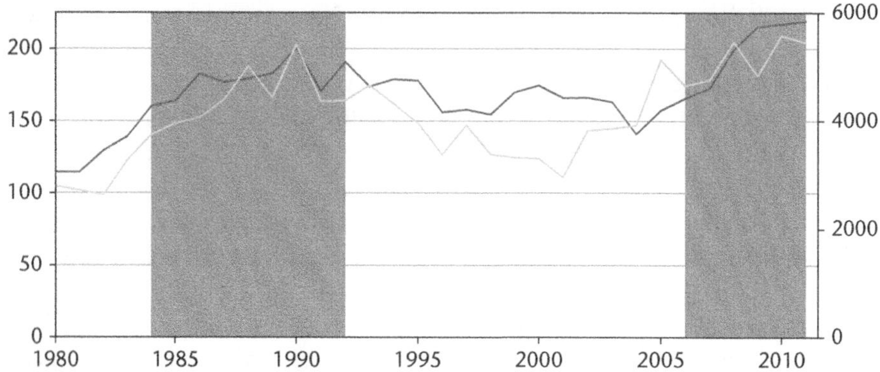

Figure 4.3. Canada's spending since 1980

IDRC expenditures (dark line, left axis) compared to Canada's official development assistance (right axis). All amounts are expressed in real terms as CA$ million adjusted to 2011. The shaded years represent time when Conservative party was in power.

IDRC Annual Reports and OECD statistics

Canada's foreign policy and science priorities: supporting local researchers during political and economic transitions in the Southern Cone, South Africa, and Southeast Asia, and positioning itself as contributing to the "internationalization" Canadian research. IDRC was both inside and outside Canada's development policy process: it could request additional funding, but was excluded from the higher-level decision making. IDRC was also outmaneuvered by the Department of Finance and by outside proposals which increasingly defined research for the developing world. The net result was an erosion of IDRC's discretion and autonomy as strategic decisions about program choice moved away from its Board of Governors and to the Cabinet and senior government officials.

In terms of *research policy*, IDRC began to argue for its effectiveness based on demand and the clients involved in its projects. IDRC adopted increasingly detailed program strategies which targeted funding to particular thematic priorities. Researchers needed to demonstrate how their work contributed to social or economic benefit, and the "utilization" of research results. Recipients were expected to identify and reach an audience of policymakers and practitioners. IDRC sought to demonstrate that its portfolio addressed real-world problems, rather than merely being motived by research interest, and that research contributed directly to development outcomes. IDRC also began to adopt competitive calls for proposals alongside its original talent-spotting practices modeled on philanthropic foundations. This brought about grant-making that paid greater attention to application deadlines as well as specifying eligibility and selection criteria, reducing the space available for the former open-ended practice of selectively responding to unsolicited proposals.

IDRC's *program theory* remained close to the Strong–Hopper vision of building the capacity of developing-country researchers. This initial emphasis meant IDRC expected that its projects would generate new skills and strengthen local institutions. Research outputs were not necessarily expected to be world-class in quality, instead IDRC was satisfied if local researchers were gaining experience and their work was useful to local audiences. Over time, projects were also expected to: incorporate interdisciplinarity into their research design, "close the loop" in terms of influencing policy in developing countries, and demonstrate how their research contributed to positive change in the lives of poor women and men. IDRC thus expected its recipients to be good communicators, reaching not only their scientific peers but also an audience of policymakers and practitioners.

Drawing on Funnel and Rogers (2011), IDRC initially pursued an empowerment theory of change, underpinned by a capacity-building archetype: supporting researchers in poor countries to exercise greater control over their own development. Such a perspective was dominant from Hopper's 1970 speech at the inaugural meeting of the Board of Governors through to Bezanson's 1991 strategy (IDRC 1991a). Under O'Neil, IDRC supplemented this core philosophy with a network theory of change underpinned by a case management archetype: recipients were encouraged to cultivate relationships toward informing policy abroad, with IDRC support adapting to the unique circumstance in each project. In contrast, the emergence of Grand Challenges Canada in 2010 exploited a gap in Canada's research landscape, embracing a diffusion theory of change.

IDRC *grantmaking* consistently favored recipients based in a range of developing countries. The role of a program officer evolved from "wandering minstrel" providing access to scientific literature and contacts not available locally, to "engaged peer" supporting the research interests of recipients. Projects were initially selected solely on their own merits, including their originality, potential contributions to a particular discipline, and perceived relevance to the developing regions of the world. Following budget cuts and restructuring in the late 1990s, staff placed greater emphasis on constructing a portfolio of projects that contributed toward a Board-approved program strategy. Programs that overlapped with donor or Canadian interest grew faster than those where IDRC was the sole investor. Yet IDRC resisted the trend among foreign aid agencies to identify a select number of focus countries. Instead IDRC consistently selected programs and projects that addressed problems common to multiple countries or that spilled across borders entirely. The majority of its projects were coded as regional in scope and included recipients working in different countries.

5

Australia

Crawford's Legacy of Partnership

The Australian Centre for International Agriculture Research (ACIAR) was created by an Act of Parliament (Australia 1982). It is a statutory authority, a public entity entrusted with a particular policy objective and established at arm's length from government. Statutory authorities are answerable to a minister for their corporate performance, but largely autonomous in terms of their day-to-day operations.

This chapter identifies three distinct periods when ACIAR was subject to different expectations and adopted different goals (Figure 5.1). During its first decade, the performance regime offered ACIAR a limited lifespan to prove its worth in terms of the potential increase in agricultural productivity stemming from the work it funded. Program theory was "doing well by doing good," seeking mutual benefits at home and abroad by mobilizing Australian talent in areas where the country was perceived to have a natural research advantage, such as on tropical, coastal, and dryland climates. Grantmaking focused on a partnership model of commissioning projects that matched state-level government scientists with local partners abroad, primarily in Southeast Asia and the Pacific, especially in countries where there was an existing pool of researchers.

During the second decade, Australia enshrined poverty reduction as the purpose of foreign aid. This policy shift coincided with ACIAR focusing more on how it contributed to real-life adoption of new technologies and techniques. Simultaneously, changes in science policy began to hollow out the capacity of state-level government and shifted the center of gravity toward university research. Program theory sought to boost rural incomes, linking poor women and men with markets beyond the farm gate and the valued added as food moved from "paddock to plate." ACIAR continued its grantmaking practice of partnerships for mutual benefits, but increasingly relied on Australian researchers in academic settings. ACIAR also modified its grantmaking to exit

Figure 5.1. Timeline of Australia case study

countries that attained middle-income status and enter countries that became a foreign policy priority.

During the third decade, the performance regime adopted whole-of-government strategies toward Australia's engagement within developing countries, particularly in response to the "war on terror" and later the global food crisis. Meanwhile, public research needed to justify itself within national priorities and program-level outcomes, such as contributing to Australia's economy and security, rather than simply pursuing individual projects based on their own merit. Program theory sought to bridge Australia's innovation system and foreign aid, emphasizing agricultural research for development as a form of science diplomacy and as promoting stability and food security abroad. While ACIAR largely retained its grantmaking practice of commissioned partnerships, the Centre placed a stronger emphasis on country strategies, giving its staff a "passport to engage" government colleagues and embassies. Responding to foreign policy priorities also led ACIAR to support work in countries with a weak or nonexistent domestic research community.

Origins

The idea for ACIAR was born as Australia reassessed its role toward the developing world. Australia saw itself as both "a Western country ... geographically isolated from the Western centres of power" and "distinctly Australian ... a multicultural society in the southern hemisphere on the very fringe of the Third World." Within international affairs, the importance of the UK was declining just as that of the developing world was rising. Growth in nearby Asia offered an opportunity "to benefit from expanding trade, to exercise political initiatives, to demonstrate our technical skills and special experience, to exercise our idealism and to enrich our culture." Australia's nascent foreign aid included calls for "applying scientific know-how to the Third World for mutual gain" (Australia 1979: 117).

The Australian public was acutely aware of the benefits of research for rural people. Each state government had established its own network of agricultural labs, research centers, and extension services. Upon forming the Commonwealth, Australian states retained and expanded these networks, tailored to the local mix of crops, livestock, and climates. Through the Commonwealth Scientific and Industrial Research Organisation (CSIRO), the national government supported some key efforts to aid farmers, including the introduction of myxomatosis virus to control rabbit populations and the introduction of dung beetles to remove breeding ground for bushflies (Collis 2002). Since the Wool Publicity and Research Act 1936, farmers and rural industries paid levies to finance research intended to benefit their industry as a whole, through enhanced productivity and advances in processing. These arrangements would subsequently become rural Research and Development Corporations. The money raised through levies was matched on a dollar-for-dollar basis with funds from the national government (Farrer 2005; Core 2009). Agricultural research already enjoyed strong support from taxpayers and industry.

The idea for ACIAR was championed by Sir John Crawford, an influential economist and civil servant. Crawford had served as the Director of Research in the government's Department of Postwar Reconstruction, and as a senior official in the departments of trade and agriculture. He then entered the Australian National University from where he contributed to the creation of the Australian Development Assistance Agency and CGIAR. In 1976, he chaired a committee which proposed that the country establish an international research assistance foundation. The committee included participants drawn from the

Department of Foreign Affairs, World Bank, and CSIRO. This committee examined examples such as the UK's IDS and France's Office de la Recherche Scientifique et Technique Outre-Mer (ORSTOM).[1]

Yet Crawford was clearly inspired by Canada's IDRC, where he had been a board member from 1970 to 1979. The committee identified a mandate for the proposed foundation that mirrored the IDRC Act, calling for a focus on developing countries "to build up their research capabilities and innovative skills as well as the institutions required to solve their problems." R4D was expected to enable developing countries to "provide food and the basic elements of decent living standards for their peoples," by enabling them "to select and... import advanced knowledge, adapt it to local conditions as necessary, and expand it through indigenous research to meet their needs" (Crawford Study 1976: 3).[2]

Yet the moment for establishing an Australian IDRC had already passed. Edward Gough Whitlam's Labor government (1972–5) had lost power after a very active period that saw the introduction of universal health care, free university education, and the opening of relations with China. In contrast, Malcolm Fraser's Liberal-led[3] government (1975–83) brought in a period of conservative policy that sought to control the costs of government. The recently established aid agency was converted into a bureau within the foreign affairs portfolio. There was very little political appetite to expand spending, and none for such a broad and apparently altruistic mandate. In the midst of this context of restraint and modest ambition, James Ingram—head of the Australian Development Assistance Bureau (ADAB)—established a Consultative Committee on Research and Development (CCRD). Once again Crawford chaired the committee, this time examining how Australia's health and agricultural research communities could contribute to the aid program.

An agricultural mission resonated with Australia's own history. Having struggled to become self-sufficient in agriculture, Australia emerged as a major exporter of food and fiber, sustaining the UK during two world wars. Australian experience was seen as relevant for developing countries seeking to feed their populations and grow their economies. Furthermore, the arid Australian landscape was comparable to conditions found in parts of the developing world. Thus crops and techniques that worked at home might help agriculture thrive abroad.

Australia already had the National Health and Medical Research Council, but lacked a comparable platform for agricultural research. The country's research

[1] In 1998, ORSTOM was renamed *Institut de Recherche pour le Développement* (IRD).

[2] IDRC contributed to ACIAR in multiple ways: the first draft of the ACIAR Act was based upon the Canadian legislation, and IDRC's David Spurgeon worked on secondment to establish ACIAR's communication division.

[3] Australia's Liberal party is politically right-of-center and akin to the conservatives in the UK and Canada.

community was fragmented among different state-level departments of agriculture and various divisions of CSIRO. Arguably there was a need to coordinate these actors if Australia was to mobilize its expertise to aid developing countries. CSIRO had already established a livestock research center in Indonesia as well as an office to market its research services to aid agencies abroad. CCRD visited the Indonesian lab and was concerned that it was isolated from both farmers and the wider national agricultural research system. The committee felt that Australia needed to mobilize expertise in CGIAR and existing institutes, rather than building new brick-and-mortar centers. Crawford and Ingram approached universities and state governments to gather support for their vision.

Their opportunity came during preparations for the 1981 Commonwealth Heads of Government Meeting. Prime Minister Fraser was keen to have an announcement and Crawford presented ACIAR as one of the short list of ideas. Fraser was himself a wool rancher who personally identified with agriculture, and his coalition government shared power with the National Country Party whose support base came from rural areas. ACIAR offered an option that both highlighted Australian leadership abroad and played well to voters at home. Shortly after the Commonwealth meeting, the draft legislation presented to Parliament focused on mobilizing Australian expertise for mutual benefit. Introducing the bill, Foreign Minister Tony Street described a mandate "to fund research by Australian persons and institutions . . . contracting research work to . . . universities, State departments of agriculture, CSIRO and suitably competent private individuals and organisations." According to the minister, Australians stood to gain in various ways including enhanced contact with overseas colleagues, increased information on problems abroad, and an expectation that "some of the solutions . . . the Centre produces will be of direct and practical benefit to Australia" (Australia 1981).

ACIAR was created in 1982 as a statutory authority, in order to attract people who understood the problems facing agriculture abroad and who had professional networks at home to address them. In introducing the Act, the minister argued that "the Centre will require the capacity to identify needs and priorities for agricultural research in developing countries . . . to monitor critically progress of the research . . . [and] staff of such stature as to command respect among scientists in Australia and in developing countries" (Australia 1981). Research program coordinators worked as brokers: conducting field visits and consultations abroad, and then scouted for talent at home that might prove useful. These coordinators worked closely with potential recipients to encourage and refine proposals, specifying objectives and responsibilities within the collaboration. Whereas government departments were seen as bureaucratic environments driven by rules and regulation, the architects and early patrons of ACIAR saw a need to create an intellectual environment driven by scientific collaboration. Early employees came from the aid bureau, CSIRO, universities,

CGIAR centers, and foreign affairs. All found that their new workplace was distinct from their previous one.

Doing Well by Doing Good

ACIAR governance included a Board of Management and a Policy Advisory Committee. The ACIAR Board included senior representatives from the academic community, the Australian aid bureau, CSIRO, state governments, and the national farmers' federation. Crawford's presence as the first Board chairman provided the gravitas to attract senior representatives and build a common perspective on what ACIAR was to become. The Policy Advisory Committee provided insights on the agricultural problems of developing countries and Australia's capacity to assist in their solution. It operated as a scientific advisor, with members selected for their knowledge of the subject matter. The Policy Advisory Committee included all the Board members, plus additional Australians drawn from universities and state governments, plus representatives from developing countries, often drawn from the agricultural science or policy departments within their national government.

ACIAR governance thus reflected the performance regime. The Board brought together the stakeholders that were vital to the Centre's success, and those that might resist if ACIAR was perceived as detrimental to their interests. The Board held formal duties for oversight and strategic direction, and served as the informal crucible for forging consensus and support among key stakeholders. All projects required Board approval, preventing ACIAR from funding an activity that might harm the interests of farmers, universities, or state governments. Meanwhile the Policy Advisory Committee gave voice to additional Australians as well as to the intended beneficiaries in developing countries. The Committee gave advice on potential priorities and partners, and debated policy guidelines, instilling in its members a sense of ownership over ACIAR's operations. In sum, the governance structure bridged national funding, talent throughout Australia, and potential partners in developing countries.

ACIAR had started operations in June 1982 with a small office within Canberra's Reserve Bank Building. Crawford continued to play a lead role as Chairman of ACIAR's Board of Management. He interviewed prospective staff members and had hired the first director, Jim McWilliam. The new staff quickly established its thematic priorities, including soil and water management, plant improvement, animal and fish production, farming systems, post-harvest technology, forestry, socio-economics, and communications. Eligible projects needed to respond to the expressed needs of developing countries, address problems of national or regional significance, involve developing-country scientists, and exploit Australian research capacity. The first project focused on pigeon pea improvement and involved participants in Thailand, Fiji, and Indonesia, alongside the University of Queensland and the International Crop Research Institute for the Semi-Arid Tropics (ICRISAT) in India.

ACIAR followed Australia's foreign policy focus on neighboring countries. The portfolio concentrated on the Pacific islands and Southeast Asia, particularly Papua New Guinea which Australia governed until 1975. ACIAR also supported work in South Asia and China, and to a lesser extent in a handful of African countries. ACIAR's Board established and monitored allocation targets for each of these regions, inspiring staff to fast-track projects in any regions that appeared to be falling behind. Project selection started with those countries with a similar climate and agricultural problems to Australia. To emphasize the point, early consultations in China and Nigeria superimposed an inverted map of Australia over these countries to demonstrate similarities in latitudes and growing conditions.

ACIAR pursued a partnership model of commissioning research. Projects sought to match countries within the aid program with areas of expertise where Australia had a "natural research advantage." In other words, it addressed problems on which Australian researchers were perceived to be at least relatively strong, if not world class. Projects aimed to boost agricultural productivity or reduce costs abroad, as well as make a contribution at home. Such pragmatism was required to entice reluctant employers to permit their scientists to participate, as working on ACIAR projects presented direct costs and opportunity costs. Employers had to contribute financial or in-kind support, as ACIAR limited its funding to 70 percent of direct project costs. Additionally, time spent overseas, or working on somebody else's problems, detracted from support to farmers at home. ACIAR needed to dispel suspicion that it "gave away" hard-earned Australian know-how, aiding Australia's competitors in export markets. Thus ACIAR unabashedly touted the benefits at home, such as improved control of pests before they reached Australian shores.

ACIAR staff actively shaped projects. They surveyed interest in working with developing countries, and drew on their networks of contacts to address needs abroad. As ACIAR became better known, researchers began to approach staff with their ideas. Concept notes describing project ideas went through an iterative in-house review process. Coordinators critiqued these ideas, deciding collectively which ones to pursue and how to enhance their design, for example identifying additional experts that could contribute to each project. The process was intensely competitive, with each coordinator viewing project ideas through the lens of their own discipline, with subtly different views as to pertinent questions, methods, and standards of evidence. For example, a crop scientist might find her or his project harshly critiqued by a soil scientist or agronomist. The resulting feedback was given to proponents who then prepared a detailed proposal specifying objectives, responsibilities, and budget.

These proposals received another round of in-house review before being recommended to the Board of Management for approval. ACIAR believed that staff needed to broker the partnerships to ensure mutual benefit for project participants at home and abroad.

While thematic priorities and selection criteria would evolve over time, these early directions would still influence practice thirty years later. On the surface, ACIAR remained remarkably consistent: a modest-sized organization that stayed true to its original purpose and design. Yet on closer examination, ACIAR was subject to changing expectations, navigated by successive managers who decided how to respond to the Canberra context.

Making Friends before Sunset

The new Centre had established its program priorities, staff roles, and grant-making practices; yet there was no guarantee that any of it would survive. The ACIAR Act contained a "sunset" clause limiting the Centre's lifespan to twelve years. ACIAR needed to convince Parliament that its work was worth renewing if it was to continue into the future. This motivated ACIAR to establish a unit focused on economic evaluation, to help identify research priorities and to assess the benefits derived from the research supported. Early studies looked at *ex ante* priorities, comparing different crops and countries, and estimating the potential benefits based on the expected gains in overall agricultural production and its likely effect on local markets.[4] This information fed into ACIAR's priority setting and was shared with partner countries and international organizations. As the first generation of projects came to completion, attention turned to *ex post* valuation of the results of that work: quantifying the value of new or increased production, or of the inputs saved—such as fertilizers or machinery—by using more efficient techniques. It was hoped that such studies would establish whether project successes justified the funds invested.

While ACIAR began with substantial political support, management soon acquired an acute sense of vulnerability. Not only did ACIAR face a possible expiration date, government had only committed funding for the first three years, totaling $25 million. From there ACIAR's fortunes were subject to the annual budgeting process and reliant on allies within the bureaucracy and Parliament. The latter eroded quickly as Bob Hawke's Labor government came to power in 1983, and Sir John Crawford passed away in 1984, depriving ACIAR of its intellectual grandfather and most powerful ally. The new government introduced an austerity budget in 1986 and reduced spending in all

[4] These studies considered changes in marginal supply and demand. Prices might decrease with increases in production, yet advances in agricultural productivity could still generate substantial overall gains.

departments, including health and public services. After four years of growth, ACIAR suddenly lost one-fifth of its budget. The honeymoon was over. Political support was no longer guaranteed and it was far from certain that a future government would renew the Centre.

ACIAR found a new ally in Derek Tribe, former dean at the University of Melbourne, fellow of the Australian Academy of Technological Sciences and Engineering (ATSE), and member of the Order of the British Empire. Tribe proposed that ATSE create a new organization dedicated to promoting agricultural research. The creation of CGIAR at the international level had revealed a need for national-level counterparts that could build awareness of its work and encourage links with domestic researchers. In 1987, Tribe's idea became the Crawford Fund for International Agricultural Research. The Fund drew financial support from governments, companies, and individuals, and engaged parliamentarians to raise awareness of Australia's support for research abroad. Whereas ACIAR focused on partnerships between Australian and developing-country researchers, the Fund provided scholarships and training abroad. More importantly, where ACIAR was part of the machinery of government, the Fund was able to lobby parliamentarians and build a domestic constituency for research abroad. It launched a series of annual seminars in Parliament House, to encourage bipartisan support by presenting how Australia benefited from such research. Doug Anthony, former leader of the National Party, agreed to serve as the Fund's chairman, and the Fund later attracted former deputy Prime Ministers Tim Fisher and John Anderson.

The end of the decade saw ACIAR's budget recover and exceed its pre-1986 level. By 1989, the Board of Management received a mid-term review of ACIAR's strengths and weaknesses. This review set the stage for the first leadership transition as George Rothschild succeeded Jim McWilliam as the ACIAR Director. The review was largely positive, yet echoed the sense of vulnerability from the 1986 budget cut and upcoming sunset review. In particular, the review suggested a need "to strengthen the mechanisms that provide parliamentary awareness" of ACIAR such as briefings with MPs (Arnold 1989: v). It also found that ACIAR's research portfolio had evolved in response to requests for collaboration, the availability of Australian expertise, staff expertise and disciplinary background, and the scientific and economic assessment of projects.

The late 1980s also saw changes in Australian research policy, aligning government support with industry. The Australian Research Council was established to fund university research, and a Chief Scientist position was created to advise government on its use of—and support for—science and technology. The Primary Industries and Energy Research and Development Act gave industry a formal role in governing and funding the rural R&D corporations (RDCs). The government introduced a 150 percent tax credit to replace direct support for industrial R&D. Meanwhile CSIRO was required to raise

30 percent of its funding from outside of its parliamentary appropriation, by selling its services to government departments or the private sector. A new program of Cooperative Research Centres (CRCs) drew together science performers from universities, industries, and government to work on priority areas. The watchwords for Australian research policy had become: priority, concentration, selectivity, accountability, and evaluation (Australian S&T Council 1990: 10).

Yet ACIAR fortunes were looking positive as Paul Keating took up leadership of the Labor government in 1991. The country had experienced the glow of its bicentennial celebrations and the mood of the country was optimistic. Derek Tribe penned an eloquent and influential argument for agricultural research abroad—entitled *Doing Well by Doing Good*.[5] Rather than a technical report, the book was an accessible read intended for politicians and farmers, responding to domestic fears that the information and benefits from Australian know-how were being given away as part of foreign aid. Tribe (1991) argued that Australia received much more than it gave, citing the use of wheat germplasm from CGIAR, which had generated over $2 billion of additional income for the Australian wheat industry.

The sunset review finally came in 1992, conducted under the parliamentary Joint Committee on Foreign Affairs, Defence and Trade. The review focused on the "effectiveness of ACIAR as an element of Australia's official development assistance" and the desirability of its continued existence. The review was exceedingly positive and praised ACIAR's work in crafting partnerships that both mobilized research expertise and improved the well-being of people at home and abroad. The committee attributed this performance to ACIAR's independence as a statutory authority, and recommended that similar organizations be established for R&D assistance in other fields, such as manufacturing and human resource development. The review even called for ACIAR to receive a fixed share of the aid budget (3.5 percent), with an additional sum (1.5 percent) dedicated to provide core funding to international agricultural research centers (Australia 1992). The government removed the sunset clause from the Act and expanded ACIAR's mandate to include project-related training. It also made ACIAR responsible for Australian funding to the international agricultural research centers, transferring this function away from the aid bureau. ACIAR thus began its second decade with a renewed lease on life.

Thus ACIAR's first decade saw the performance regime offer the Centre a limited lifespan within which to prove its worth. Program theory can be summarized under the motto "doing well by doing good," seeking mutual benefits at home and abroad by mobilizing Australian talent. Grantmaking focused on a partnership model of commissioning projects that matched

[5] Tribe wrote this short book during his time as a scholar-in-residence at Rockefeller's Bellagio Centre in northern Italy.

state-level government, CSIRO, and university scientists with local partners abroad, primarily in Southeast Asia and the Pacific, with a tendency to work where there was an existing pool of researchers able to articulate requests for collaboration and ready to work with Australian counterparts.

Renewed Mandate

ACIAR's second decade included shifts in programming and multiplying lines of work. Following the UNCED in 1992, ACIAR embraced the concept of sustainable development and began to downplay its previous emphasis on boosting agricultural yields. New work examined environmental costs with projects on conserving natural resources and minimizing impacts on the environment, such as zero-tillage planting or avoiding the use of pesticides. The decade saw ACIAR's budget double in size, yet new funding from the aid bureau was tied to specific activities rather than core funding for the Centre to allocate as it saw fit. Beyond time-limited collaborative projects, ACIAR was now responsible for allocating Australia's funding contribution among the international research centers, including CGIAR and other centers independent of the CGIAR system. ACIAR began to incubate the Centre for International Forestry Research (CIFOR), inspired by Australian expertise with tree plantations. CIFOR would eventually move to Indonesia to become part of CGIAR, and signaled the growing complexity of ACIAR's work. While thematic programs of commissioned research remained ACIAR's main line of business, the Centre developed new lines of work.

ACIAR recruited a new Board chairman and a new director, with Ross Garnaut and Bob Clements joining in 1994 and 1995. Garnaut had served as Prime Minister Hawke's senior economic advisor, as ambassador to China, and later as Chairman of Lihir Gold Ltd. Clements came from CSIRO, having led its work on tropical crops and pastures. Together Garnaut and Clements brought in strong links with government, business, and science. ACIAR moved its Canberra headquarters to Fern Hill Park in 1996, and new representatives were appointed within Australia's embassies in Papua New Guinea, South Africa, and India.

ACIAR also shifted the geographic coverage of its work, withdrawing from some rapidly growing countries and expanding further afield. Australia's aid program was involved in over sixty countries, and the government sought to scale back by exiting from—or "graduating"—those countries that could fund their own development (Australia 1997). ACIAR followed this trend and discontinued its programming in Malaysia and Thailand. Yet at the same time, the Department of Foreign Affairs and Trade (DFAT) was eager to see ACIAR expand as "a useful contribution to Australia's overall diplomatic impact" (Arnold 1989: 8). The majority of ACIAR work remained focused on neighboring countries of

Southeast Asia and the Pacific, yet the Centre began to work in the Middle East and Africa. Expansion also came at the behest of the foreign minister, who on occasion requested that ACIAR fund "something" with countries that were of interest to Australia, including North Korea or East Timor. Such requests were taken seriously and literally, leading to projects that fostered scientific collaboration as a form of "track-two" diplomacy. Within ACIAR, such efforts were seen as special projects, something outside the regular portfolio, motivated more by politics than by science. The implicit understanding in-house was that such efforts enhanced ACIAR's standing with the minister, and helped secure the funding needed to continue what ACIAR saw as its main work.

Paul Keating's Labor government (1991–6) created the Australian Agency for International Development (AusAID), giving development policy greater independence from foreign affairs. Upon coming to power, John Howard's Liberal-National government (1996–2007) commissioned the Simons Review, whose report—entitled "One clear objective"—recommended focusing foreign aid solely on reducing poverty. Yet national interests continued to figure prominently. Foreign Minister Alexander Downer argued that "it is in our self-interest to help.... [T]he aid program helps foster stability and expand trade and investment opportunities for Australia. Through aid, we are also addressing many threats to our own prosperity" (Australia 1997: para 6). In responding to the Simons Review, the government identified agriculture and rural development as a priority:

> The returns to developing countries from agricultural research and development are very high and include social and economic benefits beyond the agricultural sector. The benefits to Australia from international agricultural research are also enormous, estimated at $3 billion over the last 20 years. This is a tangible demonstration of how effective development is in our national interest.
>
> (Australia 1997: para 31)

ACIAR began to shift its *ex post* evaluation efforts to look at the diffusion of new agricultural techniques and the extent to which farmers adopted them in practice. The criteria of success became the real-world use of ACIAR work by poor women and men, rather than merely establishing the potential benefit of a technology within controlled settings of laboratories or field trials. ACIAR could control the extent to which research outcomes and training came about, yet only contributed to the outcomes now of interest, including diffusion of farming practices and improved livelihoods of poor people. In 1998, ACIAR's economic evaluation unit was renamed the "impact assessment" program. A new suite of adoption studies commissioned the principal investigators of closed projects to assign a qualitative rank describing the extent to which different audiences had taken up the findings. These adoption studies began to use a random sample of all projects, instead of the previous tendency to cherry-pick and understand the most successful projects.

Yet the argument that ACIAR generated rates of return far exceeding its costs continued to prove useful in rallying a domestic constituency. ACIAR refined the argument of how it reduced poverty abroad, linking greater yields and new crops to lower prices for staple foods and new income for rural people. These savings and income could be invested in the farm and family to acquire access to new lands, afford a better diet or health care, and support children in going to school. ACIAR also continued to refine the argument for how Australia benefited from its work, including the control of pests and diseases—such as fruit flies or guava rust—to ensure they did not appear in Australia, or at least ensuring expertise existed at home if they did. Such arguments were vital for maintaining the support of ACIAR's domestic constituency of farmers and politicians.

Competing for Talent

Meanwhile Australian research policy shifted toward shorter time horizons and reduced autonomy for researchers. Australia removed many of the agricultural subsidies at home, expecting its farmers and industry to compete with the world. This heightened the importance of the rural RDCs, which controlled $262 million in 1993–4 (Industry Commission 1994). This budget came from a levy paid by producers, matched dollar-for-dollar by the national government, plus additional funding from industry. The Department of Finance moved to limit government's liability to 0.5 percent of the gross value of production, and industry subsequently became more influential within RDC governance. A number of the RDCs were privatized to become industry-owned companies, removing government nominees from their boards and aligning more with commodity marketing corporations. The decade saw RDCs move toward shorter-term improvement of existing production techniques, rather than longer-term invention of new products and techniques. These moves signaled a shift away from the original mission of research, development, and extension, toward a new role of marketing, promotion, and industry representation (Kerin 2010).

By the mid-1990s, the national and state governments were reassessing their role in research policy. At the national level, the Industry Commission (1994) identified principles for designing public research: building on private incentives where possible, and encouraging "contestability" or ensuring that research funding opportunities were open to all researchers. Researchers were expected to compete for public funds through market-like mechanisms, yet government was seen to be a poor judge of what specific research projects needed to be done and who should perform them. To address this gap, the Prime Minister established a Science, Engineering and Innovation Council to formulate national science priorities. The state would identify higher-level themes for the national research effort, and leave the allocation of funds to peer review and industry.

At the state level, lean budgets and new priorities combined to squeeze the resources available for agricultural research. A number of states transformed their department of agriculture into departments of "primary industries," reflecting a horizontal shift to consider other sectors beyond agriculture, as well as a vertical shift to consider the value chain beyond the farm gate. Changes in government priorities, plus the rising influence of industrial funding, began to reshape research capacity at home. Government reduced the number of public servants working on agricultural research, scientists increasingly worked on industrial interests, and graduate students began to pursue new career paths. Consequently it would become more difficult for ACIAR to engage Australian researchers, as fewer of them worked on ACIAR's thematic programs or the kind of research needed in developing countries.

ACIAR continued with a matrix management approach that blended the topic and location of Centre-supported research. Projects were selected under different programs, while the budget was allocated by geographic region. Southeast Asia received more than half of ACIAR funding. The Pacific islands, China, and South Asia each received between 10 and 20 percent, while Africa received a modest 5–10 percent (ACIAR 1999). The program coordinators in Canberra were the senior staff, supported by a small number of junior representatives based in Australian embassies abroad. Nonetheless, management sensed a need to update ACIAR's approach, and commissioned an external review of the Centre's operations.

This review was once again largely positive, but recommended changes to ACIAR's program structure and staffing. Nairn et al. (1998: 67) congratulated ACIAR on its "clever mix of proactivity and reactivity in project selection, working within developing-country research priorities and matching these to Australian research strengths." Yet they feared that the program structure inhibited multidisciplinary research, and that the modest size of research projects—an average of $150,000 over three to five years—encouraged a short-term "grant mentality." ACIAR was advised to engage recipients in a longer-term dialogue regarding their research priorities and strategies. This would require an ongoing core of professional staff, rather than the existing practice of hiring program managers for a fixed term of three years—often as a secondment.

The Nairn review also identified challenges in ACIAR's grantmaking. The Centre found it difficult to work in countries where research infrastructure was weak, and grantmaking based on the partnership model encouraged ACIAR toward countries that had a local research community, ideally one that already collaborated with Australian scientists. This was relatively easy in larger, middle-income countries, yet more difficult in smaller, less developed countries. ACIAR's approach was predicated on working with local scientists, yet such talent was scarce or nonexistent in the poorest countries that increasingly dominated the aid program. The review recommended changes to ACIAR's grantmaking, including the use of open calls for expressions of interest and offering to cover the indirect costs of conducting research.

With the review in hand, the ACIAR Board of Management crafted a new policy statement to guide the Centre into the new millennium. ACIAR's mandate was reinterpreted as: (1) encouraging scientists at home use their skills for the benefit of developing countries and to resolve Australia's own problems, and (2) helping developing countries to help themselves, thus contributing to their well-being and general economic growth. ACIAR's programs were intended to contribute to food security, poverty alleviation, and natural resource management, and the Centre sought the outcomes of improved incomes, health, and skills. Research for the developing world was to contribute to these outcomes through adoptable technologies and policy influence; increases in the body of scientific knowledge; and increases in research capacity abroad. Moving forward, ACIAR's programs would address agricultural and natural resource economics, animal production, crop production, fisheries, forestry, management of land and water resources, and post-harvest technology (ACIAR 1999).

The Board also created a new Deputy Director position, to take responsibility for managing the internal process of matching country needs with Australia's scientific capacity. This freed the Director to manage external relationships with the minister and AusAID, as well as with research providers within state government, universities, and CSIRO. Whereas ACIAR used to work independently, the Centre's fortunes depended on being well connected within the Australian research community.

During ACIAR's second decade, the performance regime had enshrined poverty reduction as the purpose of foreign aid, coinciding with a shift in *ex post* evaluation to demonstrate real-life adoption of new technologies and techniques. Simultaneously, changes in Australia's research policy began to hollow out the capacity of state-level government and shift the center of gravity in Australia toward university research. Program theory sought to boost rural incomes, linking poor women and men with markets beyond the farm gate and the value added as food moved from "paddock to plate." ACIAR continued its grantmaking practice of partnerships for mutual benefits, but increasingly relied on Australian researchers in academic settings. ACIAR also modified its grantmaking to exit countries that attained middle-income status and enter countries that became a foreign policy priority.

After twenty years ACIAR remained a scaled-up version of Crawford's vision, but shifts were underway. The most obvious was the countries covered by ACIAR's programming, which evolved to follow Australia's aid program and foreign policy interests. More subtle was an evolution in program theory and evaluation criteria. ACIAR had rallied arguments based on the production added or costs averted, asserting that these contributions greatly exceeded the Centre's overall costs. ACIAR began to frame its arguments in terms of real-world impact in the lives of poor women and men, carrying out adoption studies on the extent to which research results were used in practice.

Australia experienced changes in the structure of, and incentives for, publicly funded research. Budget pressures and competing priorities within the state departments "hollowed out" their research capacity in forestry, crop sciences, and veterinary medicine. Within the RDCs, industrial representatives became more influential, and moved funding toward the shorter-term practical concerns of producers. Within the Australian research community, the center of gravity shifted toward universities, diminishing the relative weight of CSIRO and government departments. The conditions placed on these organizations required them to recover the full cost of research, rather than contributing in-kind or financial support. Meanwhile the CRCs emerged as the pre-eminent funding opportunity: offering greater prestige, larger budgets, and collaboration with industry. In short, ACIAR now needed to compete harder to gain the attention of a shrinking pool of researchers. The emerging performance regime that was beginning to surround ACIAR is depicted in Figure 5.2.

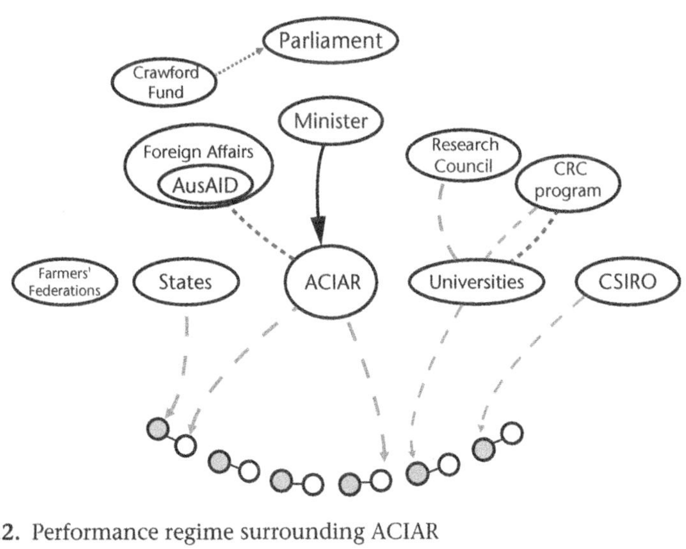

Figure 5.2. Performance regime surrounding ACIAR

Solid lines represent formal lines of authority, dotted lines describe the flow of program ideas, and dashed lines show funding relationships. Upper portion represents governance context; lower portion describes grantmaking, with shaded circles representing recipients in Australia.

Passport to Engage

The early 2000s saw ACIAR's fortunes increasingly tied to the aid program and foreign policy. Worldwide funding for agricultural research was on the decline, and Australia was drawn into the "war on terror" following the 9/11 attacks in the United States and the 2002 bombing of nightclubs on the island of Bali, Indonesia. The security agenda was ascendant in Canberra, prompting the aid program to pay greater attention to fragile states, recovery from conflict, and improved policing. ACIAR management feared the Centre was misunderstood, vulnerable, and had grown too distant from government. The relationship with the foreign minister had weakened, and ACIAR staff found it difficult to engage colleagues in AusAID and DFAT. While satisfied with ACIAR's direction, the Board of Management fretted over the prospect of "a mismatch between our program and Australian Government regional priorities... a lack of recognition by key groups of the Australian benefits from ACIAR operations; and a reduction in ACIAR's funding in the light of the above" (ACIAR 2003: 1–2).

In 2002, Peter Core was appointed as the new ACIAR Director, replacing Bob Clement. Whereas Clement was a researcher at heart, Core came from the world of public management. Core had served as Secretary of the federal departments of transport and of industrial relations, and as Deputy Secretary of the Department of Primary Industries, before managing the Rural Industries Research and Development Corporation. Core was someone in tune with government expectations and his tenure would see a number of salient changes in ACIAR. These included the adoption of an annual operational plan, greater emphasis on country programming, and reform of ACIAR's governance model.

Under Core's leadership, ACIAR adopted the government practice of preparing an annual operational plan for the year ahead. This added to the existing five-year corporate plan looking into the future, and annual reports that reflected on the past. The new operational plan described the types of activities that ACIAR intended to fund and specified key performance indicators. The plan was intended to encourage greater interaction with the minister—who signed off on it—and to focus management's discussion with the Policy Advisory Committee on reviewing the assessment of research needs abroad. The plan communicated ACIAR's priorities to potential recipients and signaled to staff where their attention should be focused, ignoring unsolicited requests from Australian researchers. Before proceeding with any project idea, staff needed to determine whether it was compatible with the priorities in the plan.

The operational plan also shifted ACIAR's budgeting process. Country strategies became the budgeting unit, replacing the past practice of regional expenditure targets. Each strategy included an analysis of the country's context and identified a few priorities of ACIAR programming. The plan provided

Australian and foreign embassies with an overview of what ACIAR intended to do in each country. Program managers were asked to specialize in a few countries, becoming knowledgeable about the research providers there. They were expected to visit Australia's diplomatic missions each time they went abroad, and link with embassies and desk officers in Canberra. The intention was to give ACIAR a passport to dialogue with the minister, AusAID, and heads of mission. Regular contact affirmed that ambassadors greatly appreciated ACIAR projects because, for relatively small amounts of money, they provided a tangible example of public diplomacy and collaboration between local people and Australians.

These changes in planning and budgeting shifted ACIAR's matrix management, strengthening the geographic axis and de-emphasizing the thematic axis. The organizational logic began to rely more on programming with particular countries and less on a particular set of problems. The shift to country-based budgets reflected the level at which the minister was involved. Given his schedule, meetings with the ACIAR Director were often restricted to just twenty minutes. The minister might request that ACIAR do more in a particular region or country, but there was no engagement in the technical aspects of the projects. While ACIAR remained focused on the Asia-Pacific, it was encouraged to further expand its work in Africa and the Middle East, including new projects in Iraq and Afghanistan.[6]

Advising the Minister

ACIAR's third decade also witnessed a change of governance, as the role of its Board diminished from one of providing strategic direction to one of advising the minister. Analogous to a Crown corporation in Canada, a statutory authority in Australia is a public entity established to pursue a specific policy objective. Whereas a line department assumes a broad set of responsibilities and is tightly bound to ministerial direction, a statutory authority has a narrow mandate and operates under its own governing board. Statutory authorities were established in areas that were seen to demand technical skills and non-partisan policy implementation, at arm's-length from ministerial direction, such as the Central Bank. While ACIAR was unique within the aid program, it was just one of over 150 statutory authorities within government.

The Department of Finance began to review the governance of statutory authorities, with an eye to incorporating insights from the private sector. Known as the "Uhrig report," this review proposed that all statutory

[6] For example, work on controlling soil salinization outside Baghdad—announced ahead of a state visit by the Iraqi Prime Minister—and on dryland wheat farming across Iraq, Syria, and Western Australia.

authorities adopt one of two options: governing board or advisory committee. The former was for organizations where the board had the power to determine and alter strategic direction, whereas the latter was for those organizations where this power remained with the minister. Advisory committees were restricted to "ensuring alignment of operations with the specified delegation and the priorities of the Minister" (Uhrig 2003: 35). While the Board of Management was originally responsible for ACIAR's directions, over time the Centre had become more and more responsive to DFAT and AusAID interests. While the motivation was to access additional funding, this pursuit unintentionally enhanced the role of the minister in setting ACIAR's directions. The Uhrig report also questioned the presence of stakeholders on a board, fearing they might "fail to produce independent, critical and objective thinking" by being more "concerned with the interests of those they represent, rather than the success of the entity they are responsible for governing" (Uhrig 2003: 43).

The Uhrig reforms coincided with pressure to rebrand public entities within the Australian government. ACIAR began to de-emphasize its old logo of three hexagons that had featured prominently on technical papers, annual reports, and website. In its place, central agencies required the coat of arms of the Commonwealth government featuring a kangaroo and emu. Some publications retained a stylized version of the old logo as a faded watermark in the background, but the Australian coat of arms soon adorned the office and business cards. It was a symbolic recognition that the performance regime was now less tolerant of independence, and ACIAR's fortunes were tied to being seen as part of—rather than apart from—the machinery of government.

The Howard government amended the ACIAR Act in 2007, converting the position of Director into a Chief Executive Officer (CEO), and transforming the Board of Management into a seven-member expert Commission. This CEO became directly accountable to the minister for administrative and financial purposes. The following annual report described the Commission's role as to ensure that ACIAR met the expectations of the minister. The Commission was to advise "the Minister on the strategic directions of ACIAR, while the CEO provides operational leadership... [and] is now directly responsible to the Minister for managing the affairs of ACIAR in a way that ensures proper use of the Commonwealth resources" (ACIAR 2008). The change in governance model had the effect of enhancing the relationship between the CEO and the minister, effectively reducing the role of the Board chairperson.

There was a short-lived experiment with a public statement to clarify what the minister expected of each statutory authority in his or her portfolio. Uhrig envisioned that "[t]his document would outline relevant government policies, including the Government's current objectives... and any expectations Government may have on how the authority should conduct its operations" (2003: 7). ACIAR staff drafted such a statement in late 2008, calling on the Centre to keep the minister "fully informed of ACIAR's activities ... and provide timely information to the Secretary of DFAT and Director General of AusAID ... to reinforce DFAT's role as the principal source of advice ... on portfolio policy and program delivery matters" (ACIAR 2008). The statement envisioned the minister receiving monthly reports on ACIAR operations, meeting annually with the new ACIAR Commission, and approving the annual operational plan as well as those projects that were in new countries or in post-conflict and post-disaster settings.

Two features of the statement were remarkable. First, it described a flow of information up to the minister, but was silent on the reverse flow back down to ACIAR management. It thus did not contain any insight on how ACIAR was expected to contribute to government policy. Second, the amount of reporting mechanisms enumerated in the statement implied a regular and deep contact with the minister. Yet such frequent contact went against history: the minister could not afford to dedicate much time to ACIAR, given the competing demands of being in Cabinet and Parliament, representing Australia's foreign policy abroad, and running the larger organizations DFAT and AusAID. It is thus hardly a surprise that the statement remained a one-time experiment. Kevin Rudd's Labor government (2007–10) subsequently discontinued any further reforms to the governance of statutory authorities.

Bridging Innovation and Foreign Aid

In 2001, a new science and technology strategy—Backing Australia's Ability—increased funding to the Australian Research Council and further boosted the portion of public research performed within universities, rather than within government. To its surprise, CSIRO was ignored in the new funding announcements. Traditionally the powerhouse of public research, CSIRO operated as a loose collection of thematic divisions, each engaged in their own projects, not unlike ACIAR. The shock of being bypassed for new funding acted as a wake-up call, prompting management to restructure CSIRO into a set of flagship programs. These were "multidisciplinary research partnerships ... [with] external collaborators to tackle big, audacious goals in areas of major national significance." For example, one program sought to achieve a ten-fold increase in the economic, social, and environmental benefits from water by 2025. These flagship programs were intended to recapture the imagination—and support—of government through ambition, relevance to national interest, and application of research findings. The reforms worked as the CSIRO benefited from new funding announced in the subsequent edition of Backing Australia's Ability in 2004. The lesson of CSIRO restructuring appeared to be "continually question your role and what your stakeholders expect of you" (Sandland and Thompson 2012: 264).

In 2002, the government identified a set of four national research priorities. These were intended to set the agenda for the country's publicly funded research and included: sustainability in the use of land, water, and energy; promoting and maintaining good health; frontier technologies for building and transforming industry; and safeguarding Australia.[7] The priorities were purposely broad, identifying themes whose importance was relatively self-evident and non-controversial. The Howard government appeared to feel that research done at public expense should contribute to the government's agenda, yet did not feel that government was well placed to select the best projects or providers. The government understood its role as setting the agenda to guide the internal self-governance with the research community that selected projects based on traditional notions of scientific excellence.

Various government agencies, including ACIAR, began to report on how their activities contributed to these priorities. Between 2002 and 2007, ACIAR's annual report tracked spending toward various sub-priorities, such as the sustainable use of soil and water, and protecting Australia from pests and disease. These priorities did not really shift ACIAR's research agenda, but allowed the Centre a new means to argue how its work contributed to the national interest beyond the aid program. ACIAR was attentive to the language of Australian research policy because it mattered to researchers at home, including universities, state government, and CSIRO. Senior managers in these organizations needed to justify their work in relation to the national research priorities, thus ACIAR recast its work in the same terms in order to mobilize in-kind and financial support for the Centre's projects.

ACIAR began to describe itself as bridging innovation and foreign aid policy, arguing that it occupied "a unique position as a funder of R&D... [and was] part of Australia's innovation system as well as part of the development assistance program" (ACIAR 2006: 9). This tactic seized upon rising government interest in promoting science as a means of enhancing the country's economy. Public research enjoyed a rising budget and prestige, while foreign aid had a stable budget and the foreign policy portfolio was increasingly focused on security. ACIAR also needed to be sensitive to the incentives shaping the willingness of researchers at home to engage with ACIAR programming. From the in-house review process to the monitoring of ongoing projects, the organizational practices within ACIAR had more in common with CSIRO or the research council than with AusAID or DFAT. ACIAR's

[7] These general themes were supported by twenty-one sub-priorities including: biotechnology, ICTs, and advanced materials, as well as "understanding other cultures" and protecting against terrorism.

routines involved crafting and managing a portfolio of research projects toward achieving change over the long term. In the 2004 annual report, ACIAR expressed intent for two-fifths of new projects to have impacts within five years, with the remainder aiming for impacts within ten-to-fifteen years.

The national research priorities were not without their critics. Government policy was based on the assumption that Australia needed to "concentrate its resources within selected areas in order to maximise benefits" (Barlow 2006: 31). Yet scale was not equally important in all scientific efforts, as evidenced by the number of Nobel prizes awarded to small teams. Furthermore, Australia's public sector would always be small compared to the amount of research performed in the private sector and in larger economies. The policy challenge was not to achieve a scale rivaling the world's largest research efforts, but to identify those projects with the potential to make a valued contribution to knowledge, technology, or skills. The task facing research funders was to assemble promising people and ideas into a portfolio that would enhance those contributions, rather than merely imposing priorities or a research agenda. Meanwhile, performance management within universities—now the heart of the public research system—was reshaped with the Research Quality Framework (RQF) introduced in 2005. The framework proposed to use narratives, examined by review panels, to assess wider benefits of publicly funded research. The intention was to assess university research from the perspectives of both an academic audience (referred to as "quality") and end users beyond academia (referred to as "impact"). The government wanted to link academic research to the concerns of industry and business (Donovan 2008).

The RQF offered mixed incentives for university researchers to work on research for the developing world. On the one hand, performance was increasingly judged based on publications. Agricultural research often adapts known techniques to the agro-climatic conditions in a specific place. Such attributes make this work less attractive to top journals seeking to describe the frontiers of knowledge on topics that interest an international readership. Furthermore, training and collaborating with colleagues abroad required time that otherwise could be invested in preparing publications. On the other hand, research for the developing world was not merely curiosity-driven, but intended to contribute to the economy and livelihoods. An ACIAR grant could serve as an example of how a researcher's work did more than merely adding to the scientific literature. It also offered an opportunity to travel overseas, see how science is performed in other countries, and expand one's network of professional contacts. University researchers appeared to respond by dividing their time between RQF criteria of "quality" and "impact": willing to participate in one or two ACIAR projects, but only after amassing a record of publications sufficient to establish their academic career.

The overall context of research policy at home offered ACIAR an opportunity to articulate with the government's agenda beyond the confines of the aid program. Under Kevin Rudd's Labor government, the national research priorities and RQF temporarily lost some of the political weight behind them. Yet these imperatives later re-emerged with a new Excellence in Research for Australia (ERA) system to measure research quality in universities and efforts to update the strategic research priorities. The new expectations of public research and the incentives they created were here to stay.

Research was also part of Australia's growing aid program. In 2005, the Howard government announced its intention to double aid by 2010 to reach over $4 billion per year, while the subsequent Labor government led by Kevin Rudd promised to double it again toward a target of 0.5 percent of GDP by 2015–16. A new review examined options for this increasing budget, recommending that AusAID country strategies become a whole-of-government framework for the delivery of Australian aid (Duncan et al. 2005). A subsequent White Paper affirmed this direction, calling for ACIAR to integrate its work into the aid agency's rural development strategy (AusAID 2006). ACIAR faced new pressure to fit within—and justify its programming choices against—cross-government strategy. AusAID was also encouraged to increase its support to research "to improve the quality and effectiveness of Australian aid" by helping to "inform where and how our own and our partners' resources can most effectively be deployed" (AusAID 2012b). In keeping with the principle of untied aid, there was new pressure to open such funding opportunities to all nationalities, through greater use of competitive calls for proposals. AusAID expected research to inform development decision-making, find solutions to global problems, and strengthen the capacity of partner countries to use research. Over the next five years, AusAID expected to increase its research funding from $30 million per year to over $106 million per year, projections that would eclipse ACIAR's budget and eventually represent more than 2 percent of aid spending.

These new investments in research for the developing world implied tension between AusAID's new approach and ACIAR's existing program theory. Yet this tension was secondary to the ongoing pressure upon the aid program to align with foreign policy. Australia's own peace and economic well-being relied on having stable neighbors—countries able to look after themselves, generate economic growth, and reduce poverty. The security agenda dominated development policy. Agricultural research was justified through convoluted logic linking insecurity to dissatisfied rural people and minorities and the need to extend to them the benefits of development. Across the aid program, the test for public spending was how to improve stability abroad and in turn enhance the safety of Australians.

Responding to Global Food Security

After twenty-five years, ACIAR found itself in a strange position. Its former independence had eroded as strategic direction increasingly originated outside the Centre. AusAID had entered the research funding business, and cast ACIAR as an add-on to its rural development strategy. Given rapid growth in the foreign aid, ACIAR was responsible for a shrinking portion of Australia's development assistance. Poverty reduction, economic growth, and international security were the watchwords of the moment, largely crowding out ACIAR's original mandate. Funding for agricultural research had decreased abroad, and the importance of agriculture had declined at home, as a boom in mining accounted for a larger share of the national economy. Agricultural science had expanded beyond field-based activities to enhance the production of crops on farms, to embrace both lab-based work in genomics and the market value-chains from "paddock to plate."[8] ACIAR also faced a tension between what researchers needed in order to maintain their academic careers and what ACIAR needed to deliver to the development agenda. Researchers needed opportunities for publication, and development practice demanded tangible improvements in the lives of poor people. ACIAR needed to maintain its credibility with both audiences, yet had less freedom to do so. Yet ACIAR's third decade still had some surprises in store.

A global crisis began in 2007–8 as food prices increased dramatically due to droughts, rising demand among middle-class consumers, low reserves within grain stockpiles, and increased prices for inputs of fuel and fertilizer. Whereas the threats of terrorism and failed states captured headlines and policy agendas early in the new millennium, the specter of hunger now garnered attention it had not seen since the 1980s. By 2011, famine once again displaced thousands of people in the Horn of Africa. Yet the understanding of food security had evolved. While humanitarian aid remained indispensable to attend to people's short-term needs, livelihoods and viable food markets were essential in the longer term.

Food security was a good fit for ACIAR and provided the basis for renewing its program theory, incorporating how its work had evolved and reframing the link with development policy. ACIAR began to argue that:

> food security is not only about providing enough food, but is also concerned with income generation driven by productivity and diversification. The flow-on effects

[8] During this period, ACIAR declined AusAID interest in funding a biosciences hub at the International Livestock Research Institute in Nairobi. The reasons appear to be a perceived mismatch in substance and modality: support for genomics research and ongoing laboratory infrastructure did not fit the business model of field-based, time-limited research projects. AusAID turned to CSIRO which eagerly accepted the funding and began an ongoing Africa–Australia collaboration with the new Centre (ironically involving former ACIAR employees).

> of increasing productivity for smallholder farmers, who represent half the world's poor, achieve other outcomes, such as education for children, access to health services and, in many cases, gender equality. Progress in achieving productivity gains and the associated benefits are central to each of the eight MDGs.
>
> (ACIAR 2010: 6)

However, the Rudd government was interested in a broader response beyond any single organization. The government's budget for 2009 included a Food Security through Rural Development initiative providing $450 million over four years, shared among AusAID country strategies, the World Food Programme, World Bank, and Asian Development Bank. To secure additional funding, ACIAR needed to identify how its work contributed to this whole-of-government strategy, rather than defending the merits of its own stand-alone programming. As Nick Austin became CEO, he inherited an ACIAR that needed to compete for attention against both the multilaterals and an international expectation that Australia would coordinate its response with other donor countries.

The commitment to reach 0.5 percent of GDP survived into Julia Gillard's Labor government (2010–13), which held on to power with the support of a handful of independent MPs. The government once again launched a review of the aid program to guide its still-growing budget. This time it called for organizing the aid program around the principle of value for money, understood as "the quality of the outcome achieved and the efficiency with which it is achieved" (Australia 2011: 46). More than ninety federal and state government agencies were engaged in spending aid dollars. This was seen as a strength "as it enhances linkages and networks across a wide range of specialised fields and is much better value-for-money than attempting to build in-house capabilities in AusAID" (Australia 2011: 28). Yet the logic of value for money also suggested Australia exit aid delivery altogether, investing instead in programs designed and managed by other donor countries. Such "delegated cooperation" arrangements were running or planned with New Zealand, the United Kingdom, the United States, Germany, and the EU. In other words, the aid budget would not necessarily go to AusAID or ACIAR. These organizations needed to demonstrate how they were better value than both multilateral organizations and the bilateral programs of other donor countries.

Once again, the aid review was favorable toward research, arguing that large successes in foreign aid involved deploying new technologies. Future development was seen to "increasingly hinge upon relevant and vibrant research . . . focused upon improving the condition of the world's poor" (Australia 2011: 20–1). The review recommended more aid funding for research by Australian and international institutions, particularly in agriculture and medicine. ACIAR seized upon this recommendation and commissioned the government's Chief Scientist, Ian Chubb, to design a framework for expanding support for international agricultural research, including its rationale, geographic focus, priorities, and models for delivery. This framework reiterated some previous arguments, noting that:

> Collaborative research with our neighbours serves our national interests, with direct benefits through improving our own agricultural productivity... and protecting crops and livestock from pests and diseases—there is a two-way flow of know-how. Furthermore, there are intangible benefits built up through the goodwill of overseas... scientists and students... similar to that derived from the Colombo Plan. (ACIAR 2011: 9)

By the end of the year, Australia came full circle. Thirty years after the 1981 announcement in Melbourne to create ACIAR, the country once again hosted the Commonwealth Heads of Government Meeting in Perth. On this occasion, the Prime Minister announced $33 million over four years to establish an Australian International Food Security Centre, to be housed within ACIAR and dedicated to improving the adoption of agricultural innovations. At first glance, it is unclear why the government would opt to establish this new center rather than simply invest in the existing one. The announcement could be dismissed as the habit of politicians to announce something of their own creation, rather than acknowledge the works of their predecessors. Yet it also signaled a lack of enthusiasm for the ACIAR approach. Compared to the scale of global food security challenges and the growing budget and ambition of the aid program, ACIAR programming was perceived to be too modest, too technical, and taking too long to contribute to development outcomes. The appetite within the aid agency had turned toward more real-time research, such as mapping of value chains and piloting of modifications in them. The aid agency determined success based on the number of farmers who gained access to agricultural technologies, and addressing food security was seen to require more than business-as-usual from ACIAR.

In summary, during this third decade the performance regime adopted whole-of-government strategies toward Australia's engagement within developing countries, particularly in response to the "war on terror" and later the global food crisis. Meanwhile, public research needed to justify itself within national priorities and program-level outcomes, such as contributing to Australia's economy and security, rather than simply pursuing individual projects based on their own merit. ACIAR's program theory sought to bridge Australia's innovation system and foreign aid, emphasizing agricultural research as a form of science diplomacy that promoted stability and food security abroad. Grantmaking continued to rely on commissioned partnerships, yet these were increasingly framed within country strategies in order to give staff a "passport to engage" government colleagues and embassies. Responding to foreign policy priorities also led ACIAR to support work in countries with a weak or nonexistent domestic research community.

Key Points

Looking across thirty years of history reveals three key ways that ACIAR both adapted and refused to adapt to changing expectations within the performance regime. On the one hand, ACIAR clearly redefined its contribution to the government's agenda, redesigning how it measured success and responding to priorities of the day with science and foreign policy. On the other hand, ACIAR responded less readily to forces reshaping the research community at home, which hollowed out the capacity of state governments that provided extension and research service for domestic farmers. ACIAR remained dedicated to its stand-alone business model of commissioning research partnerships, despite rising expectations that research be awarded through open competition and that ACIAR would fit within whole-of-government strategies.

ACIAR initially enjoyed high-level government support that had led to its creation. ACIAR's initial value proposition was to provide Australia with prestige on the world stage following its announcement at the Commonwealth Heads of Government Meeting. Yet the inclusion of a sunset clause in the Act meant that ACIAR needed to prove its worth or it would disappear after twelve years. ACIAR justified its existence using arguments based on the economic valuation of the potential to boost productivity, reduce costs, or enhance the value of commodities. These measures articulated how ACIAR benefited Australia, garnering support with farmers and the National Party. Helping agriculture in other countries was not just about helping others; it was in Australia's direct interest, as captured by Derek Tribe's phrase "doing well by doing good." ACIAR often described its cost as more than justified by the tremendous benefits stemming from a handful of projects. The weakness of this tactic was that it justified ACIAR on its own terms, but was modest in comparison to the overall aid program and disconnected from foreign policy interests. When poverty reduction became the purpose of foreign aid, ACIAR augmented its evaluation techniques to consider real-life adoption of new techniques in addition to assessing their potential benefits. ACIAR also gave more consideration to who the beneficiaries of its research were, their linkages with markets beyond the farm gate, and how additional income could enable them to overcome poverty.

Programming evolved in response to the minister's geographic priorities. Primarily focused on the Asia-Pacific, ACIAR tended to work in countries where there was an already-established research community, leading to a substantial number of projects involving India and China. Yet ACIAR also supported work in Papua New Guinea, East Timor, North Korea, Iraq, and Afghanistan. These countries had relatively weak domestic research communities and attracted less interest from the Australian scientists, and thus tended to require greater time and effort by staff. The program logic of "increasing production" initially focused ACIAR's portfolio on key staple crops in populous countries with an existing pool of domestic scientists ready and willing to collaborate with Australian counterparts. Yet the expectations of the aid program and foreign policy slowly encouraged a focus on poor farmers in smaller, less developed countries, often with a weak or nonexistent domestic research community. ACIAR's third decade saw new pressure to fit into whole-of-government strategies framing Australia's engagement within partner countries. At the same time, management repositioned ACIAR as the interface of Australia's innovation and aid agendas.

The cornerstone of the partnerships model was the existence of qualified Australian researchers with skills and knowledge that were applicable to agriculture overseas. Yet the landscape of Australian science evolved over the three decades since 1982: universities became much more prominent, accounting for a larger share of research funding and employing a greater share of scientists. In contrast, the state-level governments moved away from maintaining their own laboratories and research staff, and—like CSIRO—the capacity that remained was increasingly expected to justify itself within larger-scale priorities and program-level outcomes, rather than simply pursuing individual projects based on their own merit. Australian research policy shifted toward issues judged to be in the national interest by mobilizing capacity beyond government. Public funding moved away from supporting individual organizations based on past performance, toward funding constellations of actors based on their potential to contribute to the economy or to enhancing Australia's standing in world science. ACIAR's relative influence and ability to command the attention of Australian researchers diminished as new funding programs emerged that were more interested in practical applications at home. Involvement in ACIAR programming needed to offer Australian scientists an opportunity to get ahead in their careers. At a personal level, young researchers could find it personally rewarding to help reduce hunger in Africa rather than contribute to incremental production of sugar or beef at home. Yet work abroad is a luxury to be entertained after establishing an academic career and the required record of publications.

Within both the aid program and science policy, it is no longer sufficient to argue that taxpayers' dollars are being spent on good projects. Politicians expect that spending contributes to government's larger goals and the national interest. Once this pressure was more rhetoric than substance—a means of framing what ACIAR did rather than changing it. Yet as access to

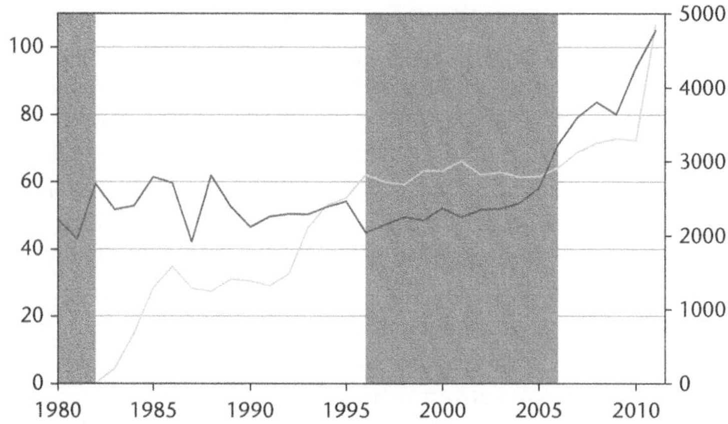

Figure 5.3. Australia's R4D spending since 1980

ACIAR expenditures (light line, left axis) compared to Australia's official development assistance (right axis). All amounts are expressed in real terms in A$ million adjusted to 2011. The shaded years represent times when the Liberal, right-of-center party was in power.

ACIAR Annual Reports and OECD statistics

new funding is tied to cross-government initiatives, ACIAR increasingly became an instrument of Australian policy, rather than merely good at what it did.

In terms of the *resources available*, ACIAR experienced three periods of rapid growth separated by two periods of relatively flat budgets (Figure 5.3). Rapid expansion lasted until Australia's austerity budget in 1986, an event that inspired the creation of the Crawford Fund to renew public and political support for R4D. After passing its "sunset review," ACIAR gained responsibility for Australia's contribution to the international agricultural research centers. Access to additional resources was contingent on demonstrating that ACIAR was aligned with the government's geographic priorities, ending programming as countries attained middle-income status and entering countries that were a foreign policy priority. Meanwhile changes in state-level departments "hollowed out" expertise in agricultural extension that were the source of ACIAR's partners. A more recent rise in ACIAR's budget was triggered by the global food crisis in 2008–9 and Australia's response to it.

In terms of *public management*, the "sunset" clause motivated ACIAR to demonstrate the benefits of its work for Australians. Over time, ACIAR shifted from estimating the potential value of enhanced production to examining real-life adoption of technologies, production techniques, and policies. Yet the ACIAR structure of thematic research programs was disconnected from foreign ministry and aid agency structure based on country desks. In its third decade, ACIAR placed a stronger emphasis on country strategies in order to provide staff with the means to engage government colleagues and embassies.

ACIAR also adopted the government practice of annual operational plans, while governance reforms converted the independent Board of Management into an advisory Commission. Both these steps reinforced ties to government and reliance upon the minister. While conceived as an autonomous statutory authority, ACIAR now justified its existence based on its fit within whole-of-government strategies and Australian foreign policy.

In terms of *research policy*, ACIAR retained its original approach, inspired by philanthropic foundations, with staff brokering partnership between developing-country researchers and their Australian counterparts. ACIAR saw "demand" as coming from developing-country governments, and its "clients" as the researchers in these countries and at home in Australia. Nonetheless, as public universities and research evaluation systems became more prominent in Australia's research system, ACIAR funding became less prestigious and attractive. Contributing to capacity abroad did not necessarily contribute to career prospects at home. Academic incentives encouraged researchers toward other funding opportunities, such as the CRCs, which multiplied inside a rising science budget. Meanwhile, decreased government funding for the rural RDCs increased the prominence of industry's goals, favoring more short-term, incremental improvements to existing techniques over longer-term strategic research. Yet CSIRO's transformation from a "university without students" into a set of audacious challenge programs shows public research can attract support by adopting a more ambitious agenda. ACIAR also began to describe its work in terms of the national research priorities, and cited science policy as an additional source of legitimacy alongside the foreign policy priorities of the day.

ACIAR's *program theory* remained rooted in the concept of mutual benefit. This reflects the political reality when the Centre was founded, which led ACIAR to emphasize benefits at home, rather than merely building capacity abroad. ACIAR started with the agricultural needs of developing countries, and developed promising project ideas if there was an Australian partner with some "natural research advantage" on the topic at hand. Australia possessed specialists in tropical coastal and dryland climates similar to conditions in parts of Asia and Africa. During its first two decades, ACIAR expanded from the productivity of single crops or species, to the more efficient use of natural resources. With the advent of poverty reduction as the main goal of Australian aid, ACIAR strengthening its work on boosting rural incomes and the value added as food moved from "paddock to plate." Drawing on Funnel and Rogers (2011), ACIAR's approach to research for the developing world combined the "diffusion" and "networks" theories of change, underpinned by "capacity" and "carrots-and-sticks" program designs: brokering partnerships between Australian and local researchers to create and share new agricultural techniques and enhance the ability of partners in the host country.

In terms of *grantmaking practice*, ACIAR remained consistent in its partnership model of commissioning projects in response to the agricultural needs abroad. Research coordinators sought out expertise at home and brokered partnerships with local institutes abroad. The ACIAR portfolio initially included a number of state-level departments of agriculture, yet evolved as the center of gravity in Australia's public research system shifted toward universities. Project approval depended on passing an in-house review that subjected proposals to cross-disciplinary critique, which could result in modifications to the research design to incorporate additional disciplines or partners. ACIAR retained a narrow set of expectations on its recipients, namely that they would do "good science," there would be some transfer of skills and experiences, and the results would be useful abroad and at home.

6

Changing Context

Public Management and Research Governance

The key argument of this chapter is that governance context matters. The changing pressures in this context encouraged funders periodically to redefine "success" and performance in terms that were favorable to different stakeholders and power holders. Chapter 2 introduced three drivers that encourage change among public research funders. The first is the availability of public resources: waves of budget growth permit funders the opportunity to become more ambitious and expand their work, while waves of budget cuts require being more focused and scaling back. The second driver is the trends in public management: funders are embedded within government and respond to waves of ideas from various sources on how to demonstrate performance and how the funder "fits" within whole-of-government initiatives. The third driver is research management: efforts to get "more" out of work funded from the public purse encouraged a shift from responsive to targeted funding and required that funders demonstrate how their grantmaking contributes to outcomes. This chapter begins by reviewing the extent to which each driver appears in the case studies.

The chapter proceeds to elaborate on the turn all three countries experienced toward emulating markets as a means to justify and direct public investment in research. Information asymmetries plague the relationship between those that fund and those that perform research. Funders surmounted these asymmetries using professional staff that are proficient in research and enjoy some standing in the scientific community. Each funder is an intermediary: simultaneously an agent to government and principal to the scientific community. Over time funders lost some of their autonomy and were pressed to align with government priorities. Decision-making shifted upwards and outwards as a wider set of actors gained influence over the definition and choice of research problems, strategies, and approaches. Yet researchers still choose whether to respond to or ignore different funding opportunities. The multiplication of research funding options at home and abroad rebalances the public research "market," as funders must compete for scarce talent as much as researchers compete for scarce funding.

Resources Available

The importance of this driver is in some ways self-evident: research funders cannot exist without money for their programs, and the rise and fall of budgets influences the scale of such programs. Less evident are the conditions placed upon access to public funding: both the expectations placed on the funder when it receives additional funding, and the scrutiny it receives in times of austerity. In all three cases, funding research for the developing world was part of the government budget for official development assistance. Each of the funders grew when there were more aid dollars, and each experienced budget cuts when aid dollars declined. Yet the relationship was by no means directly proportional. Rising aid budgets did not automatically translate into more research funding: it required active engagement—even lobbying—by managers and their allies, constantly reasserting the importance and value of such work. For IDRC and ACIAR, there was implicit competition with the relevant aid agency in how to use foreign aid dollars, plus the need to canvass the support of the foreign ministry by linking their work to the foreign policy agenda. During budget cuts, the ability to mount a campaign in favor of research—rallying friends within and beyond the bureaucracy—helped preserve funding, or at least kept the cuts proportional to those experienced by others.

Before the Second World War, the UK had firmly established programs for supporting research in and about its tropical colonies, underwriting the costs of local research facilities abroad and world-class centers of excellence at home. By mid-century, the shift to "overseas development" coincided with efforts to reduce overall costs by getting the former colonies to manage their own affairs. For research budgets, this meant scaling back support for facilities abroad and encouraging the governments of newly independent countries to assume the financial responsibility for running them. Until the 1980s, the ODA funded a number of research institutes in the UK that specialized in research on the problems of developing countries; yet it shifted from core funding to competitive work programs in part to rationalize government expenditure. Later the precipitous rise of official development assistance in the 2000s enabled an even faster rise in research funding. Yet the New Labour government applied strict controls on the resources available for staffing and other internal costs, encouraging DFID to move from "retail to wholesale," supporting larger projects. More recently, austerity budgets heightened the scrutiny placed on DFID, coinciding with a perspective that viewed research as evidence regarding the "value for money" of aid investments.

In Canada, the fortunes of IDRC rose through its first two decades, but fell in the 1990s with the government's efforts to rationalize Crown corporations and reduce the deficit. Under Bezanson, IDRC sought to reduce its reliance on government funding, contracting out its services and securing project co-funding from other sources. This helped mitigate the impact of a falling aid budget, yet meant that a share of resources was pre-committed to particular purposes. The first rise of IDRC's budget in the late 1990s was largely due to the special-purpose allocation to the Micronutrient Initiative, and much of the later rise in funding was tied to demonstrating IDRC's alignment to the government's priorities in development policy. IDRC saved itself from some of the pain of budget cuts and shared in a rising aid budget, yet both came with conditions, rather than core funding for the IDRC Board to allocate in isolation.

In Australia, ACIAR witnessed three periods of rapid growth separated by two periods of relatively flat budgets. For the first five years, ACIAR expanded to an early peak that coincided with the government's austerity budget in 1986. While cutbacks were distributed widely across government, the experience inspired the creation of the Crawford Fund to assert the case for Australian investment in agricultural research. ACIAR successfully passed its sunset review to earn a new lease on life and rising budget, including responsibility for the country's contribution to CGIAR and other international centers. Yet ACIAR also needed to align with the government's geographic priorities, ending support to countries that attained middle-income status and engaging countries that were a foreign policy priority, either as science diplomacy (North Korea) or through the war on terror (Afghanistan and Iraq). A subsequent rise in budget came as part of Australia's response to the global food crisis in 2008–9, and saw ACIAR even more tightly connected to a whole-of-government strategy on food security.

The national science budget began to rise in all three countries in the 1990s, predating a subsequent rise in official development assistance in the 2000s. Yet science spending had little direct effect on monies dedicated to research for the developing world, which came predominately from foreign aid. Despite having the fact that their business was research grantmaking, the structure of government placed DFID, IDRC, and ACIAR outside their country's science portfolio. Yet rising science budgets had an indirect impact, creating new funding programs and performance frameworks that altered the incentives available for the scientific community at home. In the UK, parts of the now emboldened research community lobbied for greater use of science within DFID. In the UK and Canada, funders enhanced their cooperation with the granting councils in order to re-engage domestic researchers after a period of focusing predominately on catering to the needs of recipients abroad. In Australia, a rising science budget exposed ACIAR to greater competition for the attention of domestic researchers. It also encouraged new fields of science and "hollowed out" more traditional ones. Furthermore, as government scaled back its investment in rural RDCs, industry funding became more prominent, favoring shorter-term tactical goals over longer-term strategic aims, further altering the incentives and careers of Australia's agricultural scientists.

Public Management

The advent of new ideas on the purpose and role of government—and how to organize it—encouraged changes in funding research for the developing world. Yet old ideas remained influential even as the governance context embraced new ones.

In the UK, Haldane's original concern following the First World War was to ensure the country was proficient in new technologies that might prove decisive to future war efforts. He introduced the idea that government departments should have a budget line for research, to commission work that could directly inform or assist government in achieving its goals. Following the Second World War, the government shifted mindset from colonial administration to overseas development. The newly created ODA was to maintain the UK science base, inheriting a diverse array of research centers specialized in the problems of tropical climates. From the 1970s, market-inspired thinking encouraged separation between those who commissioned research and those who performed it. Subsequently, Thatcher's government pressed for privatizing previously public services, and dividing policymaking from its implementation. By the early 1990s, ODA embraced these agendas and exited service delivery, progressively outsourcing research performance and spinning off its scientific units to stand on their own, merge into universities, or fold entirely. The Blair government's push—for an evidence-based approach to policy—would once again reach fruition a decade later, encouraging DFID to shift the rationale of its research from a public good to an internal service. Whereas the new millennium began with a focus on contributing to the international agenda beyond the UK, DFID subsequently focused part of its energy on informing the aid agency's actions and investments. In each shift, support for research concerning the developing world responded to an existing idea within the governance context—whether this involved separating customer and contractor or demonstrating "value for money" during times of austerity.

In Canada, the inspiration for IDRC came from the philanthropic foundations in the United States, including their independence from politics and government bureaucracy. Yet as a Crown corporation largely dependent on an appropriation from Parliament, government periodically attempted to reassert control. Before the end of its first decade, Cabinet began to question how IDRC fitted into Canada's science and foreign policy. Scrutiny by the Treasury Board encouraged IDRC to establish planning and evaluation functions, in line with then best practice in public management. The 1990s saw efforts to rationalize Crown corporations and a proposal to eliminate IDRC or convert it into a departmental corporation. IDRC avoided this fate by cultivating allies within the bureaucracy and associating itself with a new mandate to implement Agenda 21. This century emphasized alignment with the government's priorities in aid and foreign policy. Initially applied to the annual increment of a rising aid budget, this test soon applied to the entire IAE through the process of strategic reviews required by central agencies. As a Crown corporation, IDRC was both an insider and outsider to development policy and budget decisions. IDRC was allowed to make proposals and participate in discussions among bureaucrats, but was excluded from decision making among deputy ministers. At the same time, IDRC was outmaneuvered in defining "development research" as the Department of Finance promoted innovative financing mechanisms, and outside proposals gained favor with ministers. As a result, strategic decisions about program choice moved away from the Board of Governors, toward Cabinet and senior government officials.

In Australia, the ACIAR Act initially limited ACIAR to a twelve-year lifespan. This motivated management in two ways: first to continually show the benefit to Australians—both as participants and beneficiaries—and second to focus evaluation on demonstrating those benefits. In its early years, ACIAR estimated the potential value of increased productivity as a means to decide which crops represented the biggest potential gains from an investment in research. As ACIAR's first generation of projects came to fruition, attention shifted from *ex ante* estimates to *ex post* evaluation of research findings. After ACIAR passed the sunset review, evaluation increasingly examined the real-life adoption of technologies, production techniques, and policies. In this century, ACIAR found that its structure of thematic programs did not connect well to country desks within the Foreign Ministry and AusAID. Management reinforced the geographic axis of its matrix management, seeking a "passport to engage" government colleagues and embassies. Central agencies converted the independent Board of Management into a Commission to advise the minister, and ACIAR adopted the government practice of annual operational plans. Conceived as an autonomous statutory authority, ACIAR now had to justify its existence based on its fit within whole-of-government strategies and Australian foreign policy.

In all three cases, politics at home in the capital mattered. In Ottawa and Canberra, Strong and Crawford championed IDRC and ACIAR. These were high-level individuals who were well connected and well respected, adept at navigating the machinery of government in their respective countries. Both individuals were key to getting the founding legislation approved by Parliament and providing each young Centre with the autonomy to set their own program theory and grantmaking practice. They also continued to protect their creations at different times: Strong defended IDRC from proposals to change its status in 1992 and 1996, and Crawford's posthumous legacy proved instrumental to ensuring ongoing support among parliamentarians. Over time, IDRC Presidents found their job to be as much about maintaining relationships at home as it was providing direction to their Centre's program abroad. While a degree of proficiency in scientific research and knowledge of international development was useful, the CEO's most important asset was a thick Rolodex and network of contacts in key places across government, including the foreign ministry and central agencies.

In the UK, research for the developing world benefited from both external and internal champions. Outside of government, the domestic scientific community was a key stakeholder and long-time beneficiary of foreign aid spending. UK recipients accounted for 96 percent of total value of research grants made between 1990 and 1996. This portion fell to 46 percent of total value of grants between 2004 and 2010, the period when DFID untied aid and focused on the international agenda. The shift away from domestic research providers coincided with a fierce critique of the aid agency's use of science, which prompted DFID to create the position of Chief Scientific Advisor and to join the UK Collaborative of Development Sciences. Inside ODA, staff crafted each work program to ease the transition for existing recipients while moving toward competitive funding. They sought to maintain their credibility within the aid agency, as well as their own standing in the scientific community. Later each Director of DFID research drew on their own backgrounds: Paul Spray stitched together CRD out of the previous thematic programs, Gordon Conway brought in a focus on platform technologies such as ICTs and genomics, while Chris Whitty imparted a model inspired by clinical medicine to inform development investments. Each was an active policy entrepreneur within the aid agency, picking up and acting upon certain signals within the governance context.

In short, individuals and their leadership mattered. The governance context provided a setting in which these individuals found themselves, but they each played an active role in shaping how their organizations pursued research for the developing world. The performance regime and principal–agent relations influenced, but did not determine, the program theory and grantmaking practice adopted. Over time, the ideas held—and choices made—by these leaders and their successors selectively responded to outside influences, incorporating some and ignoring others. Each organization embodied and built upon the visions of its founders. It is impossible to understand DFID, IDRC, or ACIAR without acknowledging the visions of Haldane, Hopper, and Crawford. Politics at home delimited, but underdetermined, both their founding vision and the organizations' subsequent evolution from this point of departure. Individual champions were left to give life to somewhat ambiguous mandates. They were the policy entrepreneurs that mobilized support within the bureaucracy—brokering between what government wanted done and what the research community wanted to do—while staying true to an altruistic vision of research for the developing world.

Research Policy

The UK experienced the widest swings among the three countries. The work led by Haldane in the early twentieth century led to funding streams for both block grants to universities and project funding to researchers. Over time, the scientific community established a "Haldane principle" of self-governance guided by peer review and the Mertonian norms of communality, universality, disinterestedness, originality, and skepticism. Scientists saw the government as a benign benefactor, providing the resources for them to carry out their work. Yet Haldane was not catering to scientists, his aim was to ensure the country had domestic expertise in new technologies that might prove vital in world affairs. Beyond university grants and research councils, his ideas inspired research budgets within line departments for commissioning work the government needed. Rothschild later altered the governance context, introducing the market-inspired "customer–contractor" principle. Government departments were expected to become intelligent consumers, specifying exactly what they needed from the research community, and demanding a competitive price for that service. While domestic science and international development were separate portfolios, ODA and DFID held Haldane-inspired research budgets and were subject to evolving ideas regarding how government was to use this budget.

A number of shifts are particularly prominent in this evolution. First was a shift from responsive to targeted funding: from responding to the interests of the scientific community (based on their curiosity and professional consensus about original and promising avenues of work) to instead encouraging work on the interests of government (based on the department's needs or perception of public good). Second was a shift from intellectual steward to intelligent consumer. Parts of the scientific community related to a department's mandate were considered a close ally worthy of support, whether in the fields of defense, health, or development. Yet with the advent of the Rothschild principle, researchers were recast as distant consultants, to be managed through contractual relations. All three countries progressively scaled back the portion of science spending dedicated to work performed within government departments and labs, accentuating the predominance of universities as the primary location of public research.

The UK did not simply abandon Haldane in favor of Rothschild. These names provide useful shorthand for describing extremes of self-governance and market-inspired governance, yet the two coexisted, being championed and undermined by different actors at different times. Notably there were delays in implementing new policy directions. Over a decade passed between Rothschild's call for "customer–contractor" relations and ODA spinning off its scientific units and adopting competitive funding mechanisms. Even then, the relationship with the scientific community was not entirely arm's length, as the work programs initially sought to soften the blow and reduce dependency on core funding from government. Government officials also turned to researchers for assistance in identifying the government's needs and crafting the terms of references for future funding opportunities. A similar decade-long time lag separated Blair's original call for evidence-based policymaking and the fruition of this agenda under Cameron. While DFID focused inward, UK researchers looked outward. The department wanted to assess the "value for money" of its programming, while researchers needed to demonstrate their contributions to the scientific literature through publications that counted toward the Research Assessment Exercise. Tenure and publication motivated the research community, mitigating somewhat the aims of government departments.

This century was both Rothschild's triumph and Haldane's revenge: a dynamic tension between what government wanted done and what researchers were interested in doing. Government departments were a modest part of the overall funding landscape, allowing self-governance to survive and thrive. The scientific community used exit, voice, and loyalty (Hirschman 1970) when they were dissatisfied with the offerings on hand from government departments. Talented researchers would simply ignore departmental funding when the conditions were onerous or misaligned with their own interests or career goals. The scientific community used its voice to assist officials in crafting calls for proposals and to lobby Parliament for certain approaches to research policy. Finally—almost as a last resort—researchers demonstrated loyalty by aligning and evolving their efforts to what ODA or DFID required.

While most prominent in the UK, efforts to create a marketplace were also present in Canada and Australia. Over time, IDRC adopted competitive calls for proposals with explicit deadlines, eligibility, and selection criteria, in contrast to its original "foundation" approach that was more open-ended, seeking out some proposals, and selectively responding to others. ACIAR persisted with this approach, believing that staff needed to be involved in crafting the projects to ensure mutual benefit between participants at home and abroad. Yet, in a similar way to the UK, academic incentives became more influential in shaping a researcher's career prospects, making these grants less attractive relative to newer funding opportunities.

Governments sought to establish demand for research and encouraged funders to identify with "client" needs. Certain fields were selected based on their perceived relevance to national interests, or the relative strengths of the scientific community at home compared to other countries. Recipients were expected to collaborate with an audience of potential "users" and to demonstrate how their work contributed to social or economic benefit. ODA and IDRC sharpened their use of targeted programs: from an initially broad focus on particular disciplines toward a narrow set of problems. For example, funding for agriculture and health gradually evolved into specific funding envelopes for reducing micronutrient deficiency and combating specific "killer" diseases. In this way, funders sought to demonstrate that their grant portfolios addressed real-world concerns, rather than merely responding to researcher curiosity. DFID and IDRC also emphasized the uptake (or "utilization") of research results: recipients needed to identify and reach an audience of policymakers and practitioners. All three funders became progressively more explicit in arguing how the research they funded contributed to development outcomes.

In Australia, the government interpreted the increasing presence of industry funding and industrial partners as indicating "demand" for research. Yet it arguably pushed publicly funded research from longer-term strategic goals, such as developing new crops and technologies, toward shorter-term tactical goals, such as incremental enhancements to existing technologies. Initially burdened by its image as a "university without students," CSIRO improved its standing with government by restructuring around "challenge programs" with audacious goals expressed as a specific target. "Demand" was tied to national priorities, such as enhancing the efficient use of scarce water on a dry continent.

In the UK, research was originally a service to former colonies, through support to scientific units abroad and centers at home that specialized in tropical climates. Yet over two decades, the aid agency shifted from considering itself as a "proxy consumer" for developing countries, to instead becoming the "client" for the research. In contrast, neither Canada nor Australia had a historic specialization of research on the problems facing developing countries, allowing the founders of IDRC and ACIAR to shape these organizations as they saw fit. Yet the lack of a domestic constituency meant that research for the developing world was less visible and inherently vulnerable to government cutbacks. As few voters depended on IDRC or ACIAR for their livelihood, each organization needed to rally a network of allies within the bureaucracy or among parliamentarians.

Yet both organizations linked to, and were affect by, research policy. Neither IDRC or ACIAR was directly funded by their country's science budget, but found refuge in the language provided in national science strategy. In their respective annual reports, IDRC highlighted how its program choice matched the perceived strengths of Canada's research community, while ACIAR described its work in terms of national research priorities. Science policy provided an additional source of legitimacy, when foreign policy priorities of the day were less conducive to research for the development world. More importantly, research policy mattered because it reshaped the scientific community, altering the career paths available to scientists at home and the incentives for working abroad. Table 6.1 summarizes the contextual drivers

Table 6.1. Comparison of governance contexts

	Drivers that encourage funders to adjust their programs		
	Resources available	Public management	Research policy
UK	• Move away from colonial administration to reduce expenses	• Government as intelligent consumer	• Haldane principle of researcher autonomy
	• Treasury imposes controls on internal spending	• Progressive outsourcing: retain funding and privatize performing	• Rothschild principle of customer–contractor
	• Rising aid budget in 2000s	• Pressure to demonstrate value for money	• Shift from responsive to targeted funding
Canada	• Rise with aid budget and fall with cutbacks	• Adopt planning and evaluation functions	• Shift from selecting projects to designing programs
	• Earmarking funds to special purposes	• Crown corporation outside policymaking and eroding Board independence	• Pressure to show that research is applied and responds to "demand"
	• Align with aid priorities to access new funding	• Outside proposals gain traction at ministerial level	• Increased use of competitive grants
Australia	• Austerity budget in 1986 inspires Crawford Fund	• Sunset clause creates need to show results within ten years	• Industrial funding of public research pushes shorter-term tactical issues
	• Access to funds contingent on being "useful" to minister	• "Fit" within whole-of-government strategies	• Research moves from state governments to higher education
	• Follow aid policy in exiting middle-income countries and entering fragile states	• Autonomous Board converted into Advisory Commission	• Shift from responsive to targeted funding

of resources availability, public management, and research policy in each of the three countries.

Emulating Markets, Eroding Autonomy

The above changes in the resources available, public management, and research policy describe an overall shift toward more market-inspired governance. The advent of a neoliberal values as the justification for government action affected the rationale used to justify public investment in research. Official development assistance partially shielded DFID, IDRC, and ACIAR from these expectations, nonetheless each organization received an infusion of market-based vocabulary and thinking from its surroundings. By the early 2000s, existing funders found their "market share" eroding as government chose to invest its rising science and aid budgets elsewhere. All three organizations lost their monopoly over the government's funding of research for the developing world, as new mechanisms emerged and outside ideas competed for policy space and budget. In the UK, the UK Collaborative of Development Science positioned the research councils and line departments as alternative channels for delivering funds and services. Grand Challenges Canada arose as a new voice implicitly competing with IDRC, while AusAID and CSIRO bypassed ACIAR to collaborate on biosciences in East Africa.

Each funder requires a pool of candidates within the scientific community willing to apply for its grants. The funder provides a set of incentives to researchers to conduct work, at the same time individual researchers strive to define and pursue their own careers, choosing among, and drawing upon different sources of funding. A researcher's work surpasses the limits of any one project or grant, yet researchers rely on these as building blocks to construct their longer-term career path in a bricolage fashion. The increases in the budgets of the research-granting councils diminished the relative weight of DFID, IDRC, and ACIAR. Being a Canada Research Chair or part of a Cooperative Research Centre carried greater prestige and arguably fewer constraints than a grant from IDRC or ACIAR. In the UK, recipients had little incentive to, or reward from, coordinating the work of others in a consortium or consulting work that responds to the department's knowledge needs.

The UK explicitly attempted to set up a marketplace between the demand of departmental needs and the supply of presumably numerous potential providers in the scientific community. Yet the market analogy is imperfect due to a lack of competition and independence. First, by definition, there are only a limited number of providers in specialized fields of science, giving rise to a supply that is more monopsony than competitive. For extremely specialized pursuits, such as a locust control research, it was arguably more efficient to have one national or world-class center than support multiple competing efforts. Second, the research market is plagued by information asymmetries, such that government required skilled researchers to identify its knowledge needs and understand the potential opportunities for science to address them. Government officials could tender for research services blindly, but risked asking the impossible or casting researchers as mere consultants.

The three funders surmounted information asymmetries through in-house scientific expertise, staff who were themselves proficient in research and who enjoyed some standing in the scientific community. This made the funder a more "intelligent consumer," striving to be simultaneously independent of, and connected to, the scientific community. Staff had dual identities, coming from the world of research, but working "on the other side" as grantmakers. They sought to maintain their standing and credibility in the world of research, to which they might return to at a later stage in their career. In this respect, the links of principal–agent relations are not merely one-way lines of authority and control, but two-way processes of negotiation and accommodation. The scientific community could and did speak back to government, in part through funding agencies that acted as intermediaries sensitive to both sides. In this respect, the daily tasks and responsibilities of staff offered a richer set of insights than simply studying the funder's corporate strategy.

IDRC and ACIAR were initially granted the autonomy to express a distinct identity openly and proudly. Similarly, research was initially given pride of place when DFID was established. Yet the governance context surrounding all three funders progressively became less tolerant of such autonomy. The shift toward market-inspired governance eroded the political support for a distinct mandate, forcing each of these organizations to find more covert ways to pursue their work. Each funder modified their strategies and grantmaking to more closely match what was politically viable at the time. For DFID and IDRC, important shifts occurred over the 1980s and 2000s. In contrast to the IDRC Act twelve years previously, which focused on building capacity abroad, ACIAR's founding legislation focused on mobilizing the domestic research community for mutual benefit at home and abroad. This vision could more readily pass through Australian Parliament at the time than the more altruistic Canadian mandate.

Over time, each funder became increasingly embedded within government policy. Setting corporate strategy was initially an open-ended exercise under which funders largely determined their own goals and program design. Yet this autonomy eroded as central agencies reasserted control, conditions were placed on the access to new money, and funders were pressed to align with government priorities and fit their efforts within whole-of-government strategies. Decision-making shifted beyond the funder's board and management, upward toward minister's offices and outward toward other parts of the governance context. This was a gradual shift, punctuated with tipping points reflected in modifications to the founding legislation and reductions in the powers and size of board and management. This shift matches a wider trend of outside actors gaining influence over the definition and choice of research problems, strategies, and approaches supported with public money (Whitley 2011). Funders were left with reduced discretionary space and operated under constraints that limited their ability to manage strategically (Poister et al. 2010).

Yet each organization continued to pursue its vision of research, even when the policy environment was less than favorable to that vision. One means of coping was to connect to other government priorities while remaining true to their core beliefs and the integrity of their research agenda. Analogous to private companies responding to diverse consumer demands, each research funder had to choose whether to diversify its offerings or focus on its core product. ODA and DFID were very responsive: reinventing its research division and diversifying its grantmaking with changes in leadership, rising budgets, and new demands in the governance context. IDRC was moderately responsive, adding thematic programs and grantmaking mechanisms to reflect the perceived demands in developing countries and within Canadian foreign policy. As the smallest of the three case studies, ACIAR remained the most specialized, both in terms of thematic focus on agriculture and dedication to downstream application, even as the pool of Australian research providers began to privilege the upstream science of genomics.

Each funder was an intermediary: simultaneously an agent to government and principal to the research community. They formed a link in a chain of principal–actor relationships between government and the scientific communities at home and abroad. Each competed for government money against alternative uses of public funds, and competed for the attention of researchers against alternative demands for their time and ideas. This was not a passive role, as each funder actively brokered opportunities that satisfied the interests on both sides, and could not afford to alienate either side completely. Changes in performance regime occasionally inspired the funder to revise how it contributed to the government's agenda. Thus the funder catered to different actors in the governance context, alternatively finding favor within science and foreign policy priorities or among central agencies.

Each funder actively shaped a role for itself between government and the scientific community, finding allies and building a coalition that provided financial resources, political support, and an audience of grant seekers willing to engage in its programs. On the surface, the different periods of time identified in the case studies reflect a shift in funder program theory following a change in the governance context. Yet these changes also represent a realignment of coalition: the sets of actors that provided the funder with its sustenance, substance, and legitimacy. The language of market competition and demand was adopted in the governance context, and by the funders themselves. Yet the image of a discrete marketplace for research was an illusion. Funders were not independent purchasers of knowledge among perfectly competitive providers, but the political interface between government and scientific communities, at home and abroad.

Universities became the predominant location for public research as governments scaled back on the number and size of government-owned centers and labs. This introduced a tension for domestic researchers, between how performance was measured within academia and how it was assessed by DFID, IDRC, or ACIAR. These funders embraced a growing list of expectations intended to enhance "development impact," requiring grantees to do more than merely good science, in a single discipline, accepted by their peers. Best practice was redefined to incorporate insights and methods from multiple disciplines, enhance the skills of developing-country partners, communicate with lay audiences of policymakers and practitioners, and demonstrate that their work was used to benefit the lives of poor women and men. Yet the career prospects for many researchers was shaped by the need to demonstrate frequent, original, specialized, and highly cited contributions to their chosen field. Some researchers escaped this bind by working with NGOs or policy think tanks, where the expectations of their individual performance aligned with the aims of influencing policy and informing practice. Overall, where a previous generation of domestic researchers pursued a career-long specialization in the problems of the developed world, for many it is now something altruistic and fun, only to be entertained once their academic career is firmly established.

In many developing countries, funding from abroad still provides a significant share of the overall funding available for research. There is less tension between the funder's expectations of "development impact" and the interests of the local scientific community, as catering to the latter is seen as an indirect contribution to the former. This was especially so during times when funders privileged "capacity building." Yet an increasing number of developing countries have established their own granting councils and funding agencies, which provide new opportunities for local scientists and reduce their reliance on foreign funders. Whether at home or abroad, any source of funding requires researchers to balance between responding to the funder's priorities and expectations—perhaps at the cost of modifying their own research interests—or foregoing the offer of potential resources. The multiplication of research funding options at home and abroad rebalances the public research "market," requiring funders to compete for the attention of scarce talent, as much as researchers need to compete for scarce funding.

Key Points

On the surface, it appears axiomatic that funding organizations adapt to changes in the governance context. Yet the consequences of this adaptation means that program theory—the generalized understanding underpinning the funder's change model—is influenced by the performance expectations of other actors, including aid agencies, foreign ministries, other line ministries, central agencies, and even a prime minister's agenda. Evaluation theory expects a logical framework to be constructed in a step-wise fashion, starting with objectives, and proceeding to activities, outputs, and outcomes. Yet the case studies suggest that programs are partially constructed to bridge government priorities on one side and the interest of scientific communities on the other. Objectives and outcomes are predetermined by the policy process. The funder must craft a program theory that provides space for researchers to populate funding opportunities with activities that bridge these predetermined objectives and outcomes. Information asymmetries plague the relationship between those that fund and those that perform research. Funders surmounted these asymmetries using professional staff that are proficient in research and enjoy some standing in the scientific community. Each funder is an intermediary: simultaneously an agent for government and a principal to the scientific community.

All three funders faced changing expectations of their performance and eroding independence within government. The governance context turned toward emulating markets as a means to justify and direct public investment in research. Funders selectively adopted market-based thinking into their work and were exposed to greater competition in their quest to access government funding. Multiplying, and often conflicting, expectations threatened to "wag the dog" as performance management regimes circumscribed the space available to managers to pursue their mandate. Over time, funders lost some of their autonomy and were pressed to fit their efforts within "whole-of-government" strategies. Decision-making shifted upward and outward as a wider set of actors gained influence over the definition and choice of research problems, strategies, and approaches. Yet in another sense, research funders fought back, drawing legitimacy from different areas of public policy and reshaping their policy environment.

Simultaneously, researchers still choose whether to respond to or ignore different funding opportunities. The entry of more funding options for research, especially abroad, turns the public research "market" into a competition among funders for scarce talent rather than among researchers for scarce funding.

7

Looking Back

Program Theory and Grantmaking Practice

Each of the three funding organizations examined in this book adapted to changes in the governance context by altering their program theories and grantmaking practices: the "change model" of how research was understood to contribute to development, and the "action model" of how the funder supported that contribution. Chapter 6 focused on the governance context surrounding funders: changes in the resources available, public management, and research policy. Yet these drivers did not determine program theory and grantmaking practice. Funders were selective, responding to some signals and ignoring others. This chapter examines how organizations exercised their own agency in deciding whether—and how—to adapt to a changing context.

Recall the concepts of program theory and grantmaking practice introduced in Chapter 2. Program theory is the proposed causal explanation of how the organization's activities are intended to contribute to real-world results, while grantmaking practice is what actually happens in terms of everyday routines informed in part by past experience. Program theory is comparable to Chen's (2005) "change model" of the determinants understood to cause a problem the organization seeks to address, and the interventions employed by the organization to affect those determinants. Program theory is embedded in a sometimes ill-defined philosophy and ethos of how the organizations understood "research for the developing world." In contrast, grantmaking practice is related to Chen's (2005) "action model" consisting of delivery protocols, plans for arranging the organization, and efforts to ensure a supportive environment. This practice evolved over time, including shifts in who received funding, and is encoded into the daily routines of employees and the values that motivated them.

Each of the case study organizations persisted over time, adapting to substantial change in the governance context, including periods of limited resources, new ideas in public management, and a market-inspired shift in research policy. IDRC and ACIAR showed remarkable consistency in how they organized their grantmaking despite some variation in corporate strategies and priorities. This reveals an ability to preserve elements of their business even while responding to a changing context—more evolution than reinvention. In contrast, ODA/DFID fluctuated more widely, reflecting its more vulnerable position as part of a government department rather than a stand-alone, for-purpose organization.

All three organizations were active participants in the governance context shaping the policy space conducive for their mandate. These were not passive actors simply responding to the whimsical expectations of diverse stakeholders. They persisted in part due to an ability to mount arguments in favor of their way of doing business. In the UK, willingly or not, ODA/DFID was embroiled in the larger debates on research policy. In Canada, IDRC periodically formed and renewed a network of allies across the federal government reaching beyond foreign aid, to provide an early warning of policy discussions and funding decisions that might affect the Centre. In Australia, the Crawford Fund worked to renew public and political support for agricultural research in general, and ACIAR's mission in particular. Each funding organization engaged government to create a favorable policy environment. The links of principal–agent relations flow both ways, influencing both sides. In other words, the performance regime both drives, and is affected by, the funder's program theory and grantmaking practice.

Program Theory

At a corporate level, the notions of how research contributes to development were often stated in general terms and did not meet the test of an explicit theory of change (Funnel and Rogers 2011) or detailed change model (Chen 2005). Such detailed logic was often delegated to the project or program level. Yet looking at the organization as a whole, one can identify general thrusts that subsequently guided grantmaking decisions of who received funding and what their activities were expected to achieve.

An initial vision guided each of the three organizations in the period before explicit corporate strategies. In the UK, Haldane provided that government departments should have a separate line item for research, and ODA inherited the colonial legacy of a research community at home specialized in the problems of tropical climates abroad. In Canada, Strong and Hopper saw the young IDRC focus on the second part of its mandate, building the capacity of developing country researchers. In Australia, Crawford and McWilliam responded to the political reality of the times by focusing ACIAR on mutual benefit, including the application of findings at home. IDRC and ACIAR were established as for-purpose corporations, at arm's length from government, in the belief that R4D was longer term and required fundamentally different skills compared to the aid agency or foreign ministry. Each of the three funders began funding projects on general themes, yet over time adopted incrementally more detailed program theories.

At any given time, each organization had a particular perspective on what research was to contribute to the developing world and what it was expected to achieve. This broad narrative provided the umbrella for different programs to elaborate more detailed explanations of how their work contributed to change. Research for the developing world was not aimless: corporate strategies were somewhat vague, but encompassed programs in which staff invested substantial time and effort in planning, implementing, and refining. In other words, program theory tended to exist more at the program level, rather than with the corporate strategy. Such strategy provided a framework for multiple program theories that coexisted at any one time.

In the UK, the initial focus was on science at home, maintaining highly qualified people and already-established centers. Program theory evolved in response to the Rothschild expectation of being an "intelligent consumer," and began to offer competitive funding for projects toward outcomes of interest to the aid agency. Since 1997, three distinct program theories cascaded through DFID. The first saw research as a public good contributing to the global development agenda created in coordination with other donors. The second was the promise of technology—particularly genomics and ICTs—which was open to the scientific community beyond those that self-identified as working on international development. The third emulated clinical medicine, expecting research to provide evidence on what is needed and what works. Yet as each new program theory cascaded through the organization, it did not completely displace previous ones, leading to multiple grantmaking practices. For example, DFID continued to provide core funding to the ODI despite long abandoning a commitment to maintain the UK science base. Furthermore, DFID continued to fund vaccine research despite the recent focus on evidence to inform internal decision making. A growing research budget provided space for multiple program theories to coexist and thrive.

In Canada, IDRC remained close to the Strong–Hopper vision of building the capacity of developing-country researchers. After the first two decades, this emphasis was interpreted by Bezanson as "empowerment through knowledge." Underneath this consistency in goals, the Centre refined its understanding of what made a project successful in contributing to development, preferring applied and interdisciplinary research with clear plans for utilization. Consequently, IDRC moved away from basic or disciplinary research that did not appear to have an audience. Cutbacks in the 1990s triggered a substantial restructuring, dissolving the old divisions of agriculture, health, information, and social sciences and replacing them with problem-based programs related to the post-Rio agenda of "sustainable and equitable development." This move saw IDRC adopt program-level evaluation that required staff to prepare progressively more detailed program theories. The objective of policy influence subsequently took prominence over capacity building, and IDRC began to seek additional for-purpose funding from within Canada and from other donors. IDRC adopted a mantra of "innovating for development" yet continued to see its business as "grants-plus" support for developing-country researchers. The advent of the Internet shifted the program officer's role from "wandering minstrel"—providing access to scientific literature and contacts not available locally—to "engaged peer" supporting the research interests of recipients.

In Australia, ACIAR remained rooted in the concept of "mutual benefit." ACIAR started with the agricultural needs of developing countries, and elaborated on promising project ideas if there was a local partner abroad to work with, if the potential benefits outweighed project costs, and if there was an Australian partner with some advantage in the discipline. With similar coastal and dryland climates as parts of Asia and Africa, Australian experience and expertise were directly applicable for enhancing farming abroad. This was explicit in how ACIAR sought to strengthen Australia's relation to the international agricultural research centers, and to bridge between Australia's innovation system and development assistance program. The role of research coordinators was to assess the needs abroad and broker partnerships with talent at home. ACIAR expected its staff to be top minds in their respective fields, joining the Centre for a limited time—as a secondment from government departments and universities—rather than career specialists in international development. ACIAR initially focused on particular crops or species, and later evolved to support work on farming systems, soil conservation, and reducing the use of pesticides. Meanwhile ACIAR's evaluation effort shifted emphasis from estimating the potential value of improved production to measuring the real-life adoption rates of new techniques and technology. When poverty reduction became more prominent in aid policy, ACIAR strengthening its work on market chains and boosting income for the rural poor. Similar to DFID, new perspectives did not completely displace older thinking, but rather ACIAR's work combined efforts toward improved production, environmental conservation, and poverty reduction.

Grantmaking Practice

Changes in program theory translated imperfectly into grantmaking practice, or the daily routines of the organization. It is one thing to espouse a new set of priorities or program theories; it is another thing to implement them within grantmaking practices. In Chapter 2, grantmaking practice was described in terms of: selection criteria guiding the choice among potential recipients and proposals, the role of staff in the research process, the portfolio of grants made by the funder, and the implications for the research community.

In the UK, changes in program theory had direct consequences for grantmaking. ODA's initial selection criteria were based on the historic relationships with institutes at home and abroad. To rationalize these relationships, ODA shifted from core funding to project funding for institutes, which were expected to provide at least part of their own operating costs. The shift to competitive calls ought to have encouraged the entry of new actors, yet the pool of recipients contracted as some entities were merged together or with universities, and others ceased to exist. As the government rationalized the public sector, ODA's scientific units were spun off to fend for themselves. The ODA became exclusively a research funder, losing the ability for in-house research. Meanwhile the staff role of a "research advisor" evolved. Initially focused on engaging the scientific community outside of government, staff became grant managers monitoring the performance of recipients and in-house subject-matter experts within the ministry. Within DFID, a tension emerged between the London-based department responsible for research, and the bilateral programs in the field responsible for the majority of spending.

With the creation of DFID, the selection criteria initially shifted to focus on contributing to the international development agenda beyond the UK, with an increase in the funding of research abroad. Where domestic recipients accounted for 96 percent of the value of grants during 1990–6, they were just 46 percent in 2004–10. Funding followed the logic of focusing on poorer countries, emphasizing work in South Asia and eastern Africa. DFID introduced new modalities into its grantmaking. The first were Research Programme Consortia, bringing together multiple recipients at home and abroad, around a shared agenda aligned with DFID's priorities, and involving larger amounts of funding. The second was to partner with the UK research councils, which required the participation of UK scientists and saw scientific merit return to prominence in the selection criteria. Under DFID, research funding opened to a diverse set of recipients at home and abroad, including scientists who had skills that could be applied to the needs of poor people, regardless of whether they had specialized in poor countries.

Over time, recipients needed to satisfy an increasing number of expectations beyond merely producing research that was of acceptable scientific quality and relevant to the needs of developing countries. For example, agricultural sciences experienced a period in the 1980s to 1990s that privileged participatory methods involving farmers in the research process, while the health sciences witnessed a rise of a "one world" understanding of global health and universal expectations of what constituted ethical research. Beyond merely performing "good science" with the potential for development impact, recipients were to play a role in realizing that potential: becoming effective communicators to help get "research into use." Beyond generating new knowledge and technologies, projects were expected to actually deliver development, demonstrating their contribution to outcomes such as raised incomes and improved well-being. Within Research Programme Consortia, principal investigators took on a managerial role: coordinating multiple activities, involving multiple participants, across multiple institutes. Meanwhile other grants—particularly those aimed at informing DFID actions—cast researchers as consultants, synthesizing existing knowledge rather than conducting original research.

In Canada, IDRC sought to emulate the approach used by philanthropic foundations. Program officers would identify and encourage potential recipients, even engaging with them in proposal writing. IDRC also responded to unsolicited proposals submitted by researchers seeking support for their ideas. Emphasis was placed on the originality of a project idea, its potential contributions to a particular discipline, and its perceived relevance to the problems facing the developing regions of the world. After restructuring in the 1990s, staff received the delegated authority to approve projects that fit within a Board-approved program, placing the emphasis on constructing a portfolio of projects that contributed toward a defined program strategy.

IDRC consistently favored recipients based in developing countries, accounting for between 82 percent and 98 percent of grants made. The introduction of competitive calls saw IDRC express its selection criteria explicitly, including relevance to development priorities, the quality of research design and methods, and experience and qualifications of the applicants. Following cutbacks in the 1990s, the search for additional funding meant that outside interests became more influential in IDRC's program choice. Programs flourished in part due to their ability to attract support from donor agencies and philanthropic foundations, or to secure part of Canada's expanding aid budget. Yet rather than identify a select number of "focus countries," IDRC sought to address problems common to multiple countries or that spilled across borders.

IDRC also multiplied the expectations it placed on recipients. The initial emphasis on capacity building meant IDRC expected projects to generate new skills and strengthen local institutions. IDRC did not require "world-class" research outputs, but rather sought to improve local researchers through greater experience and stronger connections with—and contribution to—the international scientific community. Over time, IDRC expected projects to adopt interdisciplinary research designs, influence policy abroad, and contribute to positive change in the lives of poor women and men. IDRC further expected recipients to be good communicators: to reach policymakers and practitioners, rather than merely scientific peers.

In Australia, ACIAR remained consistent in its partnership model of commissioning projects in response to agricultural needs abroad, identified by staff in their travels and by the developing-country governments. Staff sought out expertise at home and brokered partnerships with local institutes abroad. Project approval depended on passing an in-house review process that subjected proposals to cross-disciplinary critique, leading to modifications in research design to incorporate additional disciplines or participants. ACIAR concentrated the bulk of its support in Southeast Asia and the Pacific, and privileged project development whenever a region was underrepresented in the geographic distribution of grants. ACIAR also supported projects that engaged key countries in Australia's foreign policy, including Papua New Guinea, East Timor, North Korea, Iraq, and Afghanistan.

In contrast to the other two funders, ACIAR retained a narrow set of expectations, namely that its recipients would do "good science," transferring skills and experiences and producing results that were useful abroad. ACIAR collected studies on the economic value of successful projects, and later on the adoption rates of a random sample of projects. Recipients were expected to contribute to the projects' costs both through in-kind and financial contributions. This was intended to ensure commitment on behalf of each participant, but became increasingly difficult at home as Australian researchers had less 'free' resources to invest and were encouraged to charge the full cost of their activities.

The ACIAR portfolio initially included a number of state-level departments of agriculture, yet evolved as the center of gravity in Australia's public research system shift from government to universities. ACIAR's projects tended to focus downstream on field-level applications, yet with the genomics revolution the agricultural sciences became increasingly upstream and bench-based. ACIAR relied on the altruism of Australian researchers and their interest in "doing good" abroad, yet these same researchers faced the academic requirements of "publish, patent, or perish." Dedicating substantial time and effort to working with less proficient peers abroad distracted from this imperative, forcing ACIAR to compete harder to attract the interest of Australian researchers. Table 7.1 summarizes how each of the three research funders adapted their program theory and grantmaking practice to fit with the evolving governance context.

Table 7.1. Funders as adaptive organizations

	How research was defined and funded	
	Program theory	Grantmaking practices
UK	• Maintain UK science base	• From core support to competitively tendered projects
	• Government as intelligent consumer	• Majority of funding to UK institutions
	• Contribute to development agenda	• Staff as grant administrator and in-house expert
	• New technologies and evidence to inform aid	• Multiplying expectations of recipients
Canada	• Build research capacity abroad	• Support local researcher interests
	• Empowerment through knowledge	• Majority of funding to institutions abroad
	• Influence policy abroad	• Staff as talent scout and knowledge broker
		• Multiplying expectations of recipients
Australia	• Support mutual benefit with Australia	• Partnership model of commissioned projects, involve providers at home and abroad
	• Build on "research advantage" at home	• Staff identify research problems and talent
	• Rally evidence on increased production, economic value, and adoption rates	• Comparatively narrow expectations of recipients

Changes in Grantmaking

The choices funders make affect who gets funding to do what, privileging certain lines of research over others. The advent of market-inspired governance prompted all three funders to identify a source of "demand" which encouraged shorter time horizons. This accentuated two sets of changes in their grantmaking practices. First was a shift in who received funding, moving away from governmental recipients in favor of working more with academic institutions, NGOs, international organizations, and even the private sector. Second was the point of delivery, moving away from rural field sites in the developing world, toward more work in laboratories on platform technologies and in urban capitals on policy advocacy.

Demand in the UK was defined by the needs of the government department over time. Initially this need was to sustain scientific expertise and infrastructure at home and in former colonies abroad. Subsequently, the department cast itself as a proxy client for developing countries, shaping a research agenda and purchasing knowledge and technologies that responded to perceived needs abroad. This peaked with the advent of DFID and the untying of aid, during which funding shifted from privileging fields in which the UK was perceived to excel, to instead contributing toward a global research agenda for international development negotiated through the UN, OECD, and other multilateral fora. Subsequently, DFID aimed to satisfy its own demand for evidence—becoming a direct client rather than a proxy client—to inform the design of bilateral development assistance. In the case of systematic reviews, DFID moved to purchasing a synthesis of existing knowledge, rather than funding the creation of new knowledge.

The timeframe for research activities has become compressed, and projects are expected to translate into development outcomes more quickly. Whereas the UK once funded decade-long research strategies, grants now require annual or quarterly reports demonstrating progress toward the promised results. The governance context requires quicker results from research. In terms of recipients, academic institutions continuously played a sizable role in the ODA/DFID portfolio, yet the recent emphases on platform technologies and policy influence witnessed an increased funding to laboratories and think tanks. The Chief Scientific Advisor's work with the UK research councils led DFID to engage scientists working on platform technologies—such as genomics, ICTs, and climate modeling—regardless of their experience in developing countries. Meanwhile the shift to consortia grants and funding international initiatives has favored recipients with the administrative capacity to coordinate large budgets and multiple sub-grantees.

In Canada, IDRC was founded on the conviction that local research capacity was a public good worth nurturing for its own sake. Yet over time, IDRC encouraged its recipients to respond to some form of local "demand" for research, and this became an explicit part of the selection criteria. Recipients were required to demonstrate this *ex ante* and *ex post* demand: that the problems examined were relevant to local stakeholders, and that the results of the research reached—and were used by—a local audience. This mirrored a rising expectation in Canada that publicly funded research would contribute to socio-economic benefit. IDRC also moved toward shorter time horizons, with more frequent turnover in its programs and recipients, both exiting and entering different areas of research more quickly. After restructuring during the late-1990s, IDRC adopted a regular cycle of program evaluation every five years, as well as an annual budgeting process in which the allocation to each program varied on management's assessment of its importance, quality, and the potential to make effective use of new funds.

IDRC also shifted the type of recipients it funded. While governmental institutions accounted for 24 percent of the total amount granted by IDRC during 1985–89, this portion fell to 7 percent during 2005–10. During the same period, the share of funding going to NGOs increased from 35 percent to 56 percent. A simple scan over the names of these NGOs suggests that recipients combined research with policy advocacy or the delivery of development interventions, providing a link to a potential audience and use for the funded research. In contrast, government recipients are driven by their own cycle of policy formulation and implementation, while academic recipients are constrained by their own cycles of academic publication and supervising graduate students. In both cases, the time required for these activities could easily exceed the reduced time horizons during which IDRC programs had to demonstrate results.

In Australia, demand was understood to come from farmers and governments that wanted technology and practices to boost productivity and income. ACIAR was somewhat protected from the general shift among rural RDCs toward shorter-term refinement of existing production techniques, and away from the longer-term development of novel crops and techniques with more distant and uncertain payoff. ACIAR nonetheless had to adapt to the incentives shaping the careers of research providers at home. The relative weight of state-level governance diminished as the center of gravity of public research shifted from government to universities. ACIAR projects tended to focus downstream on field-level application by farmers, yet the genomics revolution saw the agricultural sciences become increasingly upstream and lab-based. Simultaneously, ACIAR initially relied on the altruism of Australian researchers and their interest in "doing good" abroad. Yet as more and more researchers relied on universities as their institutional home, they were increasingly driven by the academic requirements of "publish, patent, or perish." Dedicating substantial time and effort to working with less proficient peers abroad distracted from this imperative, forcing ACIAR to compete harder to attract the interest of Australian researchers.

In summary, funders responded to the shift in governance context by changing time horizon, recipients, and point of delivery. In other words, there were clear changes in grantmaking regarding *how long*, *for whom*, and *for what*. The trend in all three cases was toward a compressed timeframe in which research funding was to lead to development outcomes. Where a former generation of programs aimed at achieving outcomes over a decade or longer, current programs must demonstrate success within three to five years with regular signs of progress along the way. In terms of recipients, all three organizations shifted away from funding government institutions. The UK directed a greater portion of funding to research councils at home and international initiatives abroad, as well as for-profits and non-profits of sufficient scale to administer large, complex projects. In Canada, IDRC directed a greater portion of funding to NGOs in developing countries, while in Australia, ACIAR directed more of its funds to domestic universities. In terms of point of delivery, there was a trend toward diversification. While IDRC initially favored field-based work in rural areas of developing countries, its portfolio grew over time to include laboratory-based work in Canada and abroad, as well as work performed by think tanks in urban centers. ACIAR largely retained its focus on field-based work, while part of Australia's aid budget also went to lab-based work in CSIRO and abroad. With the longest history and largest budget of the three, ODA/DFID funded research at various points of delivery, layering new grantmaking practices on to its existing portfolio with each shift in its program theory. These new practices did not completely displace older ones, and the portfolio continued to include a mix of project types and recipients.

These shifts in grantmaking practices demonstrate that research funding is an evolutionary system (Whitley 2011, Ziman 2000). Different practices represented alternative approaches to knowledge production. These variations were selectively retained because they enhance the funders' fit within the governance context, and the relationships with key stakeholder and power holders. Whitley (2011) cautions against an exclusive focus on the *ex ante* design of projects to fit public policy goals and produce expected results, warning that this can limit the range of variations and reduce the diversity of research results and knowledge claims. Fortunately, the governance context often underdetermined program theory, allowing funders to also elaborate, refine, and persist with grantmaking practices based on project monitoring and *ex post* evaluation.

Persistence in Grantmaking

The politics of the home capital influenced all three of the case study organizations in terms of the strategies they pursued and the practices used in their grantmaking. It is tempting to dismiss funders as merely responding to the whims of government policy and budgeting processes, yet their historical experience is more nuanced. All three invested substantial time and effort elaborating, enacting, and revising their program theory. Beyond formal corporate and program strategies, each held an underlining philosophy of what constituted research for the developing world and an ethos regarding their responsibilities toward researchers at home and abroad. Staff considered themselves first and foremost part of DFID, IDRC, or ACIAR: a distinct identity apart from the public service, privileging poor countries and scientific excellence over national interest and adherence to political agendas at home.

Drawing on Funnel and Rogers' (2011) typologies, each funder pursued distinct program theories and interventions. Historically, research for the developing world was described as information: providing knowledge, technology, or evidence that create new opportunities for international development (Arrow 1962, World Bank 1998, Helpman 2004, Molenaar et al. 2009). Yet the logic behind each case study reveals program theory based on the logic of diffusion, empowerment, and networks. This logic inspired grantmaking practices based on direct delivery through in-house scientific units, case management of projects tailored to particular recipients and problems, and "carrots" or incentives for the external research community.

In the United Kingdom, research for the developing world was most often based on diffusion theory, initially underpinned by direct delivery. ODA inherited a set of scientific units at home that saw government responsible for performing research. In the 1980s and 1990s, there was a slow move to competitively awarded work programs and the phasing out of direct delivery. While ODA adopted the rhetoric of the "customer–contractor" principle, it simultaneously sought to ensure that work programs provided for the transition and survival of its scientific units. With the establishment of DFID and substantial budget growth, research oscillated between diffusion and reasoned-action theories, which interpreted research as technical innovation and evidenced-based policy. In both cases, research was underpinned by a "carrots" approach of providing financial incentives to do work that benefited developing countries. DFID became more instrumental in its research funding, seeking to inform its own operations. Yet an expanding budget for research allowed space to pursue multiple program theories and grantmaking practices. Indeed, the increase in the average project budget essentially redelegated responsibility for program logic back to the research community, particularly the lead institution with each Research Programme Consortium.

In Canada, IDRC initially pursued a program theory predicated on empowerment, inspiring interventions to build capacity: supporting researchers in poor countries to exercise greater control over their own development. Such a perspective was dominant from Hopper's 1970 inaugural speech through to Bezanson's 1991 strategy (IDRC 1991b), appropriately titled *Empowerment Through Knowledge*. Under O'Neil, IDRC supplemented this core philosophy with program theory predicated on networks and case management intervention: recipients were encouraged to cultivate relationships toward informing policy abroad, with IDRC support adapting to the unique circumstance in each project. In contrast, the emergence of Grand Challenges Canada in 2010 exploited a gap in Canada's research landscape, embracing a diffusion theory of change underpinned by providing "carrots."

Meanwhile, periodic changes in program theory saw the funder switch which segments of the research community benefited most within its grant portfolio. For example, prior to the 1990s IDRC strongly favored and found support among the scientific community engaged in agriculture and health. During the decade, IDRC revised its program offerings, essentially switching its allegiance to the scientific community engaged in natural resource management and information and communication technologies. In the late 2000s, IDRC swung back to the agriculture and health segments of the research community.

In Australia, ACIAR based its program theory on a combination of diffusion and networks, leading to interventions that combined capacity building and "carrots." ACIAR brokered partnerships between Australian and local researchers to create and share new agricultural techniques and enhance the ability of partners in the host country. It also revised the countries where it worked to respond to foreign policy priorities, and consistently emphasized the benefits accruing to Australian researchers, farmers, and the Australian economy. Nonetheless, ACIAR consistently followed its model of partnerships for mutual benefits, continuing to pursue a program theory in line with Tribe's philosophy of "doing well by doing good."

Key Points

Program theory incorporates generalized notions of how research is understood to contribute to change, and is underpinned by a series of more specific programs. Over time, some programs persist or evolve as they successfully broker the world of politics and science, while other programs are ended or created to respond to the closing or opening of opportunities to strike a dynamic balance between government priority and researcher interest. Deriving funds from official development assistance, research for the developing world was much more prescriptive than funding offered to domestic researchers through the granting councils, with the expectations placed upon recipients multiplying over time in the UK and Canada. Nonetheless, funders seek to maintain their credibility within both government and the scientific community, facing challenges when it strays too far in either direction. Government occasionally requires the funder to refocus on the priorities of the day or take on new roles, such as special initiatives or science diplomacy, yet these pressures are counterbalanced by the scientific community which can ignore the funder's opportunities (exit) or lobby for change (voice).

While a funder's program theory evolves to respond to changing expectations, its grantmaking practice is more resistant to change. Canada and Australia largely persisted with their grantmaking, with IDRC conserving a project-based approach focused on supporting and networking researchers abroad, while ACIAR maintained its partnership model matching researchers abroad with talent at home. The UK experienced a wider range of grantmaking practices, yet even as new ones were added, they did not completely displace older ones, leading to a hybrid portfolio. Similarly, responsibilities were added to the job description of an IDRC program officer or ACIAR coordinator, but the core competencies and function remained. Staff needed to represent the funder's interest, verifying that recipients completed their work and accounted for their budgets. Yet staff were also expected to engage the scientific community at an intellectual level as a peer, and not merely as a bureaucrat checking up on contractual compliance.

Ultimately, funders periodically change how they define and fund research for the developing world as a means of adapting to the governance context, maintaining a dynamic balance between government and the scientific communities at home and abroad. The former provides the funder with the resources and authority required to operate, while the latter provides the real-life efforts that give the funder's programs meaning. On the surface, the funder is simultaneously an agent to government and a principal to the scientific community. Yet the relationship is not one-way, as the research community can exercise influence on the funder, and the funder actively shapes the space for its activities within government. It is thus perhaps more accurate to cast the funder as an intermediary, rather than a simple link in a chain of principal–agent relations.

8

Looking Forward

From Foreign Aid to Global Challenges

Research for the developing world is at a critical juncture. On the one hand, the policy space is closing as each donor country squeezes public expenditure, including official development assistance. As resources for foreign aid become less readily available, there is a tendency to concentrate on core priorities framed by international consensus: the successor to MDGs and on fewer, least developed, and most fragile states. On the other hand, new opportunities have opened beyond foreign aid, as donor countries diversify their relations with the developing world to include economic and trade relations, educational mobility, and science collaboration. There is also a growing middle of both participants and problems, with an increasing number of countries surpassing the low-income threshold along with an expanding set of global challenges to economy, environment, and health that affect all people. Research for the developing world is declining as the R&D of foreign aid, yet rising as part of science diplomacy and global problem solving.

This chapter begins with a brief discussion of how international development is being reimagined, shifting from foreign aid toward global challenges. The following sections describe the new rules that govern research funding, drawing on institutional design principles from scholarship on commons, or shared natural resources. In past decades, funders needed to strike a bargain between their home government and the domestic scientific community, yet developing countries increasingly determine their terms of engagement in scientific collaboration. The future of research for the developing world is one of adaptive governance, in which funders no longer shape their programs in isolation, but negotiate their role in partnerships with diverse actors at home and abroad.

Reimagining Development

The idea of "international development" is evolving. From an initial focus on the welfare of people in poor countries, the field experienced growth and specialization of scholarship and practice similar to many scientific disciplines over the past century. The field stretched to address the provision of domestic public goods (such as education and health care), international public goods (such as trade relations and biodiversity), and foreign public bads (such as terrorism and absolute poverty). Each of these threads is now pulling apart from the tapestry of "international development" to engage less with each other and more with related fields such as public policy, international relations, and subject-specific disciplines. It is tempting to simply relabel the field as global development, recognizing a change in world relations similar to the postwar period which saw "international" replace colonial or overseas development. Yet in practice the field is fragmenting into separate dialogues. With relatively few journals and academic associations to hold it together, researchers and practitioners more readily identify and interact with peers in various sub-disciplines, including economics, agriculture, and public health.

This fragmentation in scholarship coincides with a shift in discourse on international development. The field was once the realm of grand narratives explaining historic and holistic change in how society is structured and functions, embroiled in the clash between capitalist and socialist visions of such change. With the end of the Cold War, the aid community embraced the twin imperatives of poverty reduction and results-based management as the ends and means of foreign aid. More than two decades later, development thinking centers on marketing products and messages that benefit the poor, and experiments with targeted interventions in the material conditions of the most disadvantaged. The unit of "success" has shifted from the nation-state and its aggregate economic growth, toward individual citizens and their freedoms and capabilities.

The grand narratives of social change are overshadowed by frugal innovation to address the needs of poor people, including low-cost devices for energy generation, clean water, and medical diagnostics. "Successful" innovations not only demonstrate their proof of concept, but are expected to scale up into self-financing business models, largely independent of government largesse. University curricula are just as likely to emphasize methods of behavioral economics, value-chain analysis, or randomized controlled trials, as they are to impart insights from Karl Polanyi's great transformation or Robert Chambers' farmer-first approach. The rise of design, technology, and engineering to alter the material conditions of people has come at the cost of social, cultural, and political inquiry into historic change in society. Research for the developing world is now more focused on extending economic opportunity and material well-being to Collier's "bottom billion" (2007) than it is on questioning the roots of power, inequality, and justice in society.

Accompanying this shift in discourse has been an increasing attention to global challenges, problems that surpass the ability of any one country to address. This suggests a different logic for justifying investments in research for the developing world. At the risk of oversimplification, one can contrast an initial argument based on foreign aid and the new argument based on global challenges. Among other reasons, foreign aid was initially justified as a transfer of capital and technical expertise from donor countries to aid recipients, from where such resources were plentiful to places where they were scarce. Under this framing, foreign aid was intended to provide seed investment to kick-start local accumulation of capital, skilled labor, and knowledge that would allow poor countries to provide for themselves and participate more fully in world affairs. This argument holds less sway today, as fewer countries remain below the low-income threshold and foreign aid represents a decreasing share of the financial flows to the developing world.

Research for the developing world increasingly relies on an argument based on global challenges. An early wave of this argument occurred in the 1990s, as international development was briefly synonymous with environmental sustainability. The advent of the MDGs and the "war on terror" at the turn of the century refocused development on conditions abroad in poverty hotspots and failed states. Yet within a decade, the world shuddered under global shocks to finance, food, and fuel. Sudden peaks in the price of credit, grains, and oil eroded development gains in some countries and shook the foundations of advanced economies. Donor countries also began to take climate change more seriously, unlocking new financing to help developing countries cope with the impacts of hotter, drier conditions. In short, politicians and taxpayers rediscovered their own vulnerability, embracing enlightened self-interest to protect themselves against the external threats of an interdependent world.

The logic of global challenges matches how research is now organized. There has been a trend toward tying public monies for research to mission-oriented funding programs specifying the types of discoveries or breakthroughs desired. The rhetoric of challenges is intended to rally the efforts of existing research talent to ambitious, yet attainable, outcomes the value of which is supposedly self-evident. At the same time, the world of science has become less rooted as talented individuals seek to study at, and work with, renowned centers of excellence regardless of where they are located. The mobility of scientific talent does not rival that of international finance, but the dilemma facing developing countries has become less about building an autonomous research capacity, and more about plugging into the networks of global scientific collaboration (Wagner 2008).

The future of research for the developing world requires funders to move beyond foreign aid and strengthen ties with publicly funded science at home and abroad. Global challenges are problems that are clearly recognized within the language of foreign policy (used to justify action) and the language of social or natural sciences (used to guide research). This is distinct from the beginning of the millennium when a policy focus on new threats to security, governance, and fragile states was held back as social science needed to reformulate these concepts and theories. Similarly, medical science is now ahead of policy attention. Whereas decades of development sought to control infectious diseases, the burden of disease shifted toward poor diet and sedentary lifestyles as the leading causes of poor health.

Global challenges imply scale that surpasses national borders. This supranational scale may derive from the geographic footprint of the problem, the spatial distribution of suffering, or the potential scope for interventions. International public goods obviously require transboundary cooperation (e.g. climate, migration, oceans), while foreign public bads can require coordinating shared or complementary roles and responsibilities (e.g. malaria, maternal mortality, food insecurity), and even national public goods can involve opportunities for comparative learning (e.g. education, energy, mental health). In each case, global challenges imply a contribution of multiple actors in different locations, each of which brings some comparative value or assets to the collaboration such as: data, talent, funding, facilities, and access to field locations or unique phenomenon. Wagner (2008) contrasts more networked or joined-up efforts on breeding seeds or mapping genomes, to more distributed and site-based work such as mapping poverty or testing climate adaptation.

Design Principles

Research funding can be considered a common good, with a variety of stakeholders in government and within the scientific community exercising influence over how it is managed. Before being allocated to particular grants and projects, research funding is available to numerous potential beneficiaries within the scientific community. Yet it is also scarce, necessitating some means of coping with demand, and limiting or denying claims based on program design, eligibility criteria, and the quality of proposals. In the language of economics, common goods are rivalrous, meaning that their use by one beneficiary necessarily reduces the amount available for others. Common goods are also considered non-excludible, meaning that it is difficult to control their access and use. While different disciplines have various professional associations, anyone can self-identify as being a member of the scientific community and submit an application for funding.

Common goods require negotiated, cooperative use of a limited resource in a manner that avoids overexploitation or collapse. Scholarship on commons began with pasturelands and was extended to irrigation systems, water, fisheries, forestry, and information systems. Historically there was a push to enclose commons, converting them into private goods by assigning individual property titles or quotas, out of fear that individual users would tend to overexploit the resource to maximize their personal benefit. Ostrom (2005) championed empirical study that documented the real-life behavior of communities dependent on such resources, identifying a series of institutional design principles that permitted shared use of such commons.

These design principles provide useful insights for crafting research collaborations. Similar to natural resource commons, research funding involves the allocation of scarce monies and talent to generate knowledge and solutions to address social problems including poverty, hunger, and disease. Research collaboration consists of ad hoc, time-limited institutional arrangements for governing this common good (funding and talent) and common "bad" (shared public problem). Four of the design principles identified by scholarship are clearly defined boundaries, clear rules of access and use, accountability of monitors to users, and locally devised rules and shared norms among users.

First, clearly defined boundaries include membership in the community of potential applicants, and the geographic and thematic coverage of the funding programs. Once critiqued as being a club good for researchers within the field of development studies, funding opportunities have widened to a more diverse set of potential applicants and skills. This is particularly the case with open competitive calls for proposals, rather than the traditional approach of philanthropic foundations which relies on talent scouting or responding to unsolicited proposals. The recent emphasis on design, technology, and engineering has also broadened the opportunities for work on applications for use in the developing world, without necessitating a career-long specialization in such settings.

By definition, research for the developing world requires a tie to poorer, resource-constrained settings abroad, whether through the nationality of participating researchers, the location of fieldwork, or the ultimate application of the research results. Yet research funders more readily rely on thematic boundaries, crafting funding programs based on particular disciplines or problems, such as food security, maternal health, or youth employment. Researchers with skills and interests in these areas constitute the membership pool of potential applicants. Yet this membership is dynamic and changes whenever the funder closes existing programs and adopts new ones.

Second, clear access and use rules are embedded in the grantmaking practices of each funder, including selection criteria, categories of eligible expenses, and the grant agreement as a legal contract. All granting processes include a set of ex ante selection criteria which define the tests to which applications are assessed. At the core of this process is some form of merit review to assess the scientific quality of the proposed research activities, which departs from the norms of originality, significance, and contribution to existing knowledge, as well as considerations of feasibility and ethics. Yet even before reaching merit review, proposals must satisfy a host of requirements specified by the funder, which may include letters of support from the hosting institutions, participation of particular actors (e.g. the private sector or institutions based in a developing country), and plans to disseminate and promote research findings (identifying a "user" audience and how they will be reached).

A selected proposal is subjected to further scrutiny to ensure the budget compiles with guidance on eligible expenses, including acceptable rates for—and overall portion dedicated to—research expenses, staffing, training, travel, and indirect costs of the host institution. The funder then issues a grant agreement to the host institution which is a legal contract describing the provision of funding for the project and outlining the commitments the institution undertakes in accepting those funds. Grant agreements can specify conditions to be met for the continuity of funding over the duration of the project, such as the participation of key personnel and the frequency of reporting on financial and technical progress.

Third, accountability of monitors to users is seen in the ultimate feedback loop between research funders and the scientific community. Public research funders are subject to various influences within government and need to maintain their credibility within the scientific community. This community will be alienated if funding programs are too distant from researchers' interests or what can be feasibly delivered. Under such conditions, the scientific community can respond by simply ignoring the funders' attempts to rally its efforts, or exerting pressure upon government entities that can in turn influence the funder. Such instances are relatively rare due to the monitoring by research funders, not only receiving progress reports and using a milestone approach to grant management, but ongoing engagement with principal investigators, research teams, and grant administrators. Regular communication allows for early detection and resolution of difficulties encountered during project implementation. Ideally, monitoring is a form of peer-to-peer engagement, with the funding staff seen as offering useful advice rather than merely verifying compliance with the terms of grant agreements. Staff tend to be subject-matter experts, capable of understanding and critiquing the work performed, acting as intermediaries working for the funding organization while remaining part of the scientific community.

Fourth, locally devised rules and shared norms among users are vital aspects of how stakeholders self-organize to manage commons. Scientific communities have a long history of self-organizing within academia and across professional associations. While membership may be somewhat open, status within the community is defined by academic rank, professional experience, and record of publications and contributions to knowledge. Through their involvement in this community, researchers accept and perpetuate a culture of science. While the expression of this culture varies among disciplines, there is a common commitment to freedom of inquiry, the use of rigorous methods, internal and external validity in data and analysis, and subjecting findings to critique.

Research for the developing world cultivated a unique expression of this culture in the late twentieth century; one embracing further commitments to empowering southern researchers, participatory methods that involved local people in the research process, and an action-oriented approach toward the use of findings to further development outcomes. Changes to grantmaking practice eroded these norms somewhat, as funders reached out to a wider segment of the scientific community. Once tailoring themselves to the interests of development studies, development economists, and experts in tropical agriculture and medicine, funders now engage with a wider swath of the scientific community including skills in design, engineering, technology, and business.

This wider community is not only motivated by a desire to "do good" abroad, but by incentives to build a career based on responding to the pressure to publish and demonstrate the public, scientific, and commercial value of their work. Funders also became more prescriptive in detailing the structure of research collaboration, for example requiring applicants to organize themselves into consortia or mandating the participation of certain actors, such as industry, private sector, or local government. As funders sought to support larger-value grants, research projects morphed from ad hoc collections of individuals into formal arrangements among multiple institutions, with a corresponding increase in the responsibility for specifying activities, coordinating activities, and managing budgets. Beyond the opportunity to simply "do research," receiving a research grant can impose a certain burden upon principal investigators to monitor and manage the participation of others in the project.

In the past, each funding organization was autonomous in how they governed their support for research into the developing world. Funders chose their programs and refined their grantmaking practice, cognizant of the governance context at home and the interests of the scientific communities they sought to rally. These decisions formed a dynamic balance between what donor governments were willing to fund and what the scientific community was interested in working on. Funders were largely implicit with regard to how they set boundaries and rules of access and use, their accountability to the scientific community, and the shared norms among researchers. Yet as funders establish international initiatives and enter into partnerships with each other, it is necessary to explicitly identify the institutional arrangements that govern these relationships. This is particularly true with the rise of stronger research governance abroad which introduces different goals and incentives.

Rise of the South

The rules for governing research in and for the developing world are changing as more countries establish their own institutions for supporting and guiding science. A generation ago, funders such as ODA, IDRC, or ACIAR had very few counterparts in the developing world. They would engage with the foreign ministry, universities, or line ministries responsible for agriculture or health. In most developing countries, science academies and granting councils were either fairly weak or entirely absent. This has changed, with a desire to retain or regain highly qualified scientists, and policy that casts knowledge and innovation as key to global competition. The developing world has increased its investments, spurred on by high rates of economic growth and revenue from natural resources. On average, the overall amount of research funding in developing countries remains modest compared to the OECD, China, and India. Yet the creation or strengthening of science academies, granting councils, and research funds in Africa, Latin America, and elsewhere in Asia means that many developing countries now set their own research priorities, provide scholarships and funding opportunities, and shape the incentives for scientific careers.

Research governance in developing countries does not necessarily replicate the structure or practices of OECD countries nor narrowly adhere to the international development agenda. African science ministers established space sciences as a priority while Jordan's priorities include energy and information technologies. These topics do not figure among the MDGs, but are seen by policymakers as vital for the future of their countries. Akin to science policy in OECD countries, the strategic question is how to make the optimal use of scarce scientific talent, research funding, and infrastructure. While this may include new understanding and technology to benefit poor people, such considerations tend to be secondary to the imperatives of contributing to the economy, informing national policy, and enhancing links to global science. These institutions are also interlocutors for international collaboration, negotiating bilateral and regional agreements on scientific cooperation, and acting as contact points for foreign funding opportunities, such as the EU's Horizon

2020 or the United Kingdom's Newton Fund. Such institutions are getting closer to being equal partners in such arrangements, matching the funding offered by others and taking responsibility for administering such programs locally.

These institutions are crafting their own first principles regarding the purpose of research, what constitutes success, and the motivation for international collaboration. Research governance in different countries emphasizes varying notions of success ranging from peer-reviewed publications and prototype technologies, to real-world impact on policy and practice. Similar to their peers in OECD countries, funders in developing countries are embedded in a national context surrounded by diverse power holders and stakeholders that influence local ideas regarding the purpose of research and what it is expected to produce. Funders respond to these ideas when crafting different program theories and grantmaking practices. In allocating funding, they assign weight to various criteria, including: the size of an institution's teaching and research staff, a researcher's years of service or record of publications, how their work aligns with national priorities, and their engagement with policy, industry, or civil society.

Funders also vary in the attention given to the substance of research ideas proposed and the existing capacity of potential recipients. For example, Egypt offers project grants through open calls for proposals while Tunisia provides block funding to particular laboratories and research teams following a national assessment exercise. In allocating a national budget, public funders may also wish to ensure some degree of equity within the country and among recipients, as funding decisions can exacerbate existing divides between urban capitals and the hinterland, or established centers and newer start-up organizations.

The presence of science academies and granting councils in developing countries means that foreign funders must compete for the attention of the local scientific community. On the one hand, foreign funders may still have an advantage in facilitating international collaboration, particularly access to researchers back in Australia, Canada, the United Kingdom, etc. On the other hand, domestic institutions can provide incentives that shape scientific careers, the type of performance which is rewarded at home. In short, research governance abroad in developing countries is increasingly salient.

The opportunities offered by foreign funders should ideally be crafted with these drivers in mind. A funder's programs must also fit with how science is organized within developing countries. Efforts to encourage interdisciplinary work to address global challenges, such as food security, encounter a dearth of prospective applicants in settings where there is little communication or collaboration across disciplines, such as among nutritionists, sociologists, soil scientists, and agricultural economists. Collaboration is easier between countries with certain complementarity in their research landscapes. For example, Moroccan applicants were relatively successful in IDRC calls for university research chairs and for work on climate adaptation, in part drawing on existing relationships with former professors and diaspora scientists in Quebec.

Given that funders and researchers are rooted in different governance contexts, this limits their ability to buy into a shared program design. Instead it can be easier for different funders to make their own contribution toward a common agenda, but in a way that respects their individual programs and grantmaking. As the research agenda shifts toward global challenges there is arguably a need for more collaboration among like-minded funders. Yet being "like-minded" is more than having similar interests in what to fund; it also relies on having a shared understanding of what research is expected to achieve and what evidence is needed to satisfy diverse audiences who hold expectations for the funders' performance. This is a key role for research funders' collaborations, such as ESSENCE on health or the Belmont Forum on environmental change.

One alternative is simply to turn to international initiatives: for-purpose organizations and funds to support work on global challenges. A number of these came into existence over the years, including CGIAR, the Global Environmental Facility (GEF), and GAVI to name just a few. These initiatives have pursued a two-part mandate: fostering new knowledge and technology, and promoting its adoption among beneficiaries. CGIAR initially grew from four to eighteen centers between 1971 and 1993 before a period of more restricted budgets as members scaled back on funding. The food crisis in 2008–9 unlocked additional resources, yet coincided with governance reforms and restructuring which accelerated a shift to reorganize research around system-wide challenge programs. While younger, GAVI also required some degree of advocacy and personal diplomacy in member capitals to maintain funding levels. International initiatives are not immune from the politics that public funders face, and must present a set of programs that satisfy the performance expectations of different members.

Philanthropy and private funding are also important streams of support for research in developing countries. Western philanthropy remains influential, including the Rockefeller Foundation, Ford Foundation, Wellcome Trust, and the Bill & Melinda Gates Foundation. Yet these names increasingly coexist with a variety of charities, foundations, and corporate responsibility initiatives based in developing countries. The Dorbaji and Ratan Tata Trusts, Carlos Slim Foundation, Mohammed bin Rashid Al Maktoum Foundation, and Qatar Foundation are some of the better-known names, and there are literally thousands more redistributing donations from wealthy people, a growing middle class, and citizens that simply want to give back to their societies. In India, new legislation mandates that private corporations must invest 2 percent of their profits in social development.

Philanthropy and private funding often approach research differently compared to science academies and granting councils. Rather than a discrete public good in its own right, these entities tend to see research as an input into promoting social change. Whereas science academies value the creation of new knowledge, charities and social business have a more pragmatic perspective of research as feasibility studies, product innovation, and evaluation of their interventions.

Research for the developing world now requires adaptive governance, engaging these new actors abroad to foster collaboration on global challenges. Funders can no longer afford to work in isolation. Dietz et al. (2003: 1907) caution that "devising effective governance systems is akin to a coevolutionary race" as the rules crafted to fit one set of conditions erode with new social, economic, and technological developments. The reimagining of international development, decline of foreign aid, and rise of research governance abroad require funders to renegotiate their role and function in an evolving landscape. One can start with first principles of the purpose of research, what constitutes success, and the motivation for international collaboration. Funders can then negotiate a shared understanding of thematic and geographic boundaries, rules of access and use, their accountability to the scientific community, and shared norms among researchers.

Key Points

Research for the developing world is at a critical juncture. It is closing as donors concentrate on fewer, least developed, and more fragile states. Yet it is also growing with global challenges that surpass the ability of any one country to address. The idea of "international development" is fragmenting from the welfare of poor countries into separate dialogues around domestic public goods, international public goods, and foreign public bads. This fragmentation coincides with a shift from grand narratives of change in society, toward engineering and business that improves the material conditions of poor people. Refocusing on global challenges capitalizes on rising interest in international collaboration, rallying existing research talent to work on ambitious goals and plugging into the networks of global science.

As more countries join the ranks of middle-income and emerging economies, they exercise greater power and authority over the design of international research collaboration. Science academies and granting councils abroad are elaborating their own approaches to managing scarce scientific talent, research funding, and infrastructure. In short, the rules of the game are changing as research governance in the developing world becomes increasingly salient, including international initiatives, philanthropy, and private funding for research. It is no longer sufficient for northern-based funders to strike a deal between their home government and domestic scientific community, they must engage new actors abroad to renegotiate their roles and responsibilities. This means being aware of local perceptions of what research is expected to achieve and the incentives shaping scientific careers.

Research for the developing world is both evolving and returning to its roots, as science diplomacy predicated on mutual benefit. Looking back, the governance context in donor countries used to permit more autonomy and discretion for public research funders. Looking forward, the response to calls for "one world" collaboration on global challenges is constrained, as funders must remain responsive to different sets of stakeholders and power holders. As governments continue to expect "more" from publicly funded research, there is greater political demand to demonstrate how such research contributes to real-life outcomes that matter to politicians and taxpayers, at home and abroad. The recent trend was toward emphasizing short-term practical ends. In contrast, a shift toward global challenges requires moving research "up and out" toward more ambitious goals—beyond the interests of any particular researcher or country—over a longer time horizon aiming for results decades into the future.

9

Conclusion

The Quest for Research Impact

This final chapter considers three aspects of public management: leadership, performance, and impact. These concepts have particular and evolving meaning in the world of public research as reflected in the experience of funding research for the developing world. The nature of leadership evolved as research funding organizations matured and navigated an increasingly complex governance context at home and abroad. Leaders create visions of success, mobilize support, and reshape the operating space for their organizations. They define performance that satisfies external expectations, striking a balance among competing public values and ethics. Research for the developing world tended to be driven by foreign policy, yet its performance is increasingly influenced by science policy, including concerns for academic productivity and demonstrating research impact. This impact can be described as building scientific capacity, informing policy and practice, or spreading innovative technologies. How impact is understood depends on the first principles regarding the purpose of research and why science is considered useful to society. Whereas funders used to encourage "small is beautiful," with local experiments in development, today the emphasis is on "getting to scale" and delivering innovation through self-financing models.

Leadership

The nature of leadership has evolved over time, from defining and pursuing a unique approach, to instead navigating and brokering partnerships with others. Canada and Australia established for-purpose organizations with a mandate that focused exclusively on research for the developing world and a governance structure that provided substantial autonomy. Leadership for

Hopper and McWilliam was to navigate this start-up phase, experimenting with and refining a nascent business model that translated this mandate into a work culture and grantmaking practice. Within a decade, both organizations had cultivated their sense of identity which was then formalized through strategies, programs, and procedures. In contrast, leadership for Bezanson and Core was to preside over difficult eras of adjustment, as external decision making became more influential.

Public management no longer afforded these organizations the same degree of autonomy, as the powers initially invested in their boards shifted upward toward the minister, and outward toward central agencies and other parts of government. These leaders needed to demonstrate that their organizations were "fitting in" to external expectations, which required in equal parts: external engagement to cultivate and renew relationships within government, and internal change reforming the work culture to adjust to this new reality. In this sense, the leadership task began to mirror that in the United Kingdom, where research for the developing world was embedded in the aid agency and increasingly needed to renew its position within the larger science policy environment.

Individual leaders matter. Each organization initially embodied the vision of their founders and benefited from high-level champions. How each funder evolved is intimately associated with the ideas of Haldane, Rothschild, Hopper, and Crawford. Their leadership defined a vision of research for the developing world and navigated competing pressures and expectations within government. Over time, successive leaders enriched and reinterpreted these visions to keep up with and influence the governance context, selectively revising, adding, and replacing program theories as needed. The ability to shape the expectations of others, and the role of individual leaders in that process, are two key insights for the literature on public management and the study of public research funding. Leaders are entrepreneurs that create visions of success for the future, develop strategies for pursuing those visions, mobilize support (Poister 2010), and as needed reshape the operating space for their organizations (Fischer 2003).

In all three case studies, leaders guided their organizations to both retain elements of their program theory while adjusting to expectations of their performance. They were afforded this opportunity in part due to the tendency of government to underdetermine the policy space surrounding research for the developing world. Government identified priorities for international development and national research, yet provided funders with freedom to interpret these broad directions in crafting how to respond to and enact them. The governance context was more indicative than prescriptive, and although the performance expectations outside could not be ignored, and eventually gave rise to fundamental changes in program theory and grantmaking practices, leaders still had the space to mediate this process. More recently, the governance context became increasingly prescriptive, with governments determining on what, to whom, and where research funding is to be targeted. With an eroded autonomy, funders are afforded less opportunity to set and pursue their own program theory, and consequently they move closer to government and away from the scientific community.

Leaders are responsible for maintaining the credibility of their organizations, within the changing notions of performance in government and amid the evolving governance of the scientific community. Individual leaders also guided their organizations in "speaking back" to the governance context. They refused to be the passive victims of shifts in government policy and discourse, and instead actively sought to reinsert the ideas cultivated from their program theory back into the policy process. Leaders sought to inform this context with learning derived from their organization's routines and experience, including program evaluation, as well as their own vision for where and how investments in research could make a difference. They engaged powerful actors to reshape performance expectations, making the case for their way of doing business, rather than merely accepting that their grantmaking practices may no longer fit with contemporary fads in public management.

This suggests a continued need to balance competing goals, something these funders have done for over three decades. In the near-term, research funders must remain agile, nimbly adjusting their management structure and funding opportunities to maintain their relevance to, and support from, both their home government and the scientific community. There is progressively less space for multiple program theories to coexist or to preserve grantmaking practices that do not resonate with current expectations. Consequently, research funders are becoming more corporativist: streamlining themselves to concentrate a greater portion of resources into fewer, larger programs that are more tightly aligned with the assumed contribution to the world beyond. IDRC and ACIAR already witnessed their Boards' influence erode compared to outside influences.

Looking forward, research for the developing world is turning from foreign aid toward global challenges. This new reality places an even greater premium on the ability of leaders to broker new partnerships in an evolving context for research governance at home and abroad. A generation ago, funders encouraged "small is beautiful," researchers moving beyond universities and labs to work with local communities using participatory approaches. Today, international development has been reimagined as "getting to scale," working with entrepreneurs to ensure solutions are implemented widely to reduce poverty and improve lives. Whereas success used to be associated with demonstrating a proof of concept, this is now appreciated as an initial step toward prototyping, refining, and delivering innovations. The task for leaders is both to adapt and shape such visions, navigating the performance expectations of others, and reshaping programs and grantmaking as needed.

Performance

Leadership means slicing through the Gordian knot of performance expectations to craft program theory that satisfies the values and ethics underpinning public management. Leaders need to identify which actors are salient in their governance context and the means by which these actors seek to influence the performance of public organizations. Given the degree of discretion in the parliamentary systems in Australia, Canada, and the United Kingdom, one could be forgiven for assuming that public sector "performance" is merely whatever the minister and central agencies define it to be at any given time. Yet the concept of performance has deeper intellectual roots than the opinions and biases of power holders and stakeholders in the governance context.

Talbot (2010: 83) describes organizational performance from a realist perspective, drawing on historical institutionalism to analyze changing governance of that performance over time. He sees performance as both "brute facts" and socially constructed meanings attached to such facts. The dimensions of performance are epistemologically real, as are the positions, attitudes, and beliefs held by real groups and individuals. Talbot cites Moore's triad of *public value* (1995) as delivering public services, achieving social outcomes, and maintaining trust and legitimacy; as well as Fried's triad of *ethics* (1976), including responsiveness to public demand (democratic ethic), compliance with rules (legal ethic), and economy in the use of resources (work ethic). His argument is that the sum of such varied influences shapes or steers performance for specific organizations.

Over time DFID, IDRC, and ACIAR were subject to diverse performance measures, ranging across compliance with foreign policy, economy in the use of operational budgets, the spread and adoption of technology, and the number of poor people reached. Three salient observations can be drawn from the histories of these three funders. First is that any one formal system of performance measures was consolidated for a relatively brief period of time, seldom exceeding a decade. Public sector agreements under Blair in the United Kingdom, or the minister's public statement following the Uhrig reforms in Australia, ultimately faded and were replaced with newer systems which refocused attention on a different combination of values and ethics. While the public sector was buffeted by this ebb and flow of performance measures imposed from outside, they weaved into the performance story crafted by strong public leaders on the inside. Leaders provided their organizations with a sense of purpose, a description of what success looks like, and clear tests for assessment. This internal understanding of performance provides greater continuity than the external measurement systems.

Second is that research for the developing world was more sensitive to concepts of performance within foreign policy than within science policy. This followed simply from the practical realities of governmental budgeting and lines of ministerial authority. All three funders relied on the budget line for official development assistance, the policy around which formed the test for access and use of financial resources. DFID and its predecessor were particularly focused on development policy, placing its research funding in the position of serving that agenda. Meanwhile in Australia and Canada, considerations of foreign policy were more salient than notions of effective development. ACIAR and IDRC were positioned under the foreign minister, and any matters they wished to raise with the minister competed for attention with world events, ongoing diplomacy, and internal affairs of the foreign ministry. While development trumped science in formulating performance expectations, science occasionally struck back. In the United Kingdom, DFID was critiqued by the scientific community and pressed to appoint a Chief Scientific Advisor. Meanwhile changes to science policy in all three countries altered the notions of performance by hollowing out government science, assessing academic productivity, privileging partnerships beyond academia, and requiring demonstrations of research impact. Looking forward, the concept of performance is evolving as foreign aid is eclipsed by research on global challenges and scientific collaboration with the developing world.

Third is a tension between the improvement and oversight functions of performance measures. No one can argue with the desire to improve an organization's operations and achievements over time. Such a desire is not new and has inspired various tools of public management over time, including organizational mandates, corporate strategies, program evaluation, and horizontal planning. From an early stage, all three funders were required to prepare annual reports detailing how they used public resources and what was achieved. Each new edition implicitly compared recent achievements to previous years, with the intention of continuous improvement. Leaders also experimented with tailored performance measures, negotiated among management–board–minister, elaborated in-house, and ultimately discontinued when they proved unworkable or were codified in operational routines and grantmaking practices.

Yet the rise of externally imposed performance measures accompanied the slow shift from organizational autonomy toward instructions emanating from central agencies, aid agencies, and foreign ministries. Such measures formed part of the evolving governance context that pressed the funders to "fit into" and contribute to whole-of-government efforts rather than crafting their own strategies and programs. The oversight function of performance measures suggests a lack of trust in public managers and a trend toward circumscribing the space available for them to exercise leadership. At the extreme, external performance measures undermine the organization's public policy mandate, establishing a check-list of what activities are useful to others rather than encouraging a focus on the organization's raison d'être.

The performance expectations surrounding research for the developing world are encouraging a focus on demonstrating tangible results over shorter timeframes. Whereas ODA once supported a ten-year program on natural resources and sustainable agriculture, funding programs and research projects are now regularly assessed within three to five years. The potential for renewed support is partially dependent on meeting the expectations in vogue at the moment when such reviews are carried out and decisions need to be made. Over the past decade, the performance test considered the extent to which such work: contributed to development and foreign policy priorities, complied with policy directions from central agencies, and cooperated with other government entities (including foreign ministries and domestic granting councils). Today, the performance test is consolidating around the expectation that programming will scale up innovation beyond proof of concept and partner with private sectors to create self-financing models for delivering solutions. Both tests define the criteria by which funders are assessed within the governance context, helping secure access to aid budgets or retain existing resources in spending reviews. Yet such tests also threaten to "wag the dog" by fixating on ideas in good currency within government, ignoring past experience, and shifting allegiances within the scientific community.

Ultimately, attention to performance measures must not become substitutes for organizational purpose. To paraphrase one respondent, the ultimate performance test is meeting the minister. Within a few minutes, the CEO needs to provide a concise and convincing description as to what is achieved and how that is important to the minister and taxpayers. More than one CEO found this to be the first vital step. Provided the minster accepted the argument offered, the conversation would then turn to one or two opportunities to enhance operations in ways that interested the minister, such as a particular priority, theme, budget line, or bilateral relation. Yet the organization's performance story ultimately needs more than ministerial direction and signals from the governance context. Leaders provide that direction by defining performance that satisfies external expectations, strikes a balance among competing public values and ethics, and is tailored to their particular mandate.

Impact

In order to demonstrate and justify public expenditure on research, the United Kingdom and Australia elaborated assessment frameworks for research quality and excellence. While Canada has not elaborated a formal system—as higher education is a provincial rather than federal responsibility—government has nonetheless directed granting councils to privilege support to industrial partnerships and business-led research collaboration. The criteria used privilege considerations of value within academia, yet have added considerations of how research is valued by others, including actors in industry, policy, and professional practice. For example, the most recent UK framework defines impact as an effect on, change, or benefit to the economy, society, culture, public policy or services, health, environment, or quality of life beyond academia.

Penfield et al. (2014) note that the concept of impact borrows ideas from economics, such as return on investment and the time frame required for the stream of benefits to pay back the costs of the research activity. In Australia and the United Kingdom, the concept of impact distinguishes between significance and reach, intended as measures of the relative importance of the benefit derived from research impact, as well as the size and breadth of the audience affected. Bastow et al. (2014) note a tension between the two measures, as significance is easier to substantiate at a more local level, while reach rewards impact that involves larger numbers of beneficiaries or that occurs at wider spatial scales.

Assessing the impact of research is fraught with difficulty. First is the time required to achieve impact, which can vary from days to decades, and the potential for such impact to shift over time. For example, research on new vaccines or seeds requires time to pass through the phases of discovery, clinical or field trials, and widespread adoption, with different opportunities at each stage. Second is the difficulty in establishing attribution for real-world changes, as these are seldom neatly the product of a single piece of research. More often than not policy and practice evolve in response to the accumulation of knowledge over many years, including conceptual change in the ideas and theories used to frame problems and identify potential solutions. For example, recent insights into cognitive biases and behavioral economics are undoubtedly a step forward from past models based on rational actors, but emerge from a body of work rather than a particular study or project. Third is the difficulty of gathering evidence to substantiate such impact, whether through bibliometrics, altmetrics, narratives, surveys, or testimonials. Ultimately, in the words of Penfield et al. (2014: 8) "every piece of research is a unique tapestry of impact" that can span across invention, innovation, insight, and inspiration.

Research for the developing world was ahead of the curve in responding to the impact agenda for publicly funded science. Whereas science policy in Australia, Canada, and the United Kingdom increasingly embraced the goal of public funding leading to social and economic impact, this imperative was already firmly established within ACIAR, IDRC, and DFID. These funders have long had to prove their value for money, competing with aid agencies, multilateral organizations, and foreign ministries. They long abandoned any notion of funding research for its own sake, or merely catering to scientific curiosity. Before the general rise in scrutiny of domestic science policy, these funders needed to justify their spending compared to such alternative uses for official development assistance. This required a sensitivity to the changing goals of development programs, which ranged from economic growth and poverty reduction, to human freedom and women's empowerment. Research was expected to contribute toward tangible changes that advanced such goals.

The rhetoric used to describe impact evolved over time, yet tended to frame it in terms valued by both the scientific community and government backers. Notions of quality and excellence refer to methodological construct, complying with the quality standards within academia, whereas notions of utility and relevance are political constructs referring to how research is valued by—and benefits—those beyond academia (Grant et al. 2010). These terms were often interpreted as presenting certain extremes to be avoided, or trade-offs to be made in grantmaking. For example, funders tended to eschew theoretical research in favor of work with real-life applications, yet also avoid mundane pursuits which aimed simply at evaluating operations or interventions without a link to established theory and scholarship. Meanwhile the enthusiasm for methodological rigor and validity was often limited to ensuring research was of sufficient quality to justify action among or investments by intended beneficiaries, such as farmers, policymakers, or aid practitioners. Such tensions were the natural outcome of the interplay of the principal–agent relations on either side of research funders. They needed to both secure budget and authority from government, and attract interest and ideas from the scientific community. Contrasting notions of impact stemmed from the multiple ways in which each side valued research, creating the space available to craft funding opportunities and identify the results sought.

Impact is the second-order consideration, derived from the first principles regarding the purpose of research and why science is considered useful to society. Research for the developing world can be defined in various ways, including efforts to build scientific capacity abroad, to inform public policy and aid agency practice, and to design and spread the use of innovative technologies. Each offers something for both sides of the governance context in which funders operate. The impact of each can be described in various ways, including: advances in knowledge, the skills and experience embedded in highly trained people, and real-life contributions to development goals such as enhanced opportunities for income and well-being. In speaking to their governments, research funders chronicle their impact in terms of new insights and innovations nurtured, the career achievements of current and former recipients, and numbers of people positively affected by their efforts. In speaking to the scientific community, funders encourage applicants to describe a pathway to impact: why their research findings might prove important to society, how those findings might be used, and the efforts that would be taken to reach that audience of potential research users.

As research for the developing world shifted toward market-inspired governance, the criteria by which funders were judged tended toward the utility of research. Once based on its intrinsic value for empowering developing countries, research was increasingly assessed based on its instrumental value for furthering whole-of-(donor)-government strategies. This shift narrowed the research agenda by privileging those programs that resonated with foreign policy, reducing the opportunities for novel, curiosity-driven work based on local interest. The research agenda gravitated toward subjects that were politically safe, either by addressing questions of technological innovation or rooting itself in the accepted policy discourse within donor capitals. Funding opportunities also became increasingly open to a plurality of voices within the larger scientific community beyond development studies. Funders are afforded less discretion over whom and what they fund, as home governments proactively identify the themes, and even particular projects, they wish to support. At the same time, research funders are pressed to be more critical of their grants: to demonstrate the outcomes from and cost-effectiveness of their work. They have embraced measures of significance and reach, seeking not only the proof of concept and the potential for improving lives, but delivering at scale to affect with renewed programs that seek impact at scale.

Final Points

Together the three aspects of leadership, performance, and impacts form a golden braid tying together research governance. Research for the developing world is changing, fading as the R&D of foreign aid, and rising as a response to global challenges. Its future is uncertain, but its past provides key insights for public management.

The nature of leadership evolved from defining and pursuing unique approaches, toward navigating and brokering partnerships with others. The powers initially invested in governing boards shifted upward and outward, placing a premium on the ability of leaders to work within an increasingly complex context for research governance. Leaders create visions of success, mobilize support, and reshape the operating space for their organizations. Leaders provide direction by defining performance that satisfies external expectations, striking a balance among competing public values and ethics, tailored to their particular mandate.

Research for the developing world tended to be more sensitive to concepts of performance within foreign policy; yet changes to science policy heightened concern for academic productivity, partnerships beyond academia, and demonstrations of research impact. Performance measures have also been used as an oversight mechanism, circumscribing the space available for leaders and, at the extreme, undermining an organization's mandate. Where funders used to encourage "small is beautiful" with local experiments in development, success is now seen as "getting to scale," creating self-financing models to deliver innovations that eliminate poverty and improve lives.

Research impact is the second-order consideration, derived from the first principles regarding the purpose of research and why science is considered useful to society. Assessing the impact of research is fraught with difficulty, including the time required to achieve impact, establishing attribution for real-world change, and gathering evidence to substantiate such impact. As research began to shift toward market-inspired governance, the criteria by which funders were judged tended toward the utility of research. Once based on its intrinsic value for empowering developing countries, this utility was increasingly assessed based on its instrumental value for furthering donor strategies. Moving forward, the definition of impact will increasingly depend on research governance abroad and contributions toward an agenda shaped around global challenges.

References

ACIAR (2011) *Strategic Framework for International Agricultural Research within Australia's Aid Program*. Canberra: ACIAR.

ACIAR (2010) *ACIAR Annual Report 2009–2010*. Canberra: ACIAR.

ACIAR (2008) *Statement of Expectations*, received from the Minister for Foreign Affairs in September 2008. Canberra: ACIAR.

ACIAR (2006) *ACIAR and Public Funding of R&D*. Submission to productivity commission study on public support for science and innovation. Impact Assessment Series Report No. 41. Canberra: ACIAR.

ACIAR (2003) *ACIAR Annual Report 2002–2003*. Canberra: ACIAR.

ACIAR (1999) *Staying Ahead: Future Strategies for ACIAR*. Policy statement by the Board of Management following the external review. Canberra: ACIAR.

Arnold, Michael H. et al. (1989) *External Review of the Australian Centre for International Agricultural Research*. March 15 (<http://aciar.gov.au/files/node/398/Review> accessed 7 January 2015).

Arrow, Kenneth J. (1962) "Economic welfare and the allocation of resources to invention," in Richard Nelson (ed.), *The Rate and Direction of Inventive Activity: Economic and Social Factors*. Princeton, NJ: Princeton University Press.

AusAID (2012a) *AgResults: Innovation in Research and Delivery*. Draft concept note (<http://siteresources.worldbank.org/> accessed March 31, 2013).

AusAID (2012b) *AusAID Research Strategy 2012–16*. Canberra: Australia Government Publishing Service.

AusAID (2006) *Australian Aid: Promoting Growth and Stability*. A White Paper on the Australian government's overseas aid program. Canberra: Australia Government Publishing Service.

Australia (2011) *Independent Review of Aid Effectiveness*. Canberra: Australia Government Publishing Service.

Australia (1997) "Better Aid for a Better Future," the Government's Response to the Committee of Review of Australia's Overseas Aid Program given by Minister Alexander Downer on November 18. Canberra: Australia Government Publishing Service.

Australia (1992) *Government Response to the Review of the Australian Centre for International Agricultural Research*. Joint Committee on Foreign Affairs, Defence and Trade. Canberra: Australia Government Publishing Service.

Australia (1982) *Australian Centre for International Agricultural Research Act* 1982 (<http://www.comlaw.gov.au/Details/C2012C00015> accessed May 12, 2012).

Australia (1981) Speech by Minister Street on the occasion of the second reading of the ACIAR Act during the 32nd session of Parliament on October 27.

References

Australia (1979) *Australia and the Third World: Report of the Committee on Australia's Relations with the Third World*. Canberra: Australia Government Publishing Service.

Australian S&T Council (1990) *Setting Directions for Australian Research: A Report to the Prime Minister*. Canberra: Australian Government Publishing Service.

Barlow, Thomas (2006) *The Australian Miracle: An Innovative Nation Revisited*. Sydney, NSW: Pan Macmillan.

Bastow, Simon, Patrick Dunleavy, and Jane Tinkler (2014) *The Impact of the Social Sciences: How Academics and their Research Make a Difference*. London: Sage Publications.

Barney, Jay B. and Delwyn N. Clark (2007) *Resource-Based Theory: Creating and Sustaining Competitive Advantage*. Oxford: Oxford University Press.

Baum, Joel (1996) "Organizational ecology," in Clegg, S.R., C. Hardy, T.B. Lawrence, and W.R. Nord (eds.), *Handbook of Organization Studies*. Thousand Oaks, CA: Sage.

Beattie, Anthony (1994) "Experience of commissioning research and development," in Hay, R.K.M. (ed.) *Science in Government: Rise of the Intelligent Consumer*. Edinburgh: Scottish Agricultural Science Agency.

Beemans, Pierre (1999) "Re-inventing IDRC in the 1990s," presentation to SID-Ottawa Luncheon 18 May (<http://hdl.handle.net/10625/23852> accessed April 27, 2013).

Benner, Mats (2011) "In search of excellence? An international perspective on governance of university research," in Bo Göransson and Claes Brundenius (eds.) *Universities in Transition: The Changing Role and Challenges for Academic Institutions*. New York: Springer.

Boden, Rebecca, Deborah Cox, and Maria Nedeva (2006) "The appliance of science: new public management and strategic change." *Technology Analysis & Strategic Management* 18(2): 125–41.

Boden, Rebecca, Deborah Cox, Maria Nedeva, and Katharine Barker (2004) *Scrutinising Science: The Changing UK Government of Science*. Hampshire: Palgrave MacMillan.

Braun, Dietmar (2003) "Lasting tensions in research policy-making: a delegation problem." *Science and Public Policy* 30(5): 309–21.

Braun, Dietmar (1993) "Who governs intermediary agencies? Principal–agent relations in research policy-making." *Journal of Public Policy* 13(2): 135–62.

Bryson, John M. (2004) *Strategic Planning for Public and Nonprofit Organizations*. San Francisco, CA: Jossey-Bass.

Burawoy, Michael (2011) "Redefining the public university: developing an analytical framework." Social Science Research Council (<http://publicsphere.ssrc.org/burawoy-redefining-the-public-university/> accessed January 7, 2015).

Canada (2012) *Economic Action Plan 2012*, tabled by James Flaherty on March 29 (<http://www.budget.gc.ca> accessed May 8, 2013).

Canada (2010) *The Budget Plan 2010*, tabled by James Flaherty on March 4 (<http://www.budget.gc.ca> accessed March 31, 2013).

Canada (2008) *Speech from the Throne*. November 19 (<http://www.sft-ddt.gc.ca> accessed May 6, 2013).

Canada (2007) *The Budget Plan 2007*, tabled by James Flaherty on March 19 (<http://www.budget.gc.ca> accessed March 31, 2013).

Canada (2005) *The Budget Plan 2005*, tabled by Ralph Goodale on February 23 (<http://fin.gc.ca/budget05/pdf/bp2005e.pdf> accessed April 27, 2013).

Canada (2004) *Address by Prime Minister Paul Martin in Reply to the Speech from the Throne*. February 2 (<http://www.pco-bcp.gc.ca> accessed April 27, 2013).

Canada (2003) *The Budget Plan 2003*, tabled by John Manley on February 18 (<http://www.budget.gc.ca/accessed> April 27, 2013).

Canada (1995) *The Budget Plan 1995*, tabled by Paul Martin on February 27 (<http://www.budget.gc.ca/> accessed April 27, 2013).

Canada (1992a) *The Budget 1992*, tabled by Don Mazankowski on February 25 (<http://www.budget.gc.ca> accessed April 26, 2013).

Canada (1992b) *Canada's Green Plan and the Earth Summit*. Ottawa: Minister of Supply and Services Canada.

Canada (1991) *The Budget*, tabled by Michael Wilson on February 26th (<http://www.budget.gc.ca/pdfarch/1991-plan-eng.pdf>, accessed April 27, 2013).

Canada (1988) *Report of the Auditor General of Canada*, Chapter 4, Well-Performing Organizations, tabled November 1, Office of the Auditor General (<http://www.oag-bvg.gc.ca> accessed April 27, 2013).

Canada (1987) *For Whose Benefit?* Report of the Standing Committee on External Affairs and International Affairs on Canada's Official Development Assistance Policies and Programs.

Canada (1970) *International Development Research Centre Act* (<http://laws.justice.gc.ca/eng/acts/I-19/FullText.html> accessed 7 January 2015).

Canada (1968) *Memorandum to Cabinet: International Development Centre*, October 9 (<http://hdl.handle.net/10625/38415> accessed March 22, 2013).

Carden, Fred (2009) *Knowledge to Policy: Making the Most of Development Research*. Thousand Oaks, CA: Sage.

Chen, Huey-Tsyh (2005) *Practical Program Evaluation: Assessing and Improving Planning, Implementation, and Effectiveness*. Thousand Oaks, CA: Sage.

Cd 9230 (1918) *Report of Machinery of Government Committee*. London: Ministry of Reconstruction.

Cm 7656 (2009) *Eliminating World Poverty: Building Our Common Future*. White Paper on International Development. London: TSO.

Cm 6876 (2006) *Making Governance Work for the Poor*. White Paper on International Development. London: TSO.

Cm 5000 (2000) *Making Globalisation Work for the Poor*. White Paper on International Development. London: TSO.

Cm 4310 (1999) *Modernising Government*. White Paper presented to Parliament by the Prime Minister. London: TSO.

Cm 3789 (1997) *Eliminating World Poverty*. White Paper on International Development. London: TSO.

Cm 2250 (1993) *Realising Our Potential: A Strategy for Science, Engineering and Technology*. London: HMSO.

Cmnd 5046 (1972) *Framework for Government Research and Development*. London: HMSO.

Collier, P. (2007) *The Bottom Billion: Why the Poorest Countries Are Failing and What Can Be Done About It*. Oxford: Oxford University Press.

Collis, Brad (2002) *Fields of Discovery: Australia's CSIRO*. Crows Nest, NSW: Allen & Unwin.

Conway, Gordon and Jeff Waage (2010) *Science and Innovation for Development*. London: UK Collaborative for Development Sciences.

Core, Peter (2009) *A Retrospective on Rural R&D in Australia*. Canberra: Australian Government Department of Agriculture, Fisheries and Forestry.

Crawford Study Committee (1976) *A Proposal to Establish an International Research Assistance Foundation in Australia* (<http://aciar.gov.au/files/node/398/Crawford%20Study%20Committee%20Report%20201976.pdf> accessed January 7, 2015).

Daniels, Doug and Tim Dottridge (1993) "Managing agricultural research: views from a funding agency." *Public Administration and Development* 13: 205–15.

Davies, Huw T.O. and Sandra M. Nutley (2002) "Evidence-based policy and practice: rhetoric to reality." Research Unit for Research Utilisation, discussion paper 2, University of St Andrews.

Demeritt, David (2000) "The new social contact for science: accountability, relevance and value in US and UK science and research policy." *Antipode* 32(3): 308–29.

DFID (2011a) *UK Aid: Changing Lives, Delivering Results*. London: Department for International Development.

DFID (2011b) *Business Plan 2011–15*. London: Department for International Development. (<https://www.gov.uk/government/uploads/system/uploads/attachment_data/file/67658/DFID-business-plan.pdf> accessed April 18, 2015).

DFID (2009) *DFID Research 2009–2010: Providing Research Evidence that Enables Poverty Reduction*. London: Department for International Development.

DFID (2008) *Research Strategy 2008–2013*. London: Department for International Development.

DFID (2004) *Research Funding Framework 2005–2007*. London: Department for International Development.

DFID (2000a) *DFID Research: 1999/2000*. Prepared by Knowledge Policy Unit. London: Department for International Development.

DFID (2000b) *Science and Innovation Strategy 2001–2005*. London: Department for International Development.

Dietz, Thomas, Elinor Ostrom, and Paul C. Stern (2003) "The struggle to govern the commons." *Science* 302: 1907–12.

Doern, G. Bruce and Christopher Stoney (2009) *Research and Innovation Policy: Changing Federal Government-University Relations*. Toronto: University of Toronto Press.

Donovan, Claire (2008) "The Australian research quality framework." *New Direction for Evaluation* 118: 47–60.

Duncan, Ron, Meryl Williams, and Stephen Howes (2005) *Core Group Recommendations Report for a White Paper on Australia's Aid Program*. Canberra: AusAID.

Economist, The (2010) "First break all the rules: the charms of frugal innovation." April 15.

Edgerton, David (2009) "The 'Haldane principle' and other invented traditions in science policy." Wilkins-Bernal-Medawar Prize Lecture on April 20 at UK Royal Society.

Edwards, Michael (2010) "Know-how, know-what and the politics of knowledge for development." Speech at HIVOS conference Knowledge & Change: Theory and Practice of Development Dilemmas. September 29 in The Hague, Netherlands.

Ely, Adrian and Melissa Leach (2010) *Innovation, Sustainability, Development: A New Manifesto*. Brighton: STEPS Centre, University of Sussex.

Farrer, Keith (2005) To Feed a Nation: A History of Australian Food Science and Technology. Collingwood, NSW: CSIRO Publishing.

Faulker, David O. and Andrew Campbell (2003) *Oxford Handbook of Strategy*. Oxford: Oxford University Press.

Fischer, Frank (2003) *Reframing Public Policy: Discursive Politics and Deliberative Practices*. Oxford: Oxford University Press.

Fried, Robert C. (1976) *Performance in American Bureaucracy*. Boston, MA: Little, Brown & Company.

Funnel, Sue C. and Patricia J. Rogers (2011) *Purposeful Program Theory: Effective Use of Theories of Change and Logic Models*. San Francisco, CA: Jossey-Bass.

Gibbons, Michael et al. (1994) *The New Production of Knowledge: The Dynamics of Science and Research in Contemporary Societies*. Thousand Oaks, CA: Sage Publications.

Gordon, J. King (ed.) (1979) *Canada's Role in Science and Technology for Development*. Proceedings from a symposium held at the Ontario Science Centre. IDRC report 141-e.

Grace, Cheri (2010) *Product Development Partnerships (PDPs): Lessons from PDPs Established to Develop New Health Technologies for Neglected Diseases*. London: DFID Human Development Resource Centre.

Grant, Jonathan, Philipp-Bastian Brutscher, Susan Guthrie, Linda Butler, and Steven Wooding (2010) *Capturing Research Impacts: A Review of International Practice*. Cambridge: Rand Europe.

Grimpe, Christoph (2011) "Extramural research grants and scientists' funding strategies: beggars cannot be choosers?" *Research Policy* 41: 1448–60.

Guston, David H. (2000) *Between Politics and Science: Assuring the Integrity and Productivity of Research*. Cambridge: Cambridge University Press.

Habermann, Birgit and Margarita Langthale (2010) "Changing the world of development research? An insight into theory and practice." *Development in Practice* 20(7): 771–83.

Hagen-Zanker, Jessica et al. (2012) "Making systematic reviews work for international development research." Briefing paper for Secure Livelihoods Research Consortium. London: Overseas Development Institute.

Helpman, Elhanan (2004) *The Mystery of Economic Growth*. Cambridge, MA: Harvard University Press.

Hirschman, Albert O. (1970) *Exit, Voice and Loyalty: Responses to Decline in Firms, Organizations, and States*. Cambridge, MA: Harvard University Press.

Holmes, John and Brian Harris (2010) "Enhancing the contribution of research councils to the generation of evidence to inform policy making." *Evidence & Policy* 6(3): 391–409.

Hopper, William D. (1979) "Time is all important." *Mazingira* 8: 59–64.

Hopper, William D. (1973) "Research policy: eleven issues." IDRC report 14-e (<http://hdl.handle.net/10625/308> accessed August 23, 2013).

Hopper, William D. (1970) *Statement to the Inaugural Meeting of the Board of Governors of the International Development Research Centre, Ottawa, Canada, October 26, 1970*. Ottawa: IDRC. (<http://hdl.handle.net/10625/2215> accessed April 19, 2015).

House of Commons (2012) *Building Scientific Capacity for Development.* Science and Technology Committee, 4th Report of Session 2012–13, HC Report 377.

House of Commons (2004) *The Use of Science in UK International Development Policy.* Science and Technology Committee, 13th Report of Session 2003–04, HC Report 133.

House of Commons (1983) *Foreign Affairs Committee: The Overseas Development Administration's Scientific and Special Units.* London: HMSO.

House of Lords (2012) *The Role and Function of Departmental Chief Scientific Advisors.* 4th Report of Session 2010–12. HL Paper 264.

House of Lords (2010) *Setting Priorities for Publicly Funded Research.* Science and Technology Committee. 3rd Report of Session 2009–10. HL Paper 104.

IDRC (2009) *Innovating for Development: Strategic Framework 2010–2015.* Ottawa: IDRC.

IDRC (2006) *Competitive Grant Projects at IDRC.* Evaluation highlight 8. (<http://hdl.handle.net/10625/29989> accessed August 23, 2013). Ottawa: IDRC.

IDRC (2004) *Corporate Strategy and Program Framework 2005–2010.* Ottawa: IDRC.

IDRC (2002) "Closing the loop: communication for change at IDRC." (<http://hdl.handle.net/10625/21181> accessed April 26, 2013).

IDRC (2000) *IDRC Annual Report 1999–2000.* Ottawa: IDRC.

IDRC (1996) *IDRC Annual Report 1995–1996.* Ottawa: IDRC.

IDRC (1995a) *IDRC Annual Report 1994–1995.* Ottawa: IDRC.

IDRC (1995b) "1995–6 Program update." Memo from Caroline Pestieau to Board of Governors dated October 11.

IDRC (1994) *IDRC Annual Report 1993–1994.* Ottawa: IDRC.

IDRC (1991a) *Empowerment Through Knowledge: The Strategy of the International Development Research Centre.* Ottawa: IDRC. (<http://hdl.handle.net/10625/10832>, accessed April 19, 2015).

IDRC (1991b) *IDRC Annual Report 1990–1991.* Ottawa: IDRC.

IDRC (1985) *Program and Policy Review: VII 1986/87–1989/90.* Ottawa: IDRC.

IDRC (1977) "Clarification of the IDRC's role." Memo from Sylvie Plouffe to David Hopper, August 19.

IDRC (1970) "Statement to the inaugural meeting of the Board of Governors," by W. David Hopper. Ottawa, October 26. Document IDRC-002e.

Industry Commission (1994) *Research and Development.* Report no. 44, May 15. Canberra: Australian Government Publishing Service.

Jansen, Dorothea (2007) *New Forms of Governance in Research Organizations.* New York: Springer.

Jefferies, Charles J. (1964) *A Review of Colonial Research 1940–1960.* Overseas Research Publication no. 6, Department of Technical Cooperation. London: HMSO.

Kerin, John (2010) Speech on "what policy framework would I now establish for agricultural research, development and extension?" Given at University of Melbourne, May 5.

Khagram, Sanjeev et al. (2009) "Evidence for development effectiveness." *Journal of Development Effectiveness* 1(3): 247–70.

King, Kenneth and Simon A. McGrath (2004) *Knowledge for Development? Comparing British, Japanese, Swedish and World Bank Aid.* Cape Town and London: HSRC Press and Zed Books.

KPMG (2008) *Holy Grail or Achievable Goal? International Perspectives on Public Sector Performance Management*. Geneva: KPMG.

Lundvall, Bengt-Åke (1988) "Innovation as an interactive process," in Dosi, G. et al. (eds.) *Technology and Economic Theory*. London: Pinter.

Meier, G.M. (1994) "Review of development research in the UK: report to the Development Studies Association." *Journal of International Development* 6(5): 465–517.

Merton, Robert K. (1942) "The normative structure of science," in (1973) *The Sociology of Science: Theoretical and Empirical Investigations*. Chicago: University of Chicago Press.

Meyer, Michael and Matthew Kearnes (2013) "Intermediaries between science, policy and the market." *Science and Public Policy* 40: 423–9.

Mintzberg, Henry (2007) *Tracking Strategies: Towards a General Theory of Strategy Formation*. Oxford: Oxford University Press.

Molenaar, Henk, Louk Box, and Rutger Engelhard (eds.) (2009) *Knowledge on the Move: Emerging Agendas for Development-Oriented Research*. Leiden: International Development Publishers.

Moore, Mark H. (1995) *Creating Public Value: Strategic Management in Government*. Cambridge, MA: Harvard University Press.

Muirhead, Bruce and Ron Harpelle (2010) *IDRC: 40 Years of Ideas, Innovation and Impact*. Waterloo: Wilfrid Laurier Press.

Nairn, Malcom E., Gella T. Castillo, and Robert B. Dun (1998) *Staying Ahead: Report of a Review of the Australian Centre for International Agricultural Research*. Canberra: ACIAR.

Nelson, Richard R. and Sidney G. Winter (1982) *An Evolutionary Theory of Economic Change*. Cambridge, MA: Harvard University Press.

Nelson, Richard R. and Sidney G. Winter (1977) "In search of useful theory in innovation." *Research Policy* 6: 36–76.

Nutley, Sandra M., Isabel Walter, and Huw T.O. Davies (2007) *Using Evidence: How Research Can Inform Public Services*. Bristol: Policy Press.

ODM (1978) *Report on Research and Development*. Ministry of Overseas Development. London: HMSO.

ODM (1977) *Report on Research and Development*. Ministry of Overseas Development. London: HMSO.

ODM (1975) *Report on Research and Development*. Ministry of Overseas Development. London: HMSO.

ODM (1974) *Report on Research and Development*. Ministry of Overseas Development. London: HMSO.

ODA (1994) *Report on Research and Development*. Chatham: NRI.

ODA (1993) *Report on Research and Development*. Chatham: NRI.

ODA (1992) *Report on Research and Development*. Chatham: NRI.

ODA (1988) *Report on Research and Development*. Chatham: ODNRI.

ODA (1980) *Report on Research and Development*. London: Overseas Development Administration.

ODA (1979) *Report on Research and Development*. London: Overseas Development Administration.

OECD (2010) *The OECD Innovation Strategy: Getting a Head Start on Tomorrow*. Paris: OECD.

OECD (2003) *Governance of Public Research: Toward Better Practice*. Paris: OECD.
OECD (2002, 1963) *Frascati Manual: Proposed Standard Practice for Surveys on Research and Experimental Development*, 6th edition. Paris: OECD.
OECD/Eurostat (2005, 1992) *Oslo Manual: Guidelines for Collecting and Interpreting Innovation Data*, 3rd edition. Paris: OECD.
Ostrom, Elinor (2005) *Understanding Institutional Diversity*. Princeton, NJ: Princeton University Press.
Paarlberg, Laurie E. and Wolfgang Bielefeld (2009) "Complexity science: an alternative framework for understanding strategic management in public serving organizations." *International Public Management Journal* 12(2): 236–60.
Pearson, Lester B. et al. (1969) *Partners in Development: Report of the Commission on International Development*. New York, Washington, and London: Praeger.
Penfield, Teresa et al. (2014) "Assessment, evaluation, and definitions of research impact: a review." *Research Evaluation* 23: 21–32.
Pfeffer, Jeffrey and Gerald R. Salanick (1978) *The External Control of Organizations: A Resource-Dependence Perspective*. New York: Harper & Row.
Plumptre, Arthur F.W. (1968) *Memorandum to M.F. Strong from A.F.W. Plumptre on the Proposed International Development Research Institution*. January 24 (<http://hdl.handle.net/10625/39635> accessed March 22, 2013).
Poister, Theodore H. (2010) "The future of strategic planning in the public sector: linking strategic management and performance." *Public Administration Review*: S246–54.
Poister, Theodore H., David W. Pitts, and Lauren H. Edwards (2010) "Strategic management research in the public sector: a review, synthesis and future directions." *American Review of Public Administration* 40(5): 522–45.
Polanyi, Michael (1962) "The republic of science." *Minerva* 1: 54–73.
Polster, Claire (2003) "Canadian university research policy at the turn of the century: continuity and change in the social relations of academic research." *Studies in Political Economy* 71/72: 177–99.
Ravallion, Martin and Alan Gelb (2010) "Research for development: a World Bank perspective on future directions for research." *Policy Research Working Paper 5437*. Washington, DC: World Bank.
Reid, Walter V. et al. (2010) "Earth system science for global sustainability: grand challenges." *Science* 330(6006): 916–17.
Rip, Arie (2003) "Societal challenges for R&D evaluation," in P. Shapira and S. Kuhlmann (eds.), *Learning from Science and Technology Policy Evaluation*: Cheltenham: Edward Elgar.
Rip, Arie (1994) "The republic of science in the 1990s." *Higher Education* 28(1): 3–23.
Rogers, Patricia (2000) "Program theory evaluation: practice, promise and problems." *New Directions for Evaluation* 87: 5–13.
Rousseau, Denise M. (2006) "Is there such a thing as 'evidence based management'?" *Academy of Management Review* 31(2): 256–69.
Sandland, Ron and Graham Thompson (2012) *Icon in Crisis: The Reinvention of CSIRO*. Sydney: University of New South Wales Press.
Schubert, Torben (2009) "Empirical observations on New Public Management to increase efficiency in public research: boon or bane?" *Research Policy* 38: 1225–34.

Scoones, Ian and Melissa Leach (2006) *The Slow Race: Making Technology Work for the Poor*. London: Demos.

Seward, Shirley B. (1974) *The Evolution of the International Development Research Centre*. (<http://hdl.handle.net/10625/140> accessed January 7, 2015).

Shove, Elizabeth. (2003) "Principals, agents and research programmes." *Science and Public Policy* 30(5): 371–81.

Shove, Elizabeth and Michael Redclift (2001) "Steering research toward policy: the case of social science and environmental change," in Matthijs Hisschemoller et al. (eds.) *Knowledge, Power, and Participation in Environmental Policy. Policy Studies Annual Review*, Volume 12. New Brunswick, NJ: Transaction Publishers.

Singer, Hans et al. (1970) *The Sussex Manifesto: Science and Technology to Developing Countries during the Second Development Decade*. Brighton: Institute of Development Studies, University of Sussex.

Sivadasan, Suja et al. (2003) *Review of the DFID's Role in the International Research Effort* (<http://www.ibrarian.net/navon/paper/Review_of_the_Department_for_International_Develo.pdf?paperid=2155173> accessed January 7, 2015).

Slaughter, Sheila and Gary Rhoades (1996) "The emergence of a competitiveness research and development policy coalition and the commercialization of academic science and technology." *Science, Technology and Human Values* 21: 303–39.

Slaymaker, Olva et al. (1998) *The Nature of Research at IDRC, Report of Research Ad Hoc Committee of the Board*. BG 98(06)06 (<http://hdl.handle.net/10625/29892> accessed March 31, 2013).

Smillie, Ian (2011) "Learning and development: three essential books." *Development in Practice* 21(3): 441–3.

Sparrow, Malcom K. (2011) "Governing science." *New Perspectives in Policing*. Harvard Kennedy School (<https://www.ncjrs.gov/pdffiles1/nij/232179.pdf> accessed August 29, 2013).

Stephan, Paula (2012) *How Economics Shapes Science*. Cambridge, MA: Harvard University Press.

Stockdale, Peter (1995) *Pearsonian Internationalism in Practice: The International Development Research Centre*. PhD thesis in political science. Montreal: McGill University. (<http://hdl.handle.net/10625/14160>, accessed April 18, 2015).

Surr, Martin, Andrew Barnett, Alex Duncan, Melanie Speight, David Bradley, Alan Rew, and John Toye (2002) *Research for Poverty Reduction: DFID Research Policy Paper*. (<http://r4d.dfid.gov.uk/PDF/Articles/Surr_Report-Research_for_Poverty_Reduction_Policy_Paper_Annexes.pdf> accessed January 7, 2015).

Talbot, Colin (2010) *Theories of Performance: Organizational and Service Improvement in the Public Domain*. Oxford: Oxford University Press.

Talbot, Colin (2008) "Performance regimes: the institutional context of performance policies." *International Journal of Public Administration* 31(14): 1569–91.

Tribe, Derek E. (1991) *Doing Well by Doing Good: Agricultural Research Feeding and Greening the World*. Leichhardt, NSW: Crawford Fund and Pluto Press.

Truman, Harry S. (1949) "Inaugural address" (<http://www.trumanlibrary.org/whistlestop/50yr_archive/inagural20jan1949.htm> accessed April 18, 2015).

Uhrig, John (2003) Review of the Corporate Governance of Statutory Authorities and Office Holders. Canberra: Commonwealth of Australia.

UK (2011) *Science & Engineering Assurance Review of the Department for International Development.* London: Government Office for Science.

UK (2003) *Getting the Evidence: Research in Policy Making.* Report by comptroller and auditor general HC 586 session 2002–3.

UK (2002) *DFID Performance Management: Helping to Reduce World Poverty.* National Audit Office, Report by comptroller and auditor general HC 739.

UN Millennium Project (2005) *Innovation: Applying Knowledge in Development.* London: Earthscan.

UNESCO (2010) *World Social Science Report.* Paris: UNESCO.

van der Meulen, Barend (2003) "New roles and strategies of a research council: intermediation of the principal–agent relationship." *Science and Public Policy* 30(5): 323–36.

van der Meulen, Barend (1998) "Science policies as principal-agents games: institutionalization and path dependency in the relation between government and science." *Research Policy* 27(4): 397–414.

Varmus, Harold et al. (2003) "Grand challenges in global health." *Science* 302 (5644).

Wagner, Caroline (2008) *The New Invisible College: Science for Development.* Washington, DC: Brookings Institute.

Whitley, Richard (2011) "Changing governance and authority relations in the public sciences." *Minerva* 49: 359–85.

Whitley, Richard and Jochen Gläser (2007) *The Changing Governance of the Sciences: The Advent of Research Evaluation Systems.* Dordrecht: Springer.

Worboys, Michael (1996) "British colonial science policy 1918–1939," in Patrick Petitjean (ed.), *Les Sciences Coloniales: Figures et Institutions.* Paris: ORSTOM.

World Bank (1998) *World Development Report 1998–99: Knowledge for Development.* Washington, DC: World Bank.

World Commission on Environment and Development (1987) *Our Common Future.* Oxford: Oxford University Press.

Ziman, John M. (2000) *Real Science: What It Is and What It Means.* Cambridge: Cambridge University Press.

Index

African Institutes for Mathematical Sciences 90–2
agency 18, 20, 58, 142
agriculture
  food security 7, 52, 84, 87, 89, 110, 119–21, 129, 160, 164
  green revolution 4, 64
  in Australia 99–100, 107, 109, 119, 126
  rural development 107
  seeds 5, 79, 159, 174
  value chains 109, 119, 121, 157
austerity 19, 45, 53, 57, 86, 103, 124, 128–9, 136
Australia
  budget 103, 120, 124
  rural R&D corporations (RDCs) 98, 104, 108, 111–12, 125, 130, 151
  science policy 96, 123, 125
autonomy 11, 66–7, 70–1, 93, 94, 108, 125, 127, 132, 136–8, 162, 168–70

Bezanson, K. 71–7, 93, 95, 129, 144, 153, 169

Canada
  budget 60, 71, 72, 73–4, 77, 78–80, 83–6, 89, 91
  science policy 68, 77, 82–3
  Treasury Board 66, 80, 84, 131
capacity
  building 21, 42, 76, 95, 147, 154
  research 76, 101, 109–11, 150, 158, 175
CGIAR 49, 98–9, 104, 105, 106, 165
Chen, H. 21–2, 142, 143
Crawford, J. 98–9, 100, 101, 103, 143, 169
CSIRO 98–100, 111, 115–16, 119, 125, 135, 137, 152

development
  assistance 38, 43, 51, 56, 63, 79, 94, 124, 128, 157–9, 170–2, 175
  sciences 42–3, 46, 132
  studies 5, 36, 42, 45, 47, 160, 162, 176

evaluation
  adoption studies 107, 111
  ex ante 12, 103, 131, 150, 161
  ex post 12, 83, 107, 110, 131, 150, 152
  program 21–2, 170
evidence-based 38–9, 49, 57, 130, 134

genomics 47, 58, 119, 132, 139, 144, 148, 150, 151
global challenges 7, 53, 156, 158–9, 164–7, 170, 172, 176–7
governance
  adaptive 156, 166
  board 63–6, 72, 75, 92, 94, 100–1, 113–15, 131, 136, 138–9, 169, 176
  context 18–20, 22, 29–31, 36, 44, 45, 58, 78, 111, 130–40, 150, 151–2
  research 7, 9–13, 57, 163–4
  self- 10, 28, 30, 116, 133–4
government
  expectations 7, 9–10, 15–20, 38, 44, 82, 100, 112, 140, 169
  minister 36, 45, 55, 67, 78, 80, 86, 89, 100, 106–7, 111, 113–15, 136, 171–3
  priorities 11, 83–4, 92, 109, 127, 139
  science 3–4, 57, 172
Grand Challenges Canada 86, 95, 137, 153
grantmaker 138
grantmaking
  competitive calls 31, 59, 88, 134, 146–7, 160
  consortia 42, 45, 146, 153, 162
  point of delivery 151
  portfolio 18, 25, 135, 148–54
  practice 5, 16, 18, 23, 45, 59, 78, 95, 111, 126, 145–54
  recipients 7, 12, 18, 24–5, 45, 78, 111, 132, 135, 146–53
  systematic review 51–2
  time horizon 12, 108, 149–51, 167

Haldane, R. 28–9, 55, 58, 130, 133, 143
health
  clinical medicine 49–51, 132, 144
  diseases 38, 43, 108, 121, 135, 159
  vaccines 5, 6, 46, 48, 85, 144, 174
Hopper, D. 64–7, 71, 92, 143, 169

incentives
  academic 13, 48, 117, 125, 148, 162

incentives (*cont.*)
career 7, 8, 14, 44, 55, 109, 117, 119, 123, 134–8, 140, 167
information asymmetry 7, 127, 138, 141
innovation
definition 3
diffusion of 3, 21, 59, 95, 107, 153
economics of 23–4
frugal 91, 157
strategy 9, 40, 43
system 116, 121
international development
definition 157–9

market
client 35–6, 70, 94, 135, 149–50
competition 12, 31, 80, 133, 137–8, 140
consumer/customer 11, 31–3, 38, 40, 56, 130, 133–6, 138, 139, 144, 149, 153
Mintzberg, H. 20, 24

organizations
adaptive 4, 15, 20–5, 122, 141, 149
intermediary 7–8, 13, 127, 138–9, 161
mandate 8, 17, 20, 30, 38, 63, 70–4, 98, 100, 105–6, 110, 138, 141, 143, 168–9
purpose 6, 19, 20, 70, 102, 144, 165, 173
routines 9, 20, 22–4, 117, 142, 170, 172
Ostrom, E. 160
Overseas Development Administration (ODA)
scientific units 30–6, 134, 146, 153

partnership
as connecting researchers 96, 102, 115, 154
as shared funding 35, 47, 81, 87
product development 48
pattern 15, 20, 22–3
performance
assessment 9, 12
expectations 141, 165, 172, 173
management 38–9, 112, 117, 140, 141, 171–3
regime 16–19, 45, 78, 111
test 173
planning 19–20, 67, 70, 93, 136
policy
foreign 14, 18, 81, 101, 118, 159, 172
influence 5, 40, 60, 77–9, 81, 110, 149–51
principal-agent relations 7–9, 17, 127, 132, 138–9
private sector 40, 48, 85, 113, 117, 173
program
design 21, 125, 159, 165
evaluation 21–2, 150
targeted 11, 52, 94, 133, 136
theory 18, 20–2, 26–8, 95, 125, 141, 143–5, 149, 152–4, 169–70

public good 10, 36, 38, 44, 150, 157, 159
public management 19, 58, 93, 124, 130–3, 172
leadership 168–71
whole of government 19, 123, 138, 172

research
assessment exercises 40, 47, 55, 117–18, 134
councils 11, 28, 34, 45–7, 53, 77–8, 82–3, 137, 163
definition 2–3
demand 7, 41, 58–9, 135, 150
funders 7, 11, 13, 15, 19–20, 117, 128, 141, 160–1, 170
governance 9–10, 15, 133–6, 163–4, 170
impact 37, 173–6
outputs 5, 33, 95
policy 19, 58, 94, 125, 133–6
quality 6, 12, 47, 52, 117, 161, 175
university 96, 117, 165
uptake, utilization 38, 46, 76, 135, 144
resources 19, 57, 93, 124, 128–30, 136
role of staff 18, 24, 54, 59, 66, 95, 145–6
Rothschild, V. 31–2, 56, 136

science
definition 2
diplomacy 106–7, 129, 167
selection criteria 11, 18, 88, 146–7, 161
Short, C. 37–8
Shove, E. 8, 12, 24
Strong, M. 62–4, 67, 74, 76, 92, 132, 143

Talbot, C. 15, 16–18, 171
talent
competition for 9, 108–9, 128, 140
mobilize 4, 63, 65, 105, 158, 166
scout/spotting 66, 88, 94, 100, 149, 160
technology
adoption 110, 131, 145, 171
platform 58, 132, 149–50
Tribe, D. 103–5, 122, 154

United Kingdom
budget 29, 39, 45–6, 53, 57
research councils 28, 34, 37, 45–7, 53
science advisor 150
science policy 28, 29
Treasury 39, 45, 53, 57, 136

value
public value 16–17, 173
value for money 12, 39, 51, 54, 120, 134, 136, 175

Wagner, C. 4, 6, 11, 158, 159

Printed and bound by CPI Group (UK) Ltd, Croydon, CR0 4YY